THE
NEW AMERICAN GHETTO

R U T G E R S   U N I V E R S I T Y   P R E S S
N E W   B R U N S W I C K ,   N E W   J E R S E Y

THE
NEW AMERICAN GHETTO

Camilo José Vergara

Second paperback printing, 1999

Library of Congress Cataloging-in-Publication Data
Vergara, Camilo J.
   The new American ghetto / Camilo José Vergara.
    p. cm.
   Includes bibliographical references (p.)
   ISBN 0-8135-2209-9 (cloth) — ISBN 0-8135-2331-1 (pbk.)
   1. Inner cities—United States—Pictorial works.   I. Title.
HN57.V47 1995   *94-45707*
307.3´362—dc20   *CIP*

British Cataloging-in-Publication information available

Design by John Romer
Published by Rutgers University Press, New Brunswick, New Jersey
Manufactured in Hong Kong

CONTENTS

PREFACE

"LIKE CLOUDS, LIKE SHIPS, LIKE SHADOWS"
A Personal Note

"You lost or something?"

—Man surprised to see me walking along Avon Avenue in the Central Ward, Newark, 1993

"Get your damn police ass out of here, man!"

—Youth, upon seeing me photographing a building, South Side, Chicago,1994

Although I have seen thousands of ruined houses, I never saw my own. In July 1990, after an absence of over thirty years, I returned to Rengo, a small town in central Chile, only to find the house where I spent most of my childhood completely gone. It had been an L-shaped dwelling, a one-story, Spanish "casa de campo" that seemed to have grown out of the place. So thick were its adobe walls, I thought it indestructible. Along with the house, the willow trees that I had seen my father plant and that I had watched grow had also disappeared. Gone, too, were the fig, olive, laurel, and orange trees surrounding my home when we first arrived in 1951.

I knew that several families had moved in after we left. I knew there had been fires. Yet I expected to find something. It was profoundly disturbing, standing there facing only a shallow brook. Women and children passed, but I was too overwhelmed to ask questions. It did not occur to me to take photographs. Why bother about a plot of vacant land? Confused, I drove a few

blocks to where an imposing row of fragrant eucalyptus trees had stood and found half of them mutilated, reduced to a long row of stumps. By then, all I wanted was to be very far away.

The damage had been done. My return had profoundly altered my most cherished memories. Now I understood better the feelings experienced by suburbanites who visit their old urban neighborhoods, only to find them unrecognizable.

How did a book like this come to be? What motivated me to travel across a nation the size of a continent to photograph its ghettos for eighteen years? Why such a fixation with keeping a record of what was declining, disintegrating, falling into ruin? Why did I have to return to the same places, observing their fate from the same corners and the same roofs?

I can answer this only partially, by looking at my own life. My grandfather owned what was perhaps the most prosperous farm in Chile, its fruit selling as far away as Europe and the United States. The accumulated wealth of generations was visible in my early childhood in the form of beautiful houses, expensive cars, elegant furniture, and precious jewelry, which I admired and assumed would be ours forever. I had a French governess and first learned to read in French.

During my childhood and adolescence I saw this varied and seemingly endless wealth vanish, leaving me with an enduring feeling that things cannot last, and filling my mind with ghosts. The fancy crystal goblets, the silver cutlery, and the jewels went one by one to the pawnshop, or were bought by relatives and friends. Even our heavy redwood dining room table that could seat two dozen people was sold. I remember looking on somberly as it was loaded onto the back of a truck, never to be seen again. Now all that remains of our wealth is the family's white marble mausoleum containing, under the altar, my grandmother's bronze coffin with silver handles, specially commissioned from Paris.

Rich relatives rescued us from extreme destitution. They paid for private schools, gave us hand-me-down clothes and old issues of *Look*

magazine to read, and brought us staples from their farms. They came in a hurry in their chauffeur-driven cars and spoke mainly to my mother. My father, an alcoholic, would disappear from the house for weeks at a time. As an adolescent I lived in fear of abject poverty as circumstances seemed always to be getting worse. I left my house permanently when I reached the age of fifteen, and divided my time between boarding school and relatives.

Since then, I've been wary of owning and becoming attached to objects of value. Where wealth and elegance prevail, I feel out of place, nervous, and I long to leave. Things that remain the same are unsettling to me; I am attracted to what is shunned, falling apart, and changing.

In 1965, arriving in the United States to go to college at the age of twenty-one, I found myself in an immensely wealthy, self-confident, and energetic nation. I bought a camera and photographed campus life, occasionally venturing beyond the grounds of my school, the University of Notre Dame, to photograph the town of South Bend, Indiana. I drifted to the rundown neighborhoods of the city, and to the ghetto where, in addition to blacks, a few hundred Mexican families lived.

After college I moved to New York City, where for three years I did street photography. I photographed children cooling themselves off at fire hydrants, black girls amusing themselves with white dolls, Latino schoolboys cutting classes to watch dogs copulating, and poor elderly Jews standing on the stoops of their tenements on the Lower East Side. I felt pleased with the liveliness of my pictures, yet I saw myself at a dead end, retracing the steps of many others.

I returned to school, to Columbia University, to study sociology. The years as a graduate student gave me the ability to do academic research, to take a more detached view, to think historically and conceptually, and to have confidence in my vision. Using a variety of points of view, photographing over time, and striving for complete coverage, I developed a methodology to capture a monumental urban transformation underway.

Close, sustained encounters with poverty have shaped my character and driven me, perhaps obsessively, to the ghettos. I have never forgotten the places of squalor I once seemed destined to inhabit—the dark decrepit rooms housing entire families, the dirt-floor shacks built overnight, and the somewhat more affluent but tiny cottages in remote neighborhoods. In the ghetto I saw the equivalent of houses I could have lived in, and I examined them almost as part of my own life. Yet even though I live in stable middle-class neighborhoods, enjoying a life full of travel and opportunities, I feel that this comfortable existence is transitory, that my real home is in some form of ghetto.

Today, an entire generation has grown up with little direct experience of the inner city. When confronted with ruins, holes in the urban landscape, dilapidated housing, and small developments where factories, tenements, and high-rises once stood, Americans will ask how this all happened. Their curiosity will not be satisfied with intricate sagas of the welfare system, or the failure of the public schools to educate, or the epic of drugs and crime, or, on the other hand, lists of successful programs ready to be replicated in every ghetto in the nation—all accounts that leave out the urban environment itself are incomplete and misleading. The ghetto poses urgent questions I feel compelled to respond to, not with solutions but with explanations and tangible records. I am driven to publicize and preserve the memory of these environments.

Those interested in what happened to our cities will ask to *see* what happened. They will need pictures showing blocks, buildings, streets—the entire urban landscape—not just the fires, crime scenes, investigative exposés, protest marches, and politicians' visits that one is likely to find in newspaper archives and old television newscasts.

In public presentations, I direct my bleak message to young people. I derive no enjoyment from the realization that my view of this nation's ghettos finds increasing acceptance among them. Young audiences, however, are not interested in documenting the ghetto; their interest is in changing the conditions I describe. Their questions are fundamental: What can we do? How can we create an integrated society? An architecture student at Yale University expressed his

hard-boiled optimism by suggesting that buildings should be designed as temporary fortresses, with latent windows and doors that can be punched out of the walls when the neighborhood gets safer. A hopeful thought.

BOOKS, MOVIES, AND MUSIC

"I am convinced that the future is lost somewhere in the dumps of the non-historical past; it is in yesterday's newspapers, in the jejune advertisements of science-fiction movies, in the false mirror of our rejected dreams."

—Robert Smithson,
"A Tour of the Monuments of Passaic, New Jersey"

While working on this book I have been profoundly influenced by the works of writers, musicians, filmmakers, and poets whose work resonated with the cityscapes of the American ghetto. This was very important when I was groping for ideas and images to express my observations and heighten my feelings. Later I found to my surprise that others who shared my interest in the ghetto had on their own gravitated to similar works.

Two contrasting kinds of literature have attracted me: that portraying imaginary cities, such as Italo Calvino's *Invisible Cities*, and that describing real cities—Charles Dickens's London, Emile Zola's Paris, Jorge Luis Borges's Buenos Aires, Jane Addams's Chicago. My interest in realism and fantasy—in what is, what was, and what exists only in the imagination—extends to the cinema as well. Movies such as *Metropolis* by Fritz Lang, *Blade Runner* by Ridley Scott, and *Stalker* by Andrei Tarkowsky have interested me as much as the documentaries of Joris Ivens, Robert Flaherty, and Luis Buñuel.

The precise poetry that defined urban life when large, modern cities first evolved, epitomized by Charles Baudelaire's *Fleurs du mal* and *Petits Poemes en prose*, was also inspiring. And today, when reality overpowers the imagination, Edgar Allan Poe's fantastic writings about ruins and decay ("The Fall of the House of Usher," "The Mask of the Red Death") made me wish he were alive to write about the armories of New York, the derelict skyscrapers of downtown Detroit, Chicago public housing, and all of North Camden. Robert Smithson's images too, full of mystery, ambiguity, and seemingly outrageous comparisons, encouraged me to limn the shunned wonders of the contemporary cityscape.

Occasionally, metropolitan dailies issue remarkable series of articles that reveal and redefine a city. In response to the lack of information on the total number of vacant buildings in Motown, for example, the *Detroit Free Press* took on the challenge by doing its own count. In July of 1989, the *Free Press* published a number of superbly illustrated articles on abandonment and its significance. From a six-week survey conducted by five teams of staff members who drove 2,814 miles of city streets "recording each structure that was boarded up," the newspaper found 15,215 abandoned buildings, and interviewed hundreds of people, including the city's mayor, who felt worried and powerless about what to do about them.

As I moved through buildings in the ghetto, I kept an eye open for samples of anonymous writing, what a security guard in a Newark highrise called "stuff that comes from the heart." I found here the bulletin boards that reflect the daily life of young people in these neighborhoods. And riding in buses and in subways, I wrote down pieces of overheard conversations.

Sometimes even music playing on the car radio or at home while I wrote stimulated my exploration of the ghetto. Gregorian chant, with its sense of eternity, warmed the sight of urban ruins, while the tangos of Astor Piazzola brought back to me things ephemeral—youth, loves, and friendships in the working-class neighborhoods in which the tango was born.

From the cities themselves came the melodies created by those who had played in clubs located on the streets I was observing. Once John Coltrane's "A Love Supreme" seemed to be the force that pushed my car along Mack Avenue in Detroit, and the music bestowed a holiness on the city. Similarly, one Christmas, on my travels through Chicago's South Side, I heard James

Brown insistently urging Santa Claus to "Go Straight to the Ghetto." Yet another time, cruising along Springfield Avenue in Newark, I listened to Sarah Vaughan being interviewed; she replied to a question about her city of birth by repeating three times in a rich and sorrowful voice, "It looks so bad." She went on to sing love songs that hugged the ground by the projects and the empty lots.

In my struggle to give meaning to "the dumps of the non-historical past," I have pulled together disconnected ways of seeing, made an inventory of declining neighborhoods, "zones," "wastelands," and "enclaves," and assessed their significance. I have consistently documented how things end.

METHODOLOGY

"Recent developments have transformed cities, vastly altering their traditional functions, as well as their cultural, architectural, and spatial characteristics. As the tides of modernization and industrialization have receded, a startling new and complex urban landscape has been exposed . . . those neglected, worn-out and marginal buildings, sites, and structures that make up the landscape of the contemporary city. The aesthetic scrutiny of this postmodern landscape is the subject of this show ["Entropic Zones: Buildings and Structures of the Contemporary City"].

"Various artists explore the fate of structures and buildings as they move between systems of meaning (utility, abandonment, ruination, rediscovery), tracing their transmutation from what they once were into what they will soon become."

—James Dickinson,
professor of sociology, Rider University,
announcing an upcoming show at the college art gallery, 1994

The New American Ghetto is the result of an uninterrupted dialogue with poor communities, their residents, and the scholars who study them. This book grows out of the "The New American Ghetto Archive," my collection of over nine thousand color slides that I began taking in 1977 for the purpose of documenting the nation's major ghettos. Represented in the collection are the poorest and most segregated urban communities in the country, particularly those in New York City, Newark, Chicago, Los Angeles, Detroit, Gary, and Camden. My choice of locations coincides with areas called "hyperghettos"—places where at least 40 percent of the population lives below the poverty level.

Photographs function as containers of information, fragments with which we can imaginatively reconstruct lost neighborhoods. Each picture represents an instant in history. Like sensors dropped in the water by oceanographers to be regularly monitored, successive photographs of the same places serve to track change over time. These images are most revealing when used with census data, newspaper accounts, telephone directories going back several years, Sanborn maps, and everything else we can learn about the neighborhood.

I first record the changes evident from close observation of images—that is, what has been added to or has disappeared from a block; what seems to be ailing and what seems to be thriving; and what is happening to the vacant land. Secondly, I compare aspects of different cities, for example, their commercial streets. I supplement the description through interviews with those who live and work in these neighborhoods.

I have tried to produce photographs storing the maximum possible information. To get clear, readable, and stable images I use Kodachrome 64, perspective corrective lenses, high shutter speeds, and avoid dark shadows.

Until 1986 I usually shot pictures from the street level, but with crack dealers selling on every other corner, this became very dangerous. Instead of visiting the neighborhoods alone, I began to look for a local resident to escort me. My concern for security actually opened up new opportunities. I turned to public housing agencies, nonprofit developers, hospitals, and universities for help. My escorts were usually building superintendents and maintenance men well acquainted with the area and with ready access to roofs. With these people serving as guides, I began systematically to shoot from high viewpoints. Roofs are often long platforms that may

extend nearly a city block in either direction. They offer many angles from which to photograph the urban scenes below, views of what lies behind walls and windows and on the tops of buildings.

This new perspective, from above, helped me in my goal of achieving more complete and clearer documentation. Neighborhoods are represented both at street level and in bird's-eye views. Large panoramas, blocks, single buildings, and interiors are all part of a continuum.

Whenever possible, the collection has been organized into pictorial networks that begin with a panoramic shot covering several blocks. The sequence proceeds toward ever-smaller units photographed from the ground, the roof of a car, or the top of a smaller structure. Thus, we move from the panorama to shots of one of its single blocks or buildings, and then to selected details. Often I have repeated and added on to the sequence over the years, which allows the viewer to follow ongoing transformations. And this work is open-ended. By carrying on the documentation themselves, others interested in these urban areas can detect new trends as they emerge.

Although I have been using the same basic approach to documenting poor, minority communities for at least a decade and half, I have recently added new sites which, because of their size, physical structure, and my own time constraints have required a more selective strategy. The documentation begins with a different pair of questions: What are the main issues that the new territory forces us to confront? How can these be best presented? On the other hand, existing work must be continued following its own logic. Adding images to a well-covered area requires me to update views; to strengthen the weaving of pictorial networks by filling in new views; and to explore these familiar places for what is emerging.

Four years ago I decided to add Detroit (140 square miles) to the collection. Instead of doing a systematic documentation of the entire city—impossible, my being able to spend only five days a year photographing there—I choose to concentrate on the city's downtown and some of the wide commercial thoroughfares, areas

most affected by the process of disinvestment. In addition to photographing these spaces, I prowl the entire city in search of local forms of the elements that define the new ghetto: caretaking institutions, NIMBYs, ruins, graphic expressions, fortification, and enclaves.

In Chicago, I took a similar approach when I became aware that some of the worst ghettos in the city were developing to the south of the traditional Black Belt. Thus, to the south and to the west I added Englewood and South Riverdale; farther south, the small suburbs of Ford Heights and Robbins. Because these areas lack tall buildings, documentation consists mostly of views of street blocks and buildings from the roof of a car.

My thematic categories and arguments originated in the images and my experiences of the places visited. I began with essential urban themes: housing, commerce, industry, institutions, parks, and vacant land. As my work progressed, other subjects surfaced—for example, responses to the environment, expressions of cultural identity, and traces of history in the form of discarded objects. At first I regarded photographs illustrating these themes as curiosities in the collection. But later, as I encountered them frequently and in different communities, their importance became obvious, and I searched for them in visits to the field.

I study closely: 1) areas and buildings plagued by drug use and the drug trade; 2) neighborhoods chosen for the resettlement of the homeless; 3) gentrification—mainly in sections of the city selected for townhouses; 4) areas chosen for the location of NIMBYs, both institutions and facilities (particularly communities selected for homeless shelters, prisons, and drug treatment facilities); 5)"Edges"—remote neighborhoods, forgotten corners, often lacking political representation or even a name, located by railroad lines, expressways, cemeteries, and industrial areas.

In addition, the archive includes more than two hundred photographs taken inside private homes, apartments, businesses, and public areas of buildings. These record the tastes of a population whose preferences are almost always ignored. Interior photographs often show orderly, clean, and cheerful rooms that contrast with the derelict public places outside.

Often, cities have sections that are extraordinary because of the living conditions, activities, and programs that characterize them—for example, the derelict North Side of downtown Detroit, the raggedy family high-rises of the Chicago Housing Authority, and the desolate commercial streets marked by riots, such as Broadway in Camden. These also have been carefully documented.

Since the fabric of an urban area has a unique pattern, searching for characteristic images proved to be a challenge that varied according to place. This was particularly true in Gary, where most of the tall buildings were concentrated in a small section of the downtown, thus forcing me once again to rely on street-level photography to document the city. Differences in climate, the built environment, and the state of the local and regional economy add to the diversity found among these communities. Demographic distinctions also should be considered: Is the ghetto overwhelmingly African American (for example, Central Harlem, South Side Chicago, Central Ward of Newark), Latino (North Camden, East Los Angeles), or mixed, where blacks and Latinos live side by side (South Central Los Angeles and Bushwick in Brooklyn)?

Striving to approach the unattainable goal of capturing the ghettos in their entirety, I have included images that are exciting as well as those that are dull. This approach permits communities to reveal themselves despite my personal tastes and inclinations. What seemed an uninteresting view from the roof of a building, for instance, may contain revealing details, apparent only later when carefully examined or when integrated into a time-lapse sequence.

In writing the text I was guided by the people I met while photographing and by others to whom the images themselves led me. Some of these people became my advisors and I frequently called on them for their opinions. Phone numbers left on walls, names on storefronts and on vehicles, business cards given to me by cab drivers, pieces of paper I saw on bulletin boards—all provided new information and understanding.

Photographs have the power to bring back feelings and memories that are often dormant and inaccessible. As a way to orient the conversation and establish trust I approached contacts with images of their neighborhoods in hand, or I introduced a topic with a verbal description of changes that have taken place in the community.

The documentation has been enlarged and refocused by questions and suggestions that arose during the preparation of three exhibitions, more than a dozen articles, two television documentaries, and scores of public discussions and slide presentations given to diverse audiences.

Assembling pictorial networks image by image, over time, has been a most challenging puzzle. The existing body of documentation requires constant fieldwork to keep abreast of the ongoing drama of our cities. What will replace the hundreds of apartment buildings now scheduled to be demolished in Chicago? What will be the next stage in the process that has been called "Newark's Renaissance" by some, and by others a "war on poor people"? What will be the new mechanisms to isolate enclaves and protect buildings? What will the new crop of fortresses look like? What new institutions will emerge to deal with the problems of destitution?

PHOTOJOURNALISM

Photography, a natural tool to explore cities, has become ineffective at documenting change because of its rigid aesthetic conventions. After nearly a century of arousing the public's awareness to social problems, photojournalists—once those most likely to represent the ghettos—tend to produce work that is so predictable that it fails to raise concern. Images produced to illustrate an existing text, to serve the needs of a client, or to fit the conception of an editor are too narrow in scope to capture and explain urban reality.

Critic Andy Grundberg characterizes photo journalism as an activity "that combines aspects of social reform, individual heroism, and emotional compassion . . . preferring pictures that are big, graphic, and easy to understand." In 1988 John Leonard, picture editor of *Life* for a decade and a half, described the magazine's photographers as "interested in recording what people do," in using "the vagaries of circumstances as means of self-expression." Photographs depicting only an instant, lacking a sense of the whole, and constructed through dramatic light and strong compositions that hide important details shape more than record reality. Today's dazzling pictures seldom take us beyond the surface and thus cannot raise our consciousness, much less promote social change.

Ironically, even as the field is promoted and sponsored by picture agencies such as Magnum, and institutions such as The International Center of Photography, as well as hundreds of academic departments, it has lost power. Television cameras often exhaust the image-potential of a subject before photographs can be printed or even taken to the darkroom.

The cityscape of poverty is much more varied and meaningful than that captured by people-centered street photography. The speed of abandonment, the loss of neighborhoods, the growth of fortification, the spread of warehousing institutions, and changing tastes in interior decoration, graffiti, and murals are all unpredictable.

The visual and written record that I have begun enables us to mentally reconstruct neighborhoods that are disappearing and to better understand the lives of the inhabitants of shattered communities.

ACKNOWLEDGMENTS

This book would not have been possible without the support, over two decades, of my in-laws Charles, Virginia, Anthony, Gina, Gemma, and Stephen Pieroni. When I began, neither they nor I knew if this undertaking would bear fruit. They wondered who would be interested in looking at pictures of places they knew to be dangerous, ugly, and shunned, or in reading more accounts of the ghettos. Yet their doubts did not put a damper on their generosity.

My thanks go to Kea Tawana, the Ark builder of Newark, New Jersey. Tawana could find a clear and simple way to present a situation that I had photographed and felt to be important without knowing why. From her own life, she provided crucial details that helped to give concreteness to my descriptions. Lenny Hicks, a resident of the South Bronx, has been a cool, nonjudgmental, and cheerful friend.

I am fortunate to count as faithful support-

ers and friends Kenneth T. Jackson, Richard Plunz, Robert Fishman, George Carey, Herbert Gans, Sam Beck, Marshall Berman, Daniel Bluestone, and Peter Marcuse. I have repeatedly enjoyed their company on visits to poor neighborhoods, discussed with them my ideas, showed my photographs to them and their students, and recorded their responses. JoAnn Wypijewski, whose passion for older cities I share, edited sections of this book for prior publication in *The Nation*, raising difficult questions and offering valuable advice.

I wrote *The New American Ghetto* from the start as a book. Various sections have appeared, in slightly different form, in other publications, listed below, when editors found pieces interesting. *The Nation*, however, was different. JoAnn Wypijewski supported my work and style of writing, and often encouraged me to go beyond the limits I had set. She also persuaded the magazine to let me illustrate my articles, even though photographs seldom appear there.

"American Graffiti," *The Nation* (November 21, 1994).

"Archivist of Decline," *Columbia Journalism Review* (March 1995).

"Charlotte Street, South Bronx," *Assemblage* (August 1994).

"Detroit," *The Nation* (May 18, 1992).

"Downtown Detroit: American Acropolis or Vacant Land?" *Metropolis* (April 1995).

"Fleeting Images, Permanent Presences: The Visual Language of the Latino Ghetto," *Design Book Review* (Spring/Summer 1994).

"A Guide to the Ghettos," *The Nation* (March 15, 1993).

"Hell in a Very Tall Place," *The Atlantic* (September 1989).

"The New American Ghetto," *The Architectural Record* (November 1994).

"New York's New Ghettos," *The Nation* (June 17, 1991).

"178th Street and Vyse Avenue, 1980–1993," *The New York Times* (December 7, 1993).

"Our Fortified Ghettos," *The Nation* (January 31, 1994).

"Requiem for Columbus Homes: 'Dee Dee Was Here, Now She's Gone,'" *The Nation* (August 1, 1994).

"Savings & Woe: Repossessing Banks," *Metropolis* (October 1994).

"Traces of Life: The Visual Language of the Ghetto," *Print* (September/October 1993).

I am grateful to Marlie Wasserman, former editor in chief at Rutgers University Press, for her strong commitment to this book and for her clear vision of how to organize it, and to the present editor in chief, Leslie Mitchner, Marilyn Campbell, managing editor, and Tricia Politi, senior production coordinator, for their continuing commitment.

My dear wife, Professor Lisa Vergara, with her daily proximity and her firm grounding in the English language, was repeatedly pressed into confronting my prose. She was merciless when it came to the vagueness of my sentences, my tendency to repeat myself, and my groping efforts to give poetic expression to descriptions and interpretations. I was sent to look again at my photographs, to return to the sites, to rewrite my observations or to delete repetitiveness. Lisa was also extremely helpful in the selection of illustrations and the writing of captions. Her criticism sent me back to retake photographs, to replace or discard them. She made my work acceptable to magazine editors and book publishers, and for this I give thanks.

I have benefited from the generosity of the Graham Foundation (1987 and again in 1994) and the Rockefeller Foundation (1986). The Revson Foundation made me one of their Fellows in 1986, thus providing the opportunity to study for a year under the auspices of Columbia University's School of Architecture, Planning, and Preservation. I have twice been supported for this project by the Design Arts Program of the National Endowment for the Arts (1985 and 1988), for which I am deeply grateful.

"Blacks came to Gary. Whites fled—they would just as soon abandon and build someplace else than attempt to get along with blacks."

—JAMES B. LANE,

Professor of History,
Indiana University Northwest,
1994

ONE

INTRODUCTION

Sign for the Lincoln Motel in Newark, 1987. Abraham Lincoln and Martin Luther King are ubiquitous names in the ghetto for streets, cemeteries, schools, and, more recently, shelters. Malcolm X remarked in his autobiography that "in a strange city, to find the Negroes without asking where, you just check in the phone book for a 'Lincoln School.'" In Essex County, New Jersey, the largest shelters for homeless families are the Lincoln Motel in Newark and the Lincoln Motel in East Orange.

Ghettos, as intrinsic to the identity of the United States as New England villages, vast national parks, and leafy suburbs, nevertheless remain unique in their social and physical isolation from the nation's mainstream. Discarded and dangerous places, they are rarely visited by outsiders, becoming familiar to the larger population only through television and movies. Ghettos are pervaded by abandonment and ruin; they openly display crude defenses and abound in institutions and facilities that are rejected by "normal" neighborhoods. In these communities the walls have become surfaces on which to vent anger, to display models worthy of emulation, to represent African American and Latino culture, and to remember the dead.

The New American Ghetto blends description with meditation. My photographs are intended to offer a visual journey through cityscapes and interiors, accompanied by a narrative spun largely from my direct observation, accounts given by ghetto residents themselves, and historical records. Instead of starting with statistics on the number of people employed, on public assistance, incarcerated, or in school, I look at places: residential areas, vacant lots, institutions, factories, and their surroundings.

In their earnest pleas for the abolition of tenements and the construction of philanthropic housing and playgrounds, social reformers of the late nineteenth century expressed a belief in the power of urban environments to shape lives. Two generations later, architects and planners proclaimed their ability to design healthier and happier surroundings where human needs could be satisfied. Ironically, their rational designs, in the form of "towers in the park," now characterize troubled housing developments in cities

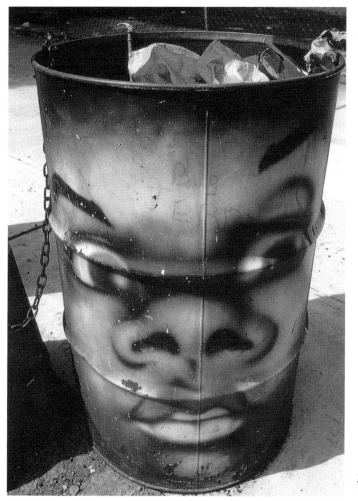

Garbage can, chain, and the face of a black youth come together in this metal drum. Central Ward, Newark, 1994.

throughout the nation. But today, when over-crowding and the deterioration of the urban fabric have re-created conditions prevalent in slums a century ago, the call to rebuild our cities lacks public resonance. Although the physical environment of the ghetto is becoming more fragmented, isolated, and hostile, we continue to neglect its influence on the people living there, and on ourselves.

For decades, poor, minority communities have been analyzed primarily through statistical data. For a more complete understanding we also need direct, sustained observation of this part of the urban ecology. Close attention to changes taking place in these settings undermines the sense of continuity that the numbers give us, revealing instead a profound transformation: the crystallization of an urbanism tolerant of ever greater inequality. Ghetto cityscapes, with their

dramatic changes in function, their starkness, and their sheer size, challenge us to ignore the human misery they represent. One inevitable conclusion of a closer look is that present policies lead to ever greater division, mistrust, and destitution.

Social justice, however, is not my only concern. I also study the emergence of new styles; discuss the ways in which ghettos contribute to our national identity; urge the development of policies regarding the clearing, preservation, restoration, and stabilization of ruins; and try to foster awareness of the loss of so much first-rate architecture. To document what is physically happening to American cities and explore the consequences, then, constitutes a realm of its own, one deserving much greater attention than it has so far received.

Martin, Ethel, and their baby were relocated from a well-run shelter to a city-managed building, one of the worst "crackhouses" in the South Bronx, 1989. Ethel "would rather be back in the shelter." A year later, a fire destroyed her apartment and she and the child went to live in a housing project with her grandmother.

A BRIEF HISTORY

"They call it a ghetto now, my old neighborhood in Newark. Ironically, it acquired that name only after the predominantly Jewish population moved out shortly after World War II. But when I was growing up, it was still a mostly Jewish community. My mother, like many of the Negro women, worked as a domestic in a Jewish home. I, like many of my black classmates, wore hand-me-downs from a well-to-do Jewish family."

—George Cureton,
"My Ghetto: A Backward Glance," 1993

Our large ghettos are the result of historical developments that have been proceeding for nearly a century. Up to World War I, urban black communities were small, and it was common for

blacks and whites to be neighbors. These mixed neighborhoods were often referred to by local names such as "New Guinea" on the tip of the North End of Boston, the "Black Belt" on Chicago's South Side, and "Bucktown" at the edge of Cincinnati's downtown. In New York City, poor white immigrant families, particularly those of Italian and Jewish heritage, often lived above black families who resided in the dark, damp cellars below. It was also common for whites and blacks to live on the same block but in separate buildings.

The character of black communities in America changed with the start of World War I. The need for unskilled labor for the expanding factories of the North, together with the mechanization of agriculture in the South and the abolition of the sharecropping system, created large masses of unemployed people, fueling a huge

Boy climbing the stairway, Columbus Homes, Newark, 1989.

migration of more than five million blacks who moved North during the seven decades starting in 1910.

Black communities in the North grew from a few thousand inhabitants to the tens and even hundreds of thousands. Chicago exemplifies these population changes. In 1910 there were no communities in which blacks made up more than 61 percent of the population, and more than two-thirds of blacks lived in areas where they composed less than 50 percent of the population. Yet this situation changed as 65,000 black migrants came to the city during the five years after 1915. By 1930 a large ghetto already had developed; now 63 percent of the black population lived in places where they constituted from 90 to 99 percent of the total residents.

Isolated from the facilities and services of the white community by distance and racial prejudice, ghettos developed their own kindergartens, orphanages, homes for the aged, settlement houses, and even hospitals. As the minority population grew, the boundaries of their settlements expanded into white neighborhoods, leading these residents to move to other areas or to form organized resistance.

The pre–civil rights ghetto in America included among its population minority professionals, affluent merchants, and middle-level entrepreneurs. Today, those who are able to flee have left. Now the vast majority of the population is unable to move elsewhere or is restricted in its movements to places they can afford, where public and subsidized housing, shelters, rooming houses, welfare offices, soup kitchens, and social services are available—that is, to other ghettos.

A new, more complex form of exclusion has developed. In a society where the suburb is

Large prison being built on the West Side of Chicago, 1991. Recent state plans emphasize the construction of shelters and prisons instead of homes.

the norm, the ghetto is now even more isolated, separated from wealthier neighborhoods either by transitional areas, or a succession of poor and blue-collar communities, or by physical barriers such as expressways, rail lines, and rivers.

In cities the distance between poor and wealthy urban areas has now been bridged, as homelessness and destitution have sent waves of beggars and wandering mentally ill people into spaces of affluence. Protected behind economic and legal barriers, and by their distance from poor communities, wealthy suburbs nevertheless continue to exclude poor and even well-off minorities. In 1993, for example, a survey of the Metro North evening trains taking corporate executives to their suburban homes in places like Rye, New York, and Greenwich, Connecticut, revealed an almost complete absence of black commuters.

THE STIGMA OF THE GHETTO

"You were born into a society which spelled out with brutal clarity, and in as many ways as possible, that you were a worthless human being. You were not expected to aspire to excellence; you were expected to make peace with mediocrity."

—James Baldwin,
The Fire Next Time, 1963

Over two decades ago, Harvard sociologist Lee Rainwater wrote eloquently about the stigmatizing and degrading effect of ghetto environments on their residents: "The physical evidence of trash, poor plumbing and the stink that goes with

6

Medical waste incinerator, South Bronx, 1991.

it, rats, and other vermin deepen [residents']
feelings of being moral outcasts. Their physical
world is telling them they are inferior and bad
just as effectively perhaps as do their human in-
teractions." According to Rainwater, childrear-
ing becomes an anxious and uncertain process:
Parents are unable to protect their children from
many miseries and even themselves may be a
source of miseries, leading children to lose faith,
and to regard their parents "as persons of relatively little consequence." Yet today, twenty-nine
years after Rainwater wrote the lines quoted
above, the influence of a physical environment
of destitution on people's lives is still neglected
by most social scientists.

Accepting the ghetto as home poses a tremendous paradox for people angry about the
condition of their surroundings yet afraid of being blamed for causing it. Many residents recol-

lect a time when the neighborhood was better.
They are often torn between fond memories of
how things once were, and their current desire to
have the problems of the place exposed. Albion,
a housing manager in Brooklyn, asked: "Who
wants to be told that they live at the very bottom,
in one of the worst places in the city, where the
police don't police, sanitation don't clean, where
there is no health department and people have a
'Wild West attitude'? If you think that of your
home, how can you keep your self-respect? What
will prevent you from committing suicide?"

Residents have developed explanations and
attitudes often characterized by resentment, anger, ambiguity, and contradictions. They usually
asked me the reason for my interest, and pre-
dicted that they'd be blamed for their circumstances. Moreover, residents mistrust outsiders
who, they believe, are likely to "trash" their

Billboard designed by the National Conference of Christians and Jews, Gary, 1991. These signs are common in Gary, Chicago, Detroit, the South Bronx, and other ghetto areas and in New York City subway stations. Since they are not displayed in white suburbs or in more affluent neighborhoods, their unintended message is that racism exists only in poor, minority communities.

neighborhoods while profiting from doing it.

In Chicago's Lawndale I ran into a young maintenance man who requested that I not use my photographs of the neighborhood against his "people." In East New York, Brooklyn, I was criticized for photographing "all the dirty spots." In Detroit I was repeatedly asked not to "make the city look grotesque," but to see ghettos in their larger contexts and to concentrate on "efforts to save the city." Upon informing a curious resident of the South Bronx that I was working on a book, he wanted to know if I was writing "the book of love or the book of hate." And, upon seeing me in Central Harlem photographing from the roof of a car, a young man expressed his mistrust by yelling: "You don't get it. You'll never get it."

At Altgeld Gardens, a Chicago Housing Authority project in South Riverdale (the city's poorest and most isolated neighborhood), I was admonished for nearly an hour by a group of elderly women, members of the local residents' council. They urged me to tell about the good things that were happening in their development. At the moment, I felt that they were trying to deny the drabness of the barrack-style buildings, the sealed-off facilities, the many boarded-up apartments, the broken-down playground decorated with characters from the Wizard of Oz, the shabby little library, empty of readers, and the extreme isolation of the project.

Yet with their arguments, they were not just overlooking an oppressive reality. They also wanted me to know that what I saw was not all there was, that it did not define them, and that, like other Americans, they aspired to and sometimes achieved a better life.

Teachers, social workers, and advocates for the poor feel uncomfortable with the word "ghetto," viewing it as a derogatory term that directs attention to violence, social disorganization, and shattered physical environments, while ignoring the energy and the "soul" that is there. The word, they argue, evokes images of victimization and social pathology, not of the institutions and the political and economic forces that have contributed so much to creating such environments. These critics prefer the terms "neighborhood" or "community," sometimes adding the qualifier "destabilized" to designate extremely disorganized and violent examples.

I find "community" misleading, however. It conveys a sense of a place like any other, masking the dreadfulness of the daily surroundings, the breakdown of social order, and the confinement, often compared to imprisonment, experienced by many residents. To Joe Moody, a lifelong resident of the Central Ward of Newark, the word "community" once meant "when everybody was concerned about everybody in the area." Today "community is the area"—that is, simply a place. Further, the term "community" suggests acceptance of these environments. The walls in such areas are often inscribed with the word "ghetto" yet never the word "community." Rappers and academics alike have fixed on the term.

Thus, although I respect others' reservations about the term "ghetto," I use it to highlight the exclusion of so many poor, minority people from mainstream society. I want to describe the size and strength of the barriers we have built to separate citizens, and also to map the changing territory, while recording the experience of living on the other side of these boundaries. My work is not directed to residents of poor, minority neighborhoods—they have lived what I chronicle—but to those unfamiliar with the ghetto.

In portraying vacant land, ruins, and fearsome structures, I do not intend to demean people, deny their strivings and successes, ignore their desire to have a regular job and a decent, safe place to live, nor to imply that they are helpless victims of circumstances, unable to shape their own lives. Rather, I believe that if we as a nation are determined to do so, we can transform poor, minority ghettos into nurturing neighborhoods.

MEMORIES AND BLAME

Ghettos are important depositories of the nation's past, containing vestiges of its former wealth, of its capacity to make possible "the good life," and of its power to shape the future. Such remains include the long broad streets of Chicago, Cleveland, and Detroit, with their imposing mansions, entertainment palaces (now sleeping like enormous turtles), or the railroad underpasses, yards, and lines that slice the city in all directions.

Among those confined to ghettos are many residents who have been displaced. Former homes, where they spent their youth and raised a family, have become ruins or vacant lots. Cora Moody, the president of the tenants' association at the Hayes Homes in the Central Ward of Newark, lived for ten years in a now-derelict building, part of the Hayes development, that she calls "a piece of my history." Contrasting with what remains—the stinking vacant structure, with its broken windows and its entrance full of garbage and excrement—is the vital community that the building once anchored: "I was pregnant with my fifth child when I moved in there. I can see my kids playing hopscotch, I can hear them outside my window, calling up for money." Pointing to a littered, overgrown spot on the grounds, she says: "There used to be a shower there. My kids would use it at all times during the summer, even at midnight, and I would not be worried. There were public telephones in here; you could use them. You could wait, you did not have to get your own phone right away. We did not have to worry about people hurting us. There was a community in there of people you could trust and got along with." Cora explains why she sees the ruined building with so much affection, saying: "You cannot shift memories to another place. These are my greatest memories. They took all that away from us when they closed the building." The present is inscribed on a wall nearby: "Shahonna Tovheedah in the motherfucking house. If you don't like it kiss my ass."

Before becoming ghettos, most of the

Mural of the IRT #6 subway on a city-owned abandoned building, Mott Haven, South Bronx, 1991. The skyline of the city of lights, a river, and the clean silvery train are sandwiched between cinder-blocked windows and a dirty sidewalk. This subway line connects the richest neighborhoods of Manhattan with the poorest sections of the South Bronx.

neighborhoods represented here had a predominantly white population. Many of those former residents with whom I spoke were hesitant to discover the present condition of their childhood homes, churches, schools, and movie theaters, places they had not visited in decades. Often they were afraid to receive confirmation that those places had vanished.

Emotions among former residents are raw. In Gary, Indiana, for example, a city that a quarter of a century ago elected one of the first black mayors in the nation, the bitterness and animosity between whites and blacks is intense. The election led to massive white flight and to the creation of a new suburb, Merrillville. The pain caused by the perceived loss of one's city was eloquently expressed by David Barrick, a Gary-born realtor, in 1976: "It seems like everyone wants to leave. I feel like an outcast in my own hometown. I don't want to live here. I don't like working here. And, most of all, I feel like they

don't want me here." I remember similar feelings of anger and exclusion expressed by a retired schoolteacher as he lead me on a tour of Gary, all along describing the heyday of places now ruined and blaming the black residents for it.

The question of blame comes up constantly. At public programs discussing my work, people in the audience repeatedly urged me to look for the perpetrators: the executives who moved their businesses from poor communities; the real estate brokers who fostered panic among white homeowners, their intention being to buy homes cheap and sell them at inflated prices to minority families; the banks and insurance companies that redlined inner city neighborhoods where blacks and Latinos were replacing exiting whites. Receiving the greatest blame, though, is the federal government, which built the highways to the suburbs, thus lowering the cost of doing business outside the city; which insured mortgages for mostly white new-home buyers,

Herd of stampeding elephants painted on the wall facing an empty lot, Finesse Arts, West Side, Detroit, 1991. A ghetto resident explains the mural: "Because of its size, its strength, and its ability, the elephant is a symbol of power. Those elephants are rampaging as they come across this empty, wasted lot. The more weeds you have growing up on the lot the more it looks like the elephants are coming through the jungle."

making the extensive post–World War II suburbanization possible; which encouraged building factories in the suburbs for reasons of national defense; which gave incentives to companies to construct new facilities and to abandon old ones before their productive life had ended.

Fortunately, these issues have been dealt with well by historians who have researched the role of the federal government in the inner cities and its support of suburbanization (Charles Abrams, Kenneth T. Jackson, Robert Fishman). Others have chronicled the rise and development of ghettos such as Harlem, Cleveland, Chicago, Philadelphia, and Gary (Jervis Anderson, Kenneth Kusmer, Arnold Hirsch, W.E.B. Du Bois, James B. Lane). And there are hundreds of accounts by journalists of real estate scandals that destabilized neighborhoods. The deindustrialization of America and its resulting loss of jobs is another well-researched topic (Barry Bluestone and Bennett Harrison). Finally, there is no issue

more pressing than the living conditions of children in these communities (Alex Klotowitz). But with the exception of urban geographers and anthropologists, social scientists have shunned the streets, wary of researching topics that are difficult to quantify and unlikely to lead to grants, academic publication, and promotion.

By recording the voices and the looks of ghettos I hope to help rescue from oblivion a part of this nation's history and to capture the world that the survivors themselves are shaping. The country needs an accurate image of the ghetto with which to devise national policies of reform, and to evaluate our progress we need to interview residents and monitor their surroundings. We need to ask from our plans and programs nothing less than the transformation of our poor, minority communities, and the breaking down of their walls.

TWO

THE GHETTO CITYSCAPE

(Above) A section of Fern Street, semi-abandoned, yet with most of its row houses still standing. North Camden, 1979.

(Center) Dirt scattered by housing demolitions give Fern Street the look of an unpaved road. Interior walls are now exposed, showing the color of the former rooms. The majority of the dwellings have been demolished and half of those remaining are abandoned. North Camden, 1988.

If you were among the nearly eleven thousand people who lived in two-story row houses in North Camden in the 1960s, you could walk to work at Esterbrook Pen, at Knox Gelatin, at RCA, or at J. R. Evans Leather. You could shop on Broadway, a busy three-mile-long commercial thoroughfare, nicknamed the "Street of Lights" because of its five first-run movie theaters with their bright neon signs.

After J. R. Evans Leather was abandoned and almost completely demolished, its smokestack stood alone in a vast field by the Delaware River, a symbol of the demise of industry in Camden. Hundreds of row houses—once counted among the best ordinary urban dwellings in America—have been scooped up by bulldozers, their debris carted to a dump in Delaware. Walking along North Camden's narrow streets, one passes entire blocks without a single structure, the empty land crisscrossed by foot-

paths. The scattered dwellings that remain are faced with iron bars, so that they resemble cages.

With nearly half of its overwhelmingly Latino population on some form of public assistance, this once thriving working-class neighborhood is now the poorest urban community in New Jersey. In 1986, former mayor Alfred Pierce called Camden a reservation for the destitute. The north section of the city has become the drug center for South Jersey, and it hosts a large state prison.

North Camden is not unique. Since the riots of the 1960s, American cities have experienced profound transformations, best revealed in the spatial restructuring of their ghettos and in the emergence of new urban forms. During the past decade, however, the "underclass" and homelessness have dominated the study of urban poverty. Meanwhile, the power of the physical surroundings to shape lives, to mirror people's

existence, and to symbolize social relations has been ignored. When scholars from across the political spectrum discuss the factors that account for the persistence of poverty, they fail to consider its living environments. And when prescribing solutions, they overlook the very elements that define the new ghettos: the ruins and the semi-ruins; the medical, warehousing, and behavior-modification institutions; the various NIMBYs, fortresses, and walls; and, not least, the bitterness and anger resulting from living in these places.

Dismissing the value of information received through sight, taste, and smell, or through the emotional overtones in an informant's voice, or from the sensation of moving through the spaces studied, has led to the creation of constructs without character, individuality, or a sense of place. And although the limitations of statistical data—particularly when dealing with very poor populations—are widely acknowledged, our great dependency on numbers is fiercely defended. Other approaches are dismissed as impressionistic, anecdotal, as poetry, or "windshield surveys."

Yet today's ghettos are diverse, rich in public and private responses to the environment, in expressions of cultural identity, and in reminders of history. These communities are uncharted territory; to be understood, their forms need to be identified, described, inventoried, and mapped.

An examination of scores of ghettos across the nation reveals three types: "green ghettos," characterized by depopulation, vacant land overgrown by nature, and ruins; "institutional ghettos," publicly financed places of confinement designed mainly for the native-born; and "new immigrant ghettos," deriving their character from an influx of immigrants, mainly Latino and West Indian. Some of these communities

The surviving houses have fenced porches and their rough sides have been smoothed out with a covering of cement. Weeds grow on the sidewalk in front of clusters of abandoned houses, and people and dogs walk in the middle of the street. This block of Fern Street, where less than 20 percent of the original houses remain occupied, exemplifies the dismantling of the city. North Camden, 1994.

15

Gang members portrayed on the stairwell wall of a housing project, Bedford-Stuyvesant, Brooklyn, 1992. Graffiti warns: "The Outlaws are Breaking Loose" and declares, next to the stalking gunman: "Animal Motherfucker Die!!" Upon seeing this image, a resident of a Brooklyn ghetto commented: "Somebody put the posse up on the wall; there is the main man at the center. It looks like a showdown, with the dude on the right setting up a drop."

have continued to lose population; others have emerged where a quarter-century ago there were white ethnic blue-collar neighborhoods; and sections of older ghettos have remained stable, working neighborhoods or have been rebuilt.

THE GREEN GHETTO: RETURN TO WILDERNESS?

Green ghettos, where little has been done to counter the effect of disinvestment, abandonment, depopulation, and dependency, are the leftovers of a society. Best exemplified by North Camden, Detroit's East Side, Chicago's Lawndale, and East St. Louis in Illinois, they are expanding outward to include poor suburbs of

large cities such as Robbins, Illinois, and are even found in small cities such as Benton Harbor, Michigan.

Residents, remembering the businesses that moved to suburban malls, the closed factories, the fires, complain of living in a threatening place bereft of jobs and stores and neglected by City Hall. In many sections of these ghettos, pheasants and rabbits have regained the space once occupied by humans, yet these are not wilderness retreats in the heart of the city. "Nothing but weeds are growing there," is a frequent complaint about vacant lots, expressing no mere distaste for the vegetation, but moral outrage at the neglect that produces these anomalies. Plants grow wildly on and around the vestiges of the former International Harvester Component Plant in West Pullman, Chicago. Derelict industrial buildings here and in other ghettos have long ago been stripped of anything of value. Large

Transition House, an early model shelter, Skid Row, Los Angeles, 1985.

In a once crowded area west of Rosa Parks Boulevard (formerly Twelfth Street) the 1967 Detroit riot began. This neighborhood in a 1987 photograph resembles the Midwestern prairie.

parcels of land lie unkempt or paved over, subtracted from the life of the city. Contradicting a long-held vision of our country as a place of endless progress, ruins, once unforeseen, are now ignored.

INSTITUTIONAL GHETTOS: THE NEW POORHOUSES

In New York City, Newark, and Chicago, large and expensive habitats—institutional ghettos—have been created for the weakest and most vulnerable members of our society. Institution by institution, facility by facility, these environments have been assembled in the most drug-infested and destitute parts of cities. They are the

complex poorhouses of the twenty-first century, places to store a growing marginal population officially certified as "not employable." Residents are selected from the entire population of the municipality for their lack of money or home, for their addictions, for their diseases and other afflictions. Nonresidents come to these institutions to pick up medications, surplus food, used clothes; to get counseling or training; or to do a stint in prison. Other visitors buy drugs and sex.

As Greg Turner, the manager of a day shelter on the Near West Side of Chicago, puts it: "They say, 'Let's get them off the streets and put them together in groups.' It is like the zoo: we are going to put the birds over here; we are going to put the reptiles over there; we are going to put the buffalo over here; we are going to put the seals by the pool. It is doing nothing to work with the root of the problem, just like they do

Sterling Street, Newark, 1980.

nothing to work with the children, to teach them things so they don't grow up and become more homeless people or substance abusers."

Although the need for individual components—for instance, a homeless shelter or a waste incinerator—may be subject to public debate, the overall consequences of creating such "campuses" of institutions are dismissed. The most important barrier to their growth is the cost to the taxpayers of building and maintaining them.

Such sections of the city are not neighborhoods. The streets surrounding Lincoln Park in south Newark, for example, an area that includes landmark houses, grand public buildings, and a once-elegant hotel, were chosen by two drug treatment programs because six of its large mansions would provide inexpensive housing for a residential treatment program. On the northwest

corner of the park, a shelter for battered women just opened in another mansion, and a block north in a former garage is a men's shelter and soup kitchen. The largest structures overlooking the park, the hotel and a former federal office building, house the elderly, who fear going out by themselves. No children play in the park; no parents come home from work. This is a no-man's-land devoted to the contradictory goals of selling drugs and getting high, on the one hand, and becoming clean and employed on the other.

NEW IMMIGRANT GHETTOS: DYNAMIC AND FLUID

In other parts of New York and Chicago a community of recent immigrants is growing up, but

Sterling Street replaced by a parking lot, 1994.

this type of ghetto is most visible in South Central Los Angeles and Compton, where the built environment is more intimate than in older ghettos, the physical structures are more adaptable, and it is easier for newcomers to imprint their identity. Here paint goes a long way to transform the appearance of the street.

The new immigrant ghettos are characterized by tiny offices providing services such as driving instruction, insurance, and immigration assistance; by stores that sell imported beer, produce, and canned goods; and by restaurants offering home cooking. Notable are the businesses that reflect the busy exchange between the local population and their native country: money transfers, travel agencies, even funeral homes that arrange to have bodies shipped home.

To get by, most residents are forced to resort to exploitative jobs paying minimum wage or less and usually lacking health benefits. For housing they crowd together in small, badly maintained apartments, in cinder-block garages, or in trailers.

Not being eligible for public or city-owned housing may in the long run prove to be a blessing for the newcomers. Although forced to pay high rents, immigrants tend to concentrate in neighborhoods that are part of the urban economy, thus avoiding the extreme social disorganization, isolation, and violence that characterize other types of ghettos. Because of the huge influx of young people with expectations that life will be better for their children and grandchildren, these ghettos are more dynamic and fluid, resembling the foreign-born communities of a century ago.

"Swing low, sweet chariot, comin' for to carry me home." Rusting black Cadillac, its heavy weight resting on flat tires, Gary, Indiana, 1990.

Busses—silvery, aerodynamic, part of a 1950s vision of the future, symbols of comfort, speed, and modernity, with the power to cross continents—since 1989 these two have sat idle in a small fenced lot in Brownsville, Brooklyn. In need of new motors and transmissions, they're up for sale, 1994.

BEHIND GHETTO WALLS, A COMMON FATE

No single ghetto is completely green, institutional, or immigrant in character. Although the overwhelming trend is toward greater waste, abandonment, and depopulation, these three models are related, channeling people and land to one another. Fires and demolitions in the green ghettos provide large tracts of cleared land where poverty institutions and other facilities can be built. By default, the most desperate people and neighborhoods become wards of the government in communities where, in the words of a Brooklyn organizer, "All the social disasters of the city are located."

If nothing is done to prevent it, within a decade more working-class communities are likely to belong to one of these types. Conversely, some institutional ghettos, such as the Near West Side of Chicago, are likely to be squeezed out by expanding sports and medical complexes. And the same forces of abandonment that open the way for the modern poorhouses can at other times free land for townhouses built for working families.

These are the "reclaimed ghettos." With their horror stories of violence, governmental incompetence, and waste, ghettos are used to provide strong moral justification for privately managed programs of redevelopment. Under the leadership of churches, community development organizations, private developers, and recent im-

Two lampposts with their lights on, and two others with their lights off, mark the perimeter of locomotive 765, Gary, Indiana, 1988. Going nowhere, standing on a few feet of tracks, but still powerful and whole, it contrasts with the broken and disappearing city. One of the original engines that hauled steel in and out of the Gary Works plant, 765 is now an outdoor sculpture.

migrants, such ghettos have kicked out most of the dependent poor and have refused to admit the institutions that serve them. Instead, they focus on attracting working families, keeping out drug dealers, and building guarded enclaves.

These communities are on the verge of melding into mainstream society. But when examining the contribution of community development corporations, we need to ask ourselves whether their efforts arc leading to the elimination of ghettos, or toward the creation of mini-cities of exclusion within the larger wasteland.

For it is at the boundaries that the individual character of ghettos reveals itself most clearly: around embattled clusters of dwellings where ethnic groups assert themselves, in blocks where strong buildings share a wall with dilapidated crackhouses, and along the perimeter of hospitals, universities, and other citadels. Bor-

ders where white meets black are stark, presenting a graphic contrast between a seemingly victorious white community and what appears to be a defeated minority community. Along Mack Avenue, as it crosses from Detroit's East Side into affluent Grosse Pointe, for example, and along Chicago's East Sixty-second Street, the border between Woodlawn and Hyde Park (home of the University of Chicago), a history of race relations has been written into the landscape. Security barriers, guards, dead-end streets, well-tended lawns on one side; on the other, vacant lots, abandoned buildings, out-of-work people hanging out.

Writers for the popular press call ghettos intractable, expressing concern about the public burden they impose. The system works for those who are motivated, many outsiders say, pointing to the presence of minorities in more affluent suburbs, to reclaimed ghettos, and to the economic success of recent West Indian, Latino, and Asian immigrants.

But among many ghetto dwellers, particularly native-born African Americans, there is growing ideological hardening and a yearning to close ranks, to reemerge from destitution and to prosper among themselves. A journalist in Gary, Indiana, a city almost completely abandoned by whites, remarked: "I don't know why people have to have white people to succeed." A Chicago construction worker called blacks who moved to the suburbs "imitation white people." A Newark woman suggested that such people have sold out, are living a lie. "They need to take a good look in the mirror," she said. Also in Newark, on the walls of the abandoned Macy's department store, graffiti by "The Natural Thebians" complains: "How can you talk about nation time and wear the underwear of your enemy!"

Echoing Malcolm X, most ghetto residents I have encountered see the devastation and violence in their communities as part of a white strategy of domination. Drugs are widely perceived as part of a monstrous plot to destroy and contain poor blacks and Latinos. A Chicago minister states: "White supremacy, a system of oppression that comes out of Western society, is the real problem." A Brooklyn artist declares: "People of color have a right to be paranoid." A national mood of desperation and resentment, expressed by words like "genocide," "concentration camps," and "apartheid," has developed to account for the conditions of our ghettos.

Within ghetto walls a new generation is growing along with new activities, ideologies, institutions, and drugs. Crack sells briskly across the street from drug treatment centers, and children walk past homeless shelters. An army of men strips cars, and hordes of scavengers push loaded shopping carts along the streets. Houses, turned into fortresses, stand alone, enclosed by fences. Dozens of cities are falling into ruin, and along their streets billboards plead for people to stop killing one another.

Today, there is renewed talk of strategies to bring jobs, to improve education, to build better housing, and to provide adequate health care for all Americans. Such developments would certainly improve the conditions in poor communities, but would not change their isolation, racial composition, and fragmentation. Ghettos would continue to expand, new ones to emerge, and the anger of their residents would remain unabated.

Public policy must also address the unique characteristics of our ghettos. A crucial step is to change policies and practices that concentrate in these communities the poor and the institutions that serve them. We need regional and national approaches to population redistribution, such as the building of low-income housing in wealthy suburbs and the elimination of the barriers that define ghettos. And as we once did in the 1960s, we need to convince ourselves that as a nation we have the power not just to improve the ghetto, but to abolish it. To do this we must go beyond the statistics and into the streets, alleys, and buildings.

In reply to those for whom dreams of a more just society have lost their power, and to those who believe that ghettos are necessary to have strong communities elsewhere, stand the haunting, defiant, and despairing words scribbled on the stairway of an East Harlem high-rise: "Help me before I die, motherfucker!"

(Above) Replica of Colleoni, *a Renaissance equestrian statue by Andrea Verrocchio, Newark, 1989. The original is still in Venice. "In the neighborhood, that is Columbus," a local resident explained. "We find the statue offensive. They should replace it with Marcus Garvey."*

(Left) Theodore Roosevelt, *"American," statue placed in front of the Congregational Church by the Benton County Republicans, Benton Harbor, Michigan, 1991.*

FRAGMENTS OF THE PAST PRESERVED

"Thomas Roosevelt, the guy that invented the telephone."

—Teenager,
identifying a statue of Theodore Roosevelt in front of the Congregational Church in Benton Harbor, Michigan, 1991

American ghettos preserve the remains of a once-powerful urban civilization, left behind when the previous residents, mostly white, moved outward. In the ghetto's industrial and domestic structures, its institutions, public spaces, and monuments, one encounters traces of a vanished power elite and outmoded forms of production. Gone, too, is the kind of energy that once brought these fragments together into cities that cohered. Churches, markers, statues, and historic houses stand as isolated ghosts of the past, survivors representing a collective identity that has long ceased to have meaning for the residents. Instead of the expensive, permanent monuments that expressed community values, today's statements are much more short-lived, taking the form of murals, graffiti, and billboards.

The True Holiness Temple, built in 1916 on the east side of Cleveland as a Christian Science church, illustrates the precarious existence of even the most solid and imposing edifices. From a church that could seat nineteen hundred people, it became—with the addition of a large stage—the home of the Cleveland Playhouse. Saved from demolition because of its landmark status, the congregation of the True Holiness Temple bought the theater a decade ago for the price of a comfortable family house. "It was the plan of the Lord for us to have it," says Bishop Dixon, the pastor. Stripping had begun, yet the

(Left) Elegant townhouse now standing alone, its edges jagged and debris scattered in the front yard, South Side, Chicago, 1980.

(Right) Simple cross placed by the highway to commemorate a tragic automobile accident that occurred there three decades ago, Gary, 1991. A plaque explaining the reason for the monument has been removed, leaving the cross standing for the dying city.

church managed to retrieve the chandeliers and a spiral staircase that had already been removed. Bishop Dixon speaks proudly of his lavish temple: "This building has the largest dome in diameter in Cleveland. The acoustics are superb. You don't even need a microphone. They have a whole lot of marble in here, they got marble going down the basement steps, so they put a whole lot of unnecessary money into it."

More often the past survives in far humbler forms. On a Brooklyn sidewalk, in Brownsville, among many reminders of the past lies a rectangular set of worn-down and broken white tiles enclosing the name of the long-demolished Palace Theatre. Lying on the ground in a park in Benton Harbor, Michigan, a marker for a tree planted to honor the memory of the Grand Army of the Republic has outlived the tree itself. In Carver Middle School, in Chicago's isolated

South Riverdale, where improvements are rare, a wall bears the following inscription from 1945: "No man who continues to add something to the material, intellectual, and moral well-being of the place in which he lives is long left without a proper reward. Booker T. Washington."

Only the largest and heaviest statues remain intact. In Newark, just three blocks west of Lincoln Park, a bronze statue of the "doughboy," a popular symbol of the American soldier in World War I, was stolen, leaving behind an empty pedestal. A resident laughingly told me: "A dude came up with a tow truck, lassoed that sucker with a piece of wire rope, and pulled it down. When they found it in a basement in Hunterdon Street, the arms and legs had been chopped and sold to the junkyard." Even the century-old statue of P. T. Barnum, Bridgeport, Connecticut's most famous resident, had its four

Former Cleveland Playhouse, built in 1916, now the True Holiness Temple, 1992.

Former headquarters of Mutual Benefit Life, later Essex Catholic High School, Newark, 1985.

bronze plaques stolen in 1992. The plaques depicted a jolly funeral procession, with schoolchildren skipping happily along.

Past ideals and present realities contrast in the once-elegant Lincoln Park section of Newark. The replica of Verrocchio's famous equestrian statue of the commanding Venetian general Colleone erected almost a century ago by the city's business elite looks down from its tall pedestal on residents of the drug treatment centers, shelters, and SROs now surrounding the park.

Prominently displayed at Detroit's main intersection, a statue from the recent past, "The Spirit of Detroit," depicts a young Caucasian male holding a family group in one hand and a globe in the other. Nicknamed "The Green Giant," the bronze statue is replicated on the doors of garbage trucks, police cars, and on the predominantly black city's official letterhead.

Buildings reveal the legacy of ethnic groups that once lived in the neighborhood. Slavs in the Hough section of Cleveland and in Gary, Indiana, have left their churches in all-black neighborhoods. These religious structures, now serving Baptist congregations, have cinder-blocked windows while keeping their picturesque green onion domes and Slavic crosses. Synagogues are everywhere, often derelict and sometimes recycled. On the facade, the Star of David, the Tablets of the Law, and Hebrew lettering coexist with the cross and signs in English. Surprisingly, in the late 1890s in the West End of Boston, the reverse process took place; as a black neighborhood was rapidly transformed into a Jewish one, the neighborhood's two black churches became temples.

In most of our large cities, German Ameri-

Colonial mansion built by Governor William Shirley in the 1740s, Roxbury, Boston, 1983.

Mark Twain's substantial Victorian house in Hartford, designed by architect Edward Tuckerman Potter and completed in 1874. The interiors were decorated by the Tiffany company. For many years the house was a branch of the Hartford Public Library, and since the early 1970s it has been a museum. Hartford, 1993.

cans have left huge ruined breweries. In Newark, for example, the Krueger Brewery, closed since Prohibition and recently dynamited, had full-size trees growing on its roof. Oddly grafted onto a minuscule section of the brewery's ground floor was a day-care center. I was reminded of the shepherd's hovels and small shops erected within the ruins of Rome's great monuments after that empire fell.

It is a strange coincidence that the homes of two of the greatest figures of American literature are in ghettos. Walt Whitman's modest two-story row house, in Camden, bought in 1884 for $1,800, is now dwarfed by the new county prison across the street. Mark Twain's Victorian mansion in North Hartford is situated on a hill in a spacious lot, now neighbor to tough Hartford High School, and two blocks away from South Marshall Street, one of the most violent streets in the city.

NATURE TAKING OVER

"This was a good neighborhood, the best neighborhood around here, there used to be stores all around, we had everything."

—Calvin Earle,
elderly resident, Camden, N.J., 1982

The most dramatic shift in most ghetto neighborhoods since the 1950s is a sharp decline in population. Detroit, which in 1950 had 1.85 million inhabitants, by the next decade had lost a quarter of a million people, and by 1990 had only one million. Patterns in individual neighborhoods are particularly startling. Two decades ago, for example, the blocks around Detroit's Twelfth Street, now Rosa Parks Boulevard, where the

Hutchins Cole, a retired construction worker originally from Georgia, is harvesting the corn crop he grows on two contiguous empty lots, Rosa Parks Boulevard, Detroit, 1987.

IRT elevated train traveling above an open field of weeds, South Bronx, 1989.

View north of the Hough section of Cleveland, 1985.

Vacant lots bordering West Madison Street, Chicago, 1988. Chicory, thistles, and Queen Anne's lace grow here. Instead of trees, billboards advertising liquor and cigarettes sprout.

(Above, left) Small children walking through the vacant lots of their ruined neighborhood, South Side, Chicago, 1988. Here the dangerous forest of classic fairy tales is replaced by the gang-ridden, decaying city.

(Above, right) Children returning from Prairie Avenue, South Side, Chicago, 1993.

(Right) Under the words "Your mother didn't raise you to be a drunk," the sweating face of a hollering black youth presides over a desolate stretch of Clinton Avenue, Central Ward, Newark, 1995. Intended by its corporate sponsors to discourage drunkenness, the void of the youth's gaping mouth echoes the empty cityscape beyond. The agitated young man in this billboard should be shouting, "My mother didn't raise me to live in a ghetto."

1967 riot started, made up the most crowded residential neighborhood in the city. In 1993, after fires, abandonment, and decades of neglectful municipal policy, it is common to see raccoons, turtle doves, and pheasants moving around in the tall grass. The elevated trains, expressways, and skyscrapers come as a surprise in these landscapes.

Residents of poor communities intensely fear and dislike empty lots, seeing them as public garbage dumps, breeding grounds for rats, places to "get high"—wasted spaces that are dark and dangerous at night. Empty land serving no useful social purpose conveys the message that people and their community are unwanted and forgotten.

Physically and psychologically residents try to separate themselves from their surroundings. Living isolated behind locked doors, bars, and tall fences, they often remain attached to the memory of a neighborhood that exists only in their minds. Although most residents are resourceful and do what they can to keep up their homes, they feel overwhelmed by the trash, abandonment, and violence surrounding them. Their lack of trust in government is often justified, yet they cling to the hope that the city will revive.

VIEWS FROM HIGH PLACES

"The surroundings have an effect on you. You see a mess here, you see a mess there and that has an effect on you."

—Reverend Bobby Wright,
Newark, 1981

Out of large, snow-covered lots rise a few surviving buildings, within sight of Chicago's skyline of giant corporate towers. Near West Side, 1989.

Under a wide sky, the landscape of the ghetto becomes part of the intricate geometry of the city. A lofty viewpoint directs our attention to the built environment. Removed from people, their voices and facial expressions, we can concentrate on the form of these communities: their borders, the movement of people and vehicles, and their proximity to lakes, rivers, parks, and the skyscrapers downtown.

The contrast between places that are abandoned and those that have been reclaimed and fenced is striking. The garbage between buildings, the cars and buses left covered by weeds on vacant lots, and the gardens hidden from the street are revealed. In these landscapes mothers walk with small children tagging along, teenagers play ball, addicts buy their drugs through holes on a wall or go into abandoned buildings to purchase them. On leveled blocks, people walk along diagonal footpaths, or down the

middle of the streets to avoid overgrown and broken sidewalks or groups of threatening teenagers. From this perspective, it is police cars, ambulances, firetrucks, and screeching elevated trains that provide the soundtrack.

History reveals itself in layers of development and redevelopment ranging from the fancy and elaborate buildings of the turn of the century to the stripped-down structures designed for the poor several generations later. Along the sides of expressways that once cut deep through the fabric of the city one can see examples of landscaping. Here, hardy shrubs, grasses, small trees, and sometimes wildflowers are planted and cared for to give pleasure to those passing through, while above in the empty lots nature grows wild.

On the South Side of Chicago, an unofficial museum of urban planning, surviving examples of various styles lie before our eyes. Scattered among patches of vacant land we can still see

North Camden, row houses, by the Delaware River, 1992. A front stoop, a brick facade, and three windows face the street. Inside are four or more rooms; in the back a yard for planting, socializing, and enjoying the breeze. A third of these dwellings, about one thousand units, have been demolished, or are burnt, stripped, and full of trash, useful only to drug dealers.

A disconnected environment: surviving townhouses and housing projects amid empty lots, South Side Chicago, 1990.

A chaotic urban landscape, Bedford-Stuyvesant, Brooklyn, 1989, consisting of vacant land, small groups of surviving frame houses, tenements, large apartment buildings, a tall Gothic church, and an abandoned school and its playground, resembles a gigantic back lot with abandoned sets waiting to be properly arranged elsewhere.

A very depressed section of Central Harlem, 1994, is nevertheless crowded with buildings, a rare example of a ghetto area with few vacant lots.

Ornate entrance to former Aidlin Automation, Inc., Brownsville, Brooklyn, 1981.

Eight years later, the same entrance, boarded up and cinder-blocked, Brownsville, Brooklyn, 1989.

Thirteen years later an attempt has been made to secure the building by installing a metal curtain, Brownsville, Brooklyn, 1994. Graffiti in Spanish says, "I am."

rows of elegant townhouses along wide avenues, followed by more modest dwellings and apartment buildings. In the distance rise the tall slabs of housing authority projects, abandoned factories, and subsidized housing for the elderly. And along Lake Michigan lies Hyde Park, with the stone neo-Gothic buildings of the University of Chicago, a fortresslike environment that escaped the devastation of its surroundings.

THE DOORS OF THE GHETTO

"These premises are protected by extreme poverty."

—Sticker from *Mad* magazine placed on the front door of an apartment in a Newark housing project, Scudder Homes, 1987

In their function of connecting street to interior, building entrances make abrupt and often jarring transitions to the inside, signaling a clash between past aspirations and present realities. The large, heavy, embellished portals of many older buildings frequently have been replaced by small, rectangular, inexpensive steel ones, with the remainder of the original entry space simply filled in.

Welcoming lions, festoons, and flowers along archways and pilasters are contradicted by the small, harsh new doors. Seashells, a classical symbol of eternity, end up around openings that have been sealed, ruined, or torn down. Urns are often found above cinder blocks or metal gates.

Seals protecting the entrances to abandoned buildings are usually broken, allowing the interiors to be used as public bathrooms, as homes for squatters, as places to sell drugs, and

(This page, left) Woman addict entering an abandoned building on Vyse Avenue, South Bronx, 1989, to go to a crackhouse in the basement.

(This page, right) Entrance to abandoned building, Brownsville, Brooklyn, 1990.

(Opposite page, left) Turnstiles are used to limit access to the courtyard of this Newark building, 1993.

(Opposite page, center) Cinderella entrance, ready to shed its rust, open its door wide, and display its former glory, Detroit, 1994.

(Oppposite page, right) Bolted iron door contrasts with the original palatial look of this building, Harlem, New York, 1992.

as gigantic garbage containers. Doorways are often littered with dead animals, tires, washing machines, kitchen equipment, mattresses, and other discarded objects.

In contrast to the middle-class dwellings handed down to the poor, the newer buildings, designed for low-income residents, have flat, linear entrances. Their bland exteriors are broken only by an abundance of graffiti, supplying, with its curves and colors, ad hoc decoration.

Housing projects and other, newer structures built with public assistance have doors that rarely lock and are often vandalized. In a Newark development, sets of metal doors brightly painted red to deter scavengers were nonetheless stolen and sold for scrap. In a South Bronx project a first-floor resident, kept awake by creaking doors, proceeded to remove them, leaving the building wide open.

In recently completed institutions, entrances are often located on the side of the building and barely visible. All wall, these "crime-proof" structures, designed like safes, appear inaccessible and hostile. In private homes and

buildings, a short locked hallway resembling a cage is added on the sidewalk to limit access to the structure and to prevent people from selling drugs or tampering with the mail. In some high-rises, access is limited by a fenced perimeter where the entrance is through guarded turnstiles.

In particularly dangerous locations, doors have so many locks that a significant part of the day must be spent searching for and turning keys. And inside, empty apartments containing evidence for drug trials are sealed with heavy chains, bolts, and locks. Bullet holes, a reminder

to residents of their deadly surroundings and of their vulnerability, mark entrances to violent buildings.

In this unpredictable environment, people frequently seek help from religion and magic. Apartment doors may be personalized with stickers, images, statues, and signs. A door in the South Bronx displays a large Sacred Heart of Jesus and a St. George Slaying the Dragon, among several other holy cards, as protection from evil; another doorway is reached through a small hallway containing a shrine.

Medical center door, Gary, Indiana, 1990.

Fence topped with razor-ribbon wire and iron gate are designed to limit access to this building to only residents and their guests, South Bronx, 1989.

Main entrance to bilingual school on Lafontaine Avenue, South Bronx, 1988.

(Left) "Doorway to Hell, enter at your own risk," a mural by Larry Rogers, Bedford-Stuyvesant, Brooklyn, 1991.

(Right) Entrance to abandoned fur salon, West Side, Chicago, 1993.

Door welded shut seals a Newark housing project awaiting demolition, Scudder Homes, Newark, May 1987

Wrought-iron cage, designed to prevent strangers from hanging out in the lobby, harassing residents, selling drugs, and stealing the mail, on the front entrance to a South Bronx apartment building, 1992.

The Adam and Eve of Detroit, 1993. The cinder-blocked entrance to abandoned Northeastern High School is decorated with crude, explicit, yet playful drawings.

(Left) A male figure is depicted upside down, balancing on one hand, his huge penis shooting upward.

(Right) A wide female figure is boxed in the door frame, her long rectangular chest resembling a "boom box," her breasts doubling as speakers.

(Above, left) Before fortification: tenement entrance in Spanish Harlem, 1973.

(Above, right) "El Porton," the big door, South Bronx, 1988.

(Right) Main entrance to the Department of Social Services, Harlem, 1996.

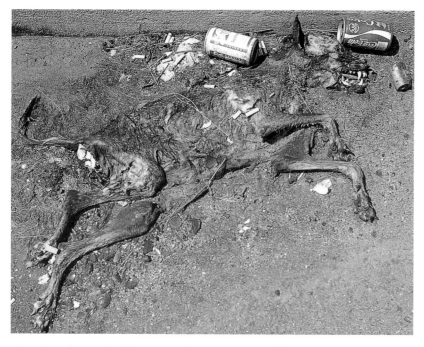

Aluminum cans, dead batteries, cigarette butts, and broken glass frame the body of a German shepherd, stretched as if running, in a South Bronx gutter, 1980.

Roaming dogs, Atlantic City, 1979.

STREET DOGS

"You can look at these dogs to learn how to survive. You can see their purpose: to get something to eat."

—Newark teenager, 1983

"Dog pound nigga!"

—Graffiti,
Central Ward, Newark, 1995

Residents of ghetto neighborhoods are often forced at great expense to keep large dogs in order to protect themselves and their property. Chained in hallways or backyards, the dogs sound an alert when strangers intrude. But when the owner dies, moves away, can no longer afford to feed the dog, lacks the time to attend to the animal, or has a house that becomes too crowded, the dog is abandoned, left to fend for itself in parks and empty lots.

These roving, emaciated animals patrol the streets, rummaging through trash for food. They lose patches of skin in fights, have their legs injured from being hit by bottles thrown at them, or hurt themselves falling down icy stairs in abandoned buildings.

Although they shy away from humans, their very presence gives a feeling of wilderness to the places they roam. At night, frightened people move out of the dogs' path, going into a hallway or crossing to the other side of the street. Elderly folks, as a way to keep children out of the streets, warn that street dogs are going to get them.

Teenagers are fond of using the word *dog* for their mark, personalizing it by preceding it with the initial of their first name: K-dog, D-dog,

Dog walking down the middle of a Newark street, 1981.

T-dog are popular. Even though *dog* is often used as a derogatory term, it also has the positive connotation of guardian. In this context the term is used to mean "homeboy," somebody local.

Rats are regarded with fear, posing a much more serious problem than street dogs. People put screens on cribs to protect their babies. Rats bite children, eat electrical cords, get into food, make messes, and carry diseases. Residents are eager to talk about these pests and to show rat holes and rat droppings to the visitor.

The ghetto is the only urban community in the United States where we can smell the pungent stench of rotten animals, which may have been left in the open for months or even longer. Local residents become used to the offensive smell of dead dogs, rats, and cats.

As the master of a vast empty lot, a street dog sits on a discarded couch, South Bronx, 1989.

*Dog surveys the street from the second-story window
of an abandoned building, South Side, Chicago 1993.*

"Today marks the beginning of a new era in the economic and social life of America. Today, we are launching an attack on the slums of this country which must go forward until every American family has a decent home."

—FRANKLIN D. ROOSEVELT,
when work began on the nation's first federally funded public housing, 1937

"People don't want housing in the South Bronx, or otherwise they would not burn it down."

—SENATOR DANIEL PATRICK MOYNIHAN,
1978

THREE

HOUSING

More than half a century later, President Roosevelt's hopes remain unfulfilled. Neglect and disinvestment and the consequent loss of buildings that characterize poor communities are worse now than ever. In Detroit during the last decade, for example, demolitions were ten times more frequent than new construction, resulting in the loss of sixty thousand dwellings. Camden, with a population of eighty thousand, demolished more than three hundred units in a three-month period in 1987 as part of a program designed to clear, in a single year, over 5 percent of all the city's dwellings. This effort, "the largest demolition program in the United States," was a source of pride to Walter Richardson, the city official responsible at the time. But William Hargrove, the contractor doing the demolition, remembered with mixed feelings having played and dined as a child in some of the houses he was razing.

In 1984, New York's governor Mario Cuomo celebrated the rehabilitation of an apartment house in the South Bronx, saying: "This building is a survivor." Yet, this was also true of most remaining structures in the area. Common in ghettos are derelict family homes, apartment buildings, and projects, which, although technically "housing," blur the distinction between having a home and being homeless. These structures are wide open, contrasting with the heavily fortified institutions and businesses that surround them. Offering a warm place to sleep and do business, these buildings function as unofficial shelters and often as drug franchises. It is common for families to double up and even for people to live on the stairway landings and the roof.

People move back and forth between the shelter system and these derelict buildings that smell of urine and excrement and that often lack heat, hot water, and electric light. Garbage is spilled in the hallways, adding to the stench; the mailboxes are vandalized; and the stairways are full of broken glass, condoms, and crack vials. Residents, lacking even minimum security, live in fear of fires, of strangers, and of each other.

"They are shelters—they are better than being in the god-damn street—a place to carry on some semblance of family life. We still had a roof over our heads; we had nails driven in the wall and an old bedsheet hung up, curtains to get some privacy. We could still function, we could still cook," said a Newark woman who lived in one of these buildings. Surprisingly, through minimal maintenance, these structures manage to survive from year to year in the same dismal shape.

The public housing program of the last years of the Depression heralded a new start. In projects, for the first time in America, improvements in living conditions sought by the nineteenth- and early twentieth-century reformers were realized on a massive scale. Instead of the atmosphere of despair pervading the slum dwellings they replaced, public housing offered space, light, sanitary plumbing, and protection against fires. They also provided the luxury of a private bathroom with a tub, and a private bedroom for adults and for every two children in the family.

In 1950, Lewis Mumford credited the vast program of slum clearance and rebuilding of the New York City Housing Authority as having done in twelve years more "to improve the living quarters of the lowest-income groups than all the earlier housing reformers did in a hundred. Acres of dark, musty, verminous, overcrowded tenements have been replaced by clean, well-lighted sanitary quarters—also overcrowded."

In 1966, sociologist Lee Rainwater stressed the superiority of the new developments over the old slums: "No matter what criticisms are made of public housing projects, there is no doubt that the structures themselves are infinitely preferable to slum housing. In our interviews in public housing projects we have found very few people who complain about the design aspects of the insides of their apartments. Though they may not see their apartments as perfect, there is a dramatic drop in anxiety about nonhuman threats within."

Today, public housing sees its own survival threatened by mismanagement, vandalism, lack of funds for maintenance, and federal guidelines designed to give preference to those most in need. Projects have become housing for destitute

Alice, standing at the entrance to her apartment in one of the row houses. New Street and Newark Street, Central Ward, Newark, March 1982.

families, those lacking the energy and resources to move elsewhere and those no other landlord will take. Another blow has been the loss of institutions that helped to make the lives of residents more pleasant, that offered them opportunities to broaden their horizons, that gave them a sense of being part of a community.

Some public housing complexes in New York City are so violent that even homeless families refuse to settle there, hoping instead to be offered an inferior apartment in a better location. And in Chicago, because of the high rate of vacancies, projects are used as the city's unofficial shelters. A program called "Homewatchers for the CHA" places homeless people who are willing to live there in vacant apartments until a family is ready to move in permanently.

Many public housing projects are isolated. In some, mail carriers refuse to deliver packages, forcing people to go to the post office. Taxi cab companies might not service them. Firefighters are reluctant to respond to alarms unless accompanied by police; the police themselves sometimes refuse to answer calls after dark—they have been insulted and hit by hard objects thrown at them by tenants.

The reputation of public housing has deteriorated to the point that to avoid being stigmatized, their residents are advised to use the word "developments," not "projects." Buildings have recently been demolished in East St. Louis, Kansas City, Detroit, Chicago, and Newark, and scores of others stand sealed, waiting to be destroyed.

A popular strategy to bring back working families to shattered inner city neighborhoods consists in building clusters of townhouses. Developments of this kind encourage home ownership by families who take care of their property, often their only investment, thus creating islands of stability.

In New York City, where space is at a premium, covering large tracts with low-density townhouses constitutes an inefficient use of valuable public land and infrastructure. And by excluding the poor, these developments force the city to concentrate the most destitute population elsewhere—typically in institutions or in badly maintained apartment buildings located in the most violent ghettos. In addition, townhouse enclaves set up barriers to defend themselves against their neighbors, resulting in the further fragmentation of these communities.

NEW YORK CITY HOUSING AUTHORITY PROJECTS

"Let us build for dignity."

—Keystone, Unity Plaza, East New York, Brooklyn, 1971

It was my need for high places from which to photograph the landscape of the ghetto that led me to approach the New York City Housing Authority (NYCHA) for permission to visit its projects. The roofs of the buildings offered excellent area views. The management was concerned enough about my safety to send an employee with me as I made my rounds; my guides were familiar with the buildings and could answer questions as we made our way to the roof. Under this arrangement I was not afraid to walk past the dealers and the addicts.

A typical visit began in the waiting room of the management office, which might be presided over by the image of a skull on a yellow background bearing the words CRACK KILLS. Other signs warned against the sale of narcotics in public housing buildings and also notified people of accidents occurring in elevators, offered aid to victims of spousal abuse, and informed residents of cultural and social activities. In this neat room, a place of official normalcy, tenants make their rent payments, request repairs, and lodge complaints. But not even here can they escape graphic reminders of the plague in their midst, the drug epidemic shaping daily life.

Sometimes to get to the management office I had to make a detour around the perimeter of

The "towers in the park" of the St. Nicholas Houses, Harlem, New York City, 1992, overpower and contain the full-grown trees on their grounds.

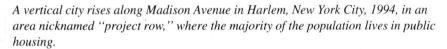

A vertical city rises along Madison Avenue in Harlem, New York City, 1994, in an area nicknamed "project row," where the majority of the population lives in public housing.

the complex; I had been warned to stay clear of the center. In the South Bronx, an administrator of the Andrew Jackson Houses told a caretaker who was to walk with me through the grounds, "Don't let him go through the projects with this [camera bag] or they'll kill him!" In Brownsville, the poorest section of Brooklyn, the supervisor of grounds loudly yelled "Move!" as I lingered to take notes in front of the northernmost tower, one of the three twenty-two-story buildings of the Langston Hughes Houses. He later explained that two of his workers had been hit by bottles hurled from the upper floors of the buildings, and had required hospitalization.

The tallest buildings and those located on corners at the perimeter of the project grounds were usually the best suited for my purposes. I visited between 10 a.m. and 3 p.m., hours when drug dealing was at a low point.

CRACK SUPERMARKETS

Entering a project during the day, accompanied by a housing authority employee, gives one a view of public housing at its best. I usually saw the buildings' public spaces soon after the caretaker had done the morning cleaning and at a time when school was in session and few children were around. My first impression was one of clean floors and quiet buildings.

But actually these massive buildings— typically they are more than twelve stories tall— are quite vulnerable. Nothing highlights this more clearly than the constant struggle to secure front doors. Entrances are constantly being forced, windowpanes are missing, and the intercoms are vandalized. Almost exclusively, tenant patrols were in buildings for the elderly and very

View of the Kingsborough Houses, Brooklyn, 1989.

Tall, wide, and isolated in 1993, the Morrisania Air Rights towers, completed in 1980 in the South Bronx, have become a symbol of misguided design.

rarely in family buildings. A young woman who was a caretaker in Brownsville reported, "Every time we put a new lock in they break it. Everybody just comes and goes, comes and goes. They don't even live in the building."

"There is only one disease here: crack," said José Rodríguez, an assistant superintendent at the Mill Brook Houses in the South Bronx. The tall, isolated, often unlocked, and overcrowded buildings of public housing complexes offer drug dealers a secure and accessible base of operations and a place to recruit employees and customers. Tenants fear to report them. In particular the tree-lined inner courtyards of these projects, hidden from the streets, which were intended as urban oases for outdoor play, picnics, and socializing, now serve as open-air drug markets. A manager of the East River Houses in East Harlem characterized the courtyard in her com-

plex as "designed for escape." According to NYCHA workers I spoke with, many of the recent killings in such projects have taken place in the courtyards.

The most effective force for keeping drugs out of the public areas of buildings is organized groups of tenants who will call the police to arrest the dealers and their customers, and are willing to testify in court against them. But organizing is becoming harder, as the most energetic and conscientious residents move out of the projects. The housing authority cannot afford twenty-four-hour security.

Maintenance personnel are perhaps the closest and most knowledgeable observers of the present crack epidemic. They know in detail the history, mechanics, and social costs of addiction in their work areas. When asked why drugs are so popular, these people give answers that fit into

45

Door used for target practice, Bushwick Houses, Brooklyn, 1989.

three categories. Some lay the blame for addiction on the tenants' bleak prospects for the future. They argue that many turn to drugs for relief, particularly discouraged youths who are prone to depression. Others cite peer pressure: "Everybody is doing it." Young people use drugs first to be like their friends and later because they have become addicted. Still others bitterly blame the welfare system and the idleness it fosters: "People here don't have to strive. They clothe them; they feed them—this make them lose their self-respect. You see grown-ups just hanging around the lobbies all day with nothing to do, except maybe going to the check-cashing place; always the same crowd, and they make fun of the people going to work. If they were busy doing something, they would not take drugs."

A popular theory among maintenance per-

sonnel is that the federal government allows drugs to be sold openly in ghetto neighborhoods. I was repeatedly told that the U.S. army and navy have the power to stop the drug trade, and that since they do not use it, important people must be involved, making profits. Housing authority workers complain that outsiders, by coming to the projects to buy, encourage drug dealing. They rightly feel that the police would not tolerate such blatant commerce in middle-class neighborhoods.

Many open lobbies of public housing buildings have become crack supermarkets. A caretaker at the Seth Low Houses, in Brownsville, sadly pointed to the building he is responsible for and said, "This place is distinctive. You go to the lobby and there is nothing but junkies down there. You see a lot of crackheads moving back and forth." He drew attention to the broken

The early ideals of public housing are represented in this bronze sculpture of healthy children playing, Johnson Houses, Harlem, New York City, 1989.

windows and missing signs, saying that addicts sometimes steal the front doors of buildings to sell as scrap metal.

The ubiquitous drug addicts often die, or go to jail or the hospital; their bony faces and starved bodies are soon replaced by others on street corners, in lobbies, behind buildings, and on stairways. Their strange, dematerialized presence is a constant reminder of death.

THE GAUNTLET

A long, slow elevator ride in complete darkness is a dreaded experience associated with the worst housing projects; muggers, a maintenance man explained, "put the elevator lights out to rob you." In entryways I found elderly tenants patiently waiting for somebody they trusted to accompany them on the elevators to their apartments. Besides being unsafe, the elevators are slow and sometimes need carefully placed kicks and a helping hand to get started. Their walls are full of bumps and sometimes bullet holes: signs of rough treatment. Less menacing, but still annoying, elevator walls are often covered with a layer of oil (to facilitate the removal of graffiti), which has the side effect of ruining people's clothes.

Reaching one's floor unharmed does not necessarily mean that one is safe: muggings occur frequently in the corridors. A maintenance man at the J. Weldon Johnson Houses, in East Harlem, explained that if tenants see addicts on their floor, they will often go back down and call the police. Some mothers even fear being robbed by their own drug-addicted children. To protect themselves, they request that their door locks be changed. Forced out of their homes, the teenagers move in with friends or share the public spaces of their buildings with other homeless people. At a project in Brooklyn a mother locked her four addicted children out of her top-floor apartment; to get in, her sons made a hole in the roof.

The stairway walls serve as bulletin boards. There, in the E. R. Moore Houses in the South Bronx, "K.C." choose to announce that after eight years he was "back from jail, 1-25-89." On the fourteenth-floor landing of one of the buildings of the notorious Marcus Garvey Houses in Brownsville, someone had written, "Bob and I was walking down the Ave. smoking on a blunt and we saw this crab. The crab walked up and this is what she said: 'Give me five dollars and I buff your head.' " Another inscription, in the Bronxchester Houses, in the South Bronx, warned, "Crack is wack. You use crack today, tomorrow you be bumming. That's word experience talk." Yet another, in the Patterson Houses in the South Bronx, consisted of this cryptic sentence: "Misty blue is the place to be." Many of the steps and landings were strewn with empty crack vials, used condoms, human excrement, and carefully hidden bundles containing the belongings of homeless people who sleep there.

When opening the top-floor doors leading to the roof, caretakers spoke loudly, started singing, or banged the door, to warn of our coming. A maintenance man at the Polo Grounds Towers, in Harlem, went ahead of me, explaining, "I have to watch and see if somebody is smoking crack." The wisdom of this became apparent when I saw people up there sleeping, reading, sitting, and talking, with empty vials and syringes next to them.

The roofs of projects showed many signs of drug activity, and there are often bullet holes in the vandalized metal doors and ventilation systems. At the Abraham Lincoln Houses, in Harlem, I saw a U.S. army manual describing how to take apart and clean a high-powered rifle. At the Bushwick Houses, in Brooklyn, I found a door with a life-sized drawing of a deranged-looking man on it that had been used for target practice. A caretaker at the Albany Houses, in Brooklyn, explained to me that gun sellers take their clients to the tops of buildings to demonstrate their wares. If the customer can hit something in a nearby building, the gun fetches a higher price.

"BROWNSVILLE, NOT THE WALDORF ASTORIA"

NYCHA workers with whom I spoke were almost unanimous that crime in their projects was getting worse and their job was getting more difficult. For thirty-five years William Monroe, a housing authority maintenance man, has lived and worked at the Marcy Houses, in the Bedford-Stuyvesant section of Brooklyn. He has seen many industries in the area move away and once-busy factories reduce their activities so much that their buildings look deserted. "No work, no money, except from what comes from welfare, Social Security, and drugs," he says, and then asks, "How can you run a city without money?" Today, he observes, even the army is not taking the youngsters most in need of work—the high school dropouts. He calls the neighborhood "dead man's city." He has seen the children he coached in baseball and took on field trips grow discouraged. Yet William Monroe is proud of having raised nine children in the Marcy Houses, not one of whom has become an addict. "It can be done," he says.

At the Samuel J. Tilden Houses, in Brooklyn, I overheard a caretaker complaining, "With all the crack and stuff that is going on, you only can do the best you can. This is Brownsville, not the Waldorf Astoria." Several caretakers told me that they would not live in the complexes where they work even if they got a rent-free apartment. One said that he would rather take his chances in the Bowery than live there. Others complained that NYCHA was rehabilitating additional buildings in the neighborhood instead of concentrating in improving the troubled projects. A caretaker at the Patterson Houses felt that the only solution would be to sell the apartments as co-ops. In a few exceptional projects, maintenance men told me that during the past year or so conditions had improved: their front doors now locked and fewer killings had occurred.

Despite their pessimistic outlook, however, workers and officials made lists of things that needed to be done, picked up garbage left behind by careless residents, and addressed tenants politely. Although many long for retirement, not one expressed the desire to look for other work. As they passed by the crackheads and the pushers, the housing authority employees did not look at them, perhaps to avoid a confrontation, or perhaps as a sign that the public areas of the buildings were out of their control.

A MONUMENT TO MOSES

New York City's public housing is a precious resource, especially in the present housing crisis. Yet the conditions in most projects remain unstable and are often worsening. NYCHA buildings, maintenance people report, are only as good as the neighborhoods they are in. During 1990, the last year the agency has figures for, more than thirty-eight thousand families were sharing apartments without authorization, and thousands of people were sleeping on roofs, on stairways, in basements, and even in elevators. In this way public housing, at a great cost to itself, helps contain the flood of homelessness.

Beginning in the mid-1930s, the NYCHA projects were seen as a vast improvement over the crowded, unsanitary tenements and decrepit wooden houses they replaced. The projects boasted fireproof construction and sunny, ventilated apartments with hot and cold running water. Life in them had, moreover, a provisional character: The complexes were designed to provide decent, sanitary housing for families until rising income and an increasing supply of private housing permitted them to move to more desirable dwellings.

In 1995, however, life in public housing is vastly different from what it was expected to be. The projects of the NYCHA are increasingly becoming like those in the rest of the nation: permanent residences for the indigent.

Most of the developments in ghetto areas of the city are part of the legacy of Robert Moses, New York City's construction coordinator from 1946 to 1960. They reflect his preference for large complexes of more than a thousand units and of towers seven or more stories high. Arnold Vollmer, his long-time associate, told me that Moses had wanted "a project that would not be swamped, that could have an impact in the area." Vollmer said that Moses's view was "if you cannot do something that is really substantial, it is not worth doing." Moses's policies led to great concentrations of public housing. NYCHA became a model for the nation, with similar complexes arising from St. Louis to Boston.

Even after Moses's influence waned, NYCHA continued to build new complexes near existing ones, resulting in clusters of as many as half a dozen housing projects. Today, more than a quarter of a century after their completion, these modern agglomerations are surrounded by fortified schools, libraries, post offices, police precinct houses, Medicare mills, and stores. More recently, the idle land and abandoned buildings surrounding the projects have been saturated with NIMBY projects, making public housing part of institutional ghettos.

In the poorest and most crime-ridden and devastated areas of the city, NYCHA has more than ninety thousand apartments, constituting more than 50 percent of its total stock. This is more than twice as many apartments as the Chicago Housing Authority, the second largest public housing agency in the country, has altogether. And the poverty of the residents will continue to grow, since of the 132,270 families on the waiting list, 49 percent are welfare recipients.

It is unfair to ask landlords to solve problems like homelessness, drug addiction, and crime, all of which have devastating effects on public housing, said Joseph Shuldiner, the general manager of NYCHA in 1989 and now assistant secretary of HUD responsible for public housing. The agency would not consider evicting the thirty-eight thousand doubled-up families in order to improve living conditions in projects.

The main source of funding for public housing, the federal government, supports almost no new construction. The cuts in funding for services and community centers have worsened the health, education, employment, recreation, and safety problems faced by public housing residents. The dwindling resources that Washington still provides are directed toward the poorest of the poor, thus accelerating a change in tenants from a mixed-income, mostly working population to dependent female-headed families. Working families, lacking subsidies of any kind and perceiving that the "market rate" rents they pay for their apartments in dangerous surroundings are already too high and are increasing, are moving to private housing in better neighborhoods.

UP ON THE ROOF

On the roof of these projects I see blankets, mattresses, large pieces of cardboard, even tables and chairs. During the winter people prefer to sleep inside the building, or inside the shed that holds the elevator machinery, referred to as the penthouse. People also live beneath the water tanks, where they arrange their belongings in a small space as if it were their private bedroom. The buildings being accessible to all, this practice has become accepted as inevitable. At the Bushwick Houses, for instance, a homeless man told the caretaker to stop placing new light bulbs on the stairway landing where he sleeps. "You put a light there and I will bust it. This is my house and I don't want a light there," he said.

Most homeless people taking shelter in public housing buildings come at night and leave early in the morning, so as not to be found by maintenance workers. But at the Patterson Houses a suddenly awakened man threatened me with a large knife, which he held by the blade as he sprang from a top-floor landing. After a quick

retreat the caretaker with me commented, "We surprised him, and surprise brings out the devil in people." At the Jefferson Houses, in Manhattan, while accompanied by two supervisors, I encountered a sleeping man on the roof landing. One of the supervisors, while he was ordering the man out of the building, held a knife ready halfway out of his coat pocket. Weapons are increasingly among the tools of the public housing trade; maintenance workers carry knives, heavy wrenches, golf clubs, and on payday, I was told, even guns.

About half a dozen men live on each roof of the Polo Grounds public housing complex— four thirty-story buildings. Located between the bluffs of Washington Heights and the Harlem River, in a stirring natural setting, these giant buildings offer a breathtaking view of Manhattan, its pointed skyline, misty parks, and silvery bodies of water. From the top of the buildings one can see the backs of hawks and seagulls as they fly below. Spanning the river are several magnificent bridges, and on highways along the perimeter of the project, thousands of vehicles move rapidly by.

Contrasting with the panorama of the city are the sights that greet a caretaker who told me he visits these roofs in the early morning: He sees a line of men defecating along a wall and others sleeping nearby. In this, the richest of cities in the richest of countries, in buildings of advanced late twentieth-century technology, men who own nothing sleep under the open sky on a windswept roof three hundred feet above the ground.

CHICAGO HOUSING AUTHORITY PROJECTS

"The hate-mongers are determined to confine the Negro population of Chicago within a walled city."

— *Chicago Defender,* 1950

Poverty and public policies contributed to making the facade of this building, part of the Cabrini-Green housing project, Chicago, 1990, into a collective work of folk art. Trash fires have turned entrances into dark holes. Within the rectangular perimeter of the structure, a geometric composition of window coverings—curtains, plastic, garbage bags, blankets, newspaper, Plexiglas, and painted boards— form a varied pattern controlled by a multitude of concrete frames. The colors, textures, and glimpses of people and plants impart a gentle rhythm to these American quilts, one block long and half a block tall.

"Kids Chores

Mon. Wed. & Friday Vincent do dishes

Tues. & Thurs. & Saturday Kenny do dishes

Mon. Wed. & Friday Kenny clean bathroom

Tues. Thurs. & Saturday Vincent clean bathroom

TOGETHER THEY WILL TAKE OUT

Garbage, do their room, straighten out their Play.

They will also clean the refrigerator on Sundays

CLEAN PLAY ROOM EVERY NIGHT before going to bed

Who Says!

Your Mama Says!

—Note attached to a refrigerator,
Robert Taylor Homes, Chicago, 1989

At the office of the Washington Park Houses on the South Side, on a winter day, Mr. Jenkins and another man known as "The Greek" tried to dissuade me from going to the roofs of their buildings. My shoes, they said, were of the wrong type, "they had no grip like those they sell at Sears." On the windy, icy roofs of the projects I could easily go sliding off their unprotected perimeter. Recently, I twice had nightmares where I went feet first down the side of one of these monoliths and had waked up as I dangled 160 feet above the ground. The Greek made me relive these nightmares by depicting with his hand a person sliding down the roof.

He was still shaken from having been mugged a few days before. In the middle of the day, in the office parking lot, next to a family who watched and did nothing, a man put a knife to his throat.

With great apprehension and feeling foolish, I approached a building on Prairie Avenue, one of the worst of this South Side complex. As I parked the car across the street and faced the

A teenager looks out through the iron grate of the corridor, sixteenth floor, ABLA Houses, Chicago, 1989.

The most visible stretch of poverty in the United States, three miles of high-rises belonging to the Chicago Housing Authority, 1991. Stateway Gardens on the right and the Robert Taylor Homes are separated from white ethnic neighborhoods by the Dan Ryan Expressway.

massive sixteen-story structure I could feel the stares of a group of men standing on the ground floor. Randolph, my guide, said that they were selling cocaine and added that he knew them all because he had worked in that building. With him, he said, I was safe. I tagged along with Randolph, afraid of being left alone.

On the ground floor, we stopped at the maintenance room where the caretaker had cooked a pot of pigs' ears in a brown sauce on a hot plate. He offered us one to put between two pieces of white bread. Randolph eagerly made himself a sandwich and ate it on our way to the elevators. The hearty food, filling with aroma the small and warm maintenance room, contrasted with the stench and threat of violence in the public spaces of the high-rise.

The outside corridors of these tall buildings are surprisingly dark—unlighted, blackened by the smoke of countless trash fires, obscured by overlapping graffiti, cluttered with uncollected garbage. They resemble subterranean caverns instead of the light, airy spaces one would expect in buildings conceived as "towers in the park." Adding to the underground feeling is the sound of dripping water forming pools in empty apartments. The walls between vacant units are perforated with holes made by gangs for quick passage.

On the way to the roof I passed through a dark penthouse where large, outmoded elevator machinery sparked and sizzled as it was turned on and off. The ceiling leaked and hot water dripped from pipes. The room resembled a setting for a horror film; yet it felt surprisingly warm and comfortable compared to the exposed roof that lay behind a metal door.

Outside the penthouse, the roof was clear of ice and seemed safe, except for the wind that pushed from all directions. Around me lay an

High-rise building, part of the Henry Horner Homes, West Side, Chicago, 1991. The dark brown of the walls merges with the darker brown of the window seals, contrasting with the white sheets used as curtains in most of the occupied apartments.

Sixteen-story building, part of the infamous Robert Taylor Homes, Chicago, 1989. When completed in the 1960s, buildings like this were nicknamed "Congo Hiltons."

extraordinary landscape of contrasting wealth and poverty: surviving gray stone Victorian mansions, snow-covered empty lots, black glass downtown towers with the world's tallest building among them, the Gold Coast, public housing projects. Only the hissing of the wind and the creaking of the elevated trains as they curved on their way to and from downtown broke the silence. An immense, freezing Lake Michigan lay to the east.

Misery spreads for miles along streets such as State or West Madison. There is so much empty land that in places the city seems to have ceased to exist. The most destitute of all communities are the Chicago Housing Authority (CHA) projects, whose 85,500 official residents are nearly 90 percent black. Public housing even in an era of homelessness contains many thousands of empty units, with their boarded-up windows contributing to a sense of desertion. The CHA

has 16 percent of its units vacant and has been losing apartments at a rate of several hundred units a year for the last five years ("Statistical Profile," CHA, 1991–1992).

Many CHA buildings are "consolidated," meaning that their upper floors have been sealed as residents move or are relocated to the lower floors. The empty floors are closed off, their windows covered with Plexiglas or plywood to stop gangs from stealing aluminum window frames, pipes, and cabinets or from moving into the empty units. Apartments on these floors are strewn with furniture and garbage, the former residents' possessions sometimes being of so little value that they did not even bother to take them when they left.

Even though there are more dangerous and more derelict developments in Chicago than the Robert Taylor Homes, this complex has become the most infamous public housing project in the nation, "the worst in ghetto living," to borrow a phrase of sociologist Lee Rainwater. Here the failures of the system are magnified. The twenty-eight sixteen-story buildings of the Taylor Homes are among the tallest, its tenants are among the poorest, and in its four thousand apartments live the largest number of families of any single development in the United States. A monument to racial segregation, this project is nevertheless visible to the multitudes driving by its two miles of buildings east of the Dan Ryan Expressway. For three decades, the Robert Taylor Homes have been an important defining element of the city.

Aware of the Taylor Homes' reputation as an extremely violent environment, I was concerned about my safety and that of my photographic equipment, so I asked for advice. I was told to act natural and not to show fear; not to condescend to, condemn, or to in any way offend the residents; and finally not to see what one is not supposed to see. A security man at the Stateway Homes gave me the following recommendation: "It is always good to look around. You may walk into someone ready to shoot somebody." I asked him what he would do if he found himself in that situation, and he said he did not know. Mr. Wilson, the locksmith of the Washington Park Homes, suggested that residents would welcome me if I let them think that I was there to improve their building.

I visited the Taylor Homes in the company of Curtis Smith, a maintenance worker with a quarter-century of experience in the development. On the way to one of the buildings, Curtis told me a story that has the simplicity and the horror of myth. He referred to it as "heavy action." A decade and half ago, a white plumber came to work in the development. Said Curtis: "He had an arrogant attitude. He did not like black people. He called children 'niggers.' With that attitude you can't make it, it makes no difference who you are. He did not last long. One day they took him to the basement, to the mechanical room, and kicked his eyes out. He went to the hospital, and when he got out he shot himself in a forest preserve."

Perhaps to balance the rawness of the story, Curtis explained that several white maintenance men had worked at the Taylor Homes for decades without experiencing any problems. One was remembered for his willingness to come alone to fix boilers in the middle of the night. Another, an old painter, Curtis said, "would be seen strolling through the parking lot holding a little black girl's hand. When they see that they aren't going to bother him and they are not going to let anybody else bother him. It is all a matter of attitude."

The open, friendly lobbies of the management offices are the most attractive spaces in CHA complexes. Here, unlike in the lobbies of many other housing authorities, employees do not address residents through Plexiglas windows or buzz them through locked doors when they need to go inside for an interview. The decor includes potted plants and pictures on the walls. One office displayed a print of a graceful young black woman, "the West Indian girl," wearing a simple white dress—a vision of innocence and promise. There are snapshots of small flower gardens planted on the grounds, and the popular portrait of the late mayor Harold Washington with his grandfatherly smile.

Yet, residents waiting in the lobbies look frustrated and prepared for a long wait. During my June 1989 visit to Cabrini-Green, Mrs. Jackson was wearing a T-shirt inscribed "Same Shit Different Day." Children played with household objects made into toys: a boy, for example, made sailor knots in a long black extension cord and placed it on his head for a crown. Carrying an aluminum window frame with some broken glass still in it, a teenager complained that "a kid" had thrown a brick through his third-floor window. A woman sat looking at a questionnaire about basic skills; while another held in her hand a letter from the Illinois Department of Public Aid, the source of support for about nine-tenths of the families in the project.

At Cabrini-Green I saw very few residents until noon, when the grounds, paths, and lobbies started to become busy with people. "Things are jumping here at 7 p.m. and there is a lot of activity even past midnight, particularly in the summer," explained a security guard.

According to Curtis Smith, "Many are depressed; they have nothing; they feel the world is against them. They say, 'This is the land of plenty' and ask, 'Why can't I get a piece of it?' People say: 'I am going to sit and let the system take care of me.' " Smith stresses, however, that not all people are like this; some are self-motivated, manage to raise themselves above their circumstances, and move to better places.

Although their raggedy exteriors were familiar to me, the state of the project buildings' interiors came as a shock after the projects of the New York City Housing Authority. At a distance one cannot smell the stench of the garbage, see the dark hallways, or feel claustrophobic in the lobbies and small elevator cabs. Here the atmosphere was very different from that of the management office. Graffiti on the walls of Stateway Gardens sets the tone: "All is well, go to hell." Mayor Washington, depicted alive and protective in the management office of the Cabrini-Green Houses, is all but written off inside one of the buildings, where a sign on the wall says: "Harold is dead, white man is the boss."

In a typical building there is a long wait for the elevator in a foul-smelling lobby made more depressing by the sight of vandalized mailboxes. The scene repeats itself minus the mailboxes on every floor along the way. Elevators are unbearably slow and often broken. About a third have no light, the bulbs repeatedly smashed, their filaments exposed.

Small children long for the ground. During the warm weather they gravitate to the elevators, which represent a way out of the confines of their apartments, as well as a hope that the doors will open on family members returning from jobs or errands to care for them. As the elevator doors open on each floor along the way children are waiting, sometimes alone, sometimes following their parents. Often they get pushed back into the hallways, where they stand staring after their parents or other grown-ups as the metal doors close. But as soon as they reach school age, and sometimes even earlier, children move around the complexes, keeping elevators in constant use.

In one of the buildings of the Henry Horner Homes I saw an elderly man with three children get off the elevator at the fourteenth floor, where they were the sole residents. They walked through the dark hallway to their apartment, avoiding the pools of water on the floor. First the man opened a set of iron gates and then the front door to his apartment. As he turned on the light, the white appliances inside the bare, undecorated kitchen gave off a surreal glow.

While I was in the lobby of the management office of the Horner Homes, there entered a furious, disheveled man named Nathaniel, looking half derelict, half prophet, accompanying a small elderly woman coming to complain about a leak in her apartment. The woman remained silent while he yelled, "They want us to have diseases, they want us to die out." After their departure, the receptionist explained that he was a drug addict and alcoholic, and she blamed the tenants for the terrible conditions of the buildings. She also expressed her views loudly and angrily: "The women sit by the windows and throw out Pampers, bloody napkins, and pipes. You have to have four people on the grounds but only three can work, since the fourth has to look up all the time to warn the others about things coming out of the windows. Nobody wants to come here and work in this hellhole. I think this is the worst development in Chicago."

CHA buildings accumulate messages, scribblings, and drawings. Years of compressed script become part of an endless collective text, shadows of a history that will remain unwritten. Most popular are nicknames, for example: Lil-Roach, Lil-Nell (nicknames kept from childhood), Creep #1, Chilly, Kid-Fresh, Laty, A-Dog, D-Dog, Nike-Dog, T-Bone, Bongo, Solid World, Shot Gun, Terrible Taurus, and Lord Radar. Many of the residents have first names unknown in white America, for example: Bakarus, Shaterse, Marshon, Jevale, Dijo, Demida, Kentaro, Martee, Tomal, Davetta, Deshay, Lamario, and Toimail. Names and nicknames like these fill every exterior wall and stairway in most highrises. People claim a spot for themselves in the places they hang out by writing their names there. According to Randolph, of the Washington Park Houses, other residents respect this because "there is plenty of room in the building for all to write."

As chairman of the CHA since 1988, Vincent Lane has inspired widespread trust. His policies designed to reclaim the CHA buildings from gangs and drug dealers have received almost unanimous praise. Lane's first priority is to secure the most crime-ridden buildings by restricting access to residents and their guests. Visitors must be accompanied by a resident, must sign a book at a twenty-four-hour security office in the lobby, and are not permitted to stay overnight unless they check in with security. Armed guards are visible patrolling the grounds. Only after the buildings are secured are they painted and repaired. Lane originally received funds from HUD to rid the city's most troubled high-rises of gangs and drugs.

A maintenance man who supports Lane's efforts recommends caution, saying, "He's no miracle worker." And the *Chicago Tribune*, in a July 1, 1989, editorial, paid tribute to Lane's initiatives, yet found them wanting. The newspaper came out against fixing the buildings, urging instead the emptying and destruction of troubled CHA high-rises and their replacement by scattered new housing on city-owned land. What project residents needed, the *Tribune* opined, was "nothing less than a complete overhaul of the social, economic, and moral climate of their communities." Such a revolution is clearly beyond Lane's power. Even to attempt this huge, difficult task would require strong, sustained public support and expenditures of billions of dollars.

Since the riots of the late sixties, tens of thousands of black families have fled the Chicago ghettos for nearby suburbs. Left behind are more than half a million others less able to move out, overwhelmingly single mothers and their children. Peter Marcuse, a Columbia University professor of urban planning, explains the sense of confinement and despair experienced by many who remain: "Poor people need to have some evidence that what they do makes a difference. In the Taylor Homes they don't have that, and in the most segregated ghettos in New York they don't have that." The cause of the problems, according to Marcuse, is "the involuntary segregation of people with limited life chances in environments in which their limitations are reinforced by everything that they see and they do and hear and smell."

To be viable the CHA needs to become a more manageable and more selective agency. Its buildings must provide a good environment to raise families. Will HUD continue to back the CHA's reclamation program or allow the buildings already secured to return to their former state?

Unlike his predecessors, Lane enjoys the confidence of HUD. Funds for building rehabilitation, long frozen, have been released under his administration. Expenditures for modernization have risen to about $179 million a year, ten times their level under the previous chairman. Additional funding to secure the buildings has come from the federal government under the aegis of the war on drugs. Lane is trying to show that a new start is possible. To bear this out he has dozens of clean, fully occupied, and secured buildings and the CHA is in the process of rehabilitating many more. Yet the majority of the family high-rises are still in bad shape and the residents remain as poor as before, even though the expenses to keep the buildings safe are huge. Now it is up to HUD and ultimately to Congress to decide whether to pay the price to continue the Chicago program and to expand it to other cities.

"FAILED BUILDINGS," THE SCUDDER HOMES, NEWARK

"They were light apartments; the rooms were adequate size; the kitchens were complete. They were very nice apartments. If the building was lifted and put in Chicago, or Manhattan, or Los Angeles they would have been very expensive. Those people who made the decision to tear down the buildings say that will solve our problem. Maybe it will, maybe it won't. It is easy to blame a high-rise for a socio-economic problem."

—Thomas C. Lehman,
*an architect with the firm that designed
the Scudder Homes, Roseland, N.J., 1987*

The Edward W. Scudder Homes, with sixteen hundred apartments, were formerly the largest public housing project in New Jersey. Completed in 1963 in the Central Ward of Newark, during the "New Frontier" of the Kennedy administration, they symbolized a time when the abolition of poverty seemed both desirable and attainable.

The project consisted of eight thirteen-story buildings, built of red brick and reinforced concrete, each longer than one city block, and each with two hundred apartments. The units varied in size from one to five bedrooms, and all included a living room–dining room and a bathroom with a tub. Contrasting with the dark, wooden tenements they replaced, the rooms had large windows that allowed sunlight and fresh air to enter.

Scudder Homes were originally intended as temporary housing for a racially mixed, low-income population. After the 1967 riots, businesses and stores moved out of the area. The deteriorating projects became housing of last resort for a black, predominantly female population on public assistance. Extreme violence became characteristic. In 1984, for example, a family of four had a 75 percent chance of a member's becoming the victim of a serious crime during the course of a year.

The 1968 annual report of the Newark Housing Authority mentions a large number of organizations in which the tenants participated, among them the Boy Scouts, the Police Athletic League's recreation program, and the Newark Churches Volunteer Service Program, which offered a day camp with arts, crafts, games, sports, swimming, and field trips to the Newark Museum, public library, and airport. There was a blood bank, a tenants' association, programs for the elderly, and a regular newsletter, "a factor of social cohesion." A dozen years later, when four of the buildings were being emptied, no traces could be found of these organizations or the newsletter. A new addition was a methadone clinic located on the ground floor of one of the high-rises.

In 1981 the housing authority got $23 million from the federal government for the comprehensive modernization of the Scudder Homes; yet it never intended to rehabilitate them. For six years, until their demolition in 1987, two of these buildings stood broad, tall, isolated, and useless, their doors welded shut along well-traveled Springfield Avenue. They were an embarrassment to the city. Another two buildings were slowly emptied, the fixtures removed as apartments became vacant, their entrances finally sealed.

Housing Authority officials, realizing that the destruction of eight hundred apartments in a time of widespread homelessness was bound to attract criticism, publicized the demolition as a spectacular way of obliterating blight. Public relations experts prepared a press package entitled "A New Beginning" in which the destruction of four of the derelict buildings was presented as a way to break ground for one hundred townhouses. But Newark Councilman Donald Tucker, noting the lack of low-income housing, opposed the demolition, calling the celebration of the building's destruction "obscene."

Roaming through the buildings, right before the blast, I encountered the only inhabitants, nesting pigeons. The smell of their droppings filled the apartments; their nests were in closets and on the floors of the rooms. The birds' flight followed by a crash against the windows broke the silence and never ceased to startle me. The apartments on the lower floors were full of rocks that had been hurled through the windows.

The buildings contained scattered remains, a lingering presence of the former tenants and their successors, the squatters. The late 1970s was recalled by images and inscriptions painted on walls, by books, letters, cards, and other discarded objects. Thousands of rooms, miles of corridors, and stairways allowed glimpses into the everyday life that filled these projects.

Newspaper and magazine clippings taped on walls included portraits of Elijah Muhammad, Malcolm X, and Huey P. Newton—rarely Rev. Martin Luther King, Jr. The emblem of Islam, the star and the crescent, was much more popular than the cross. Islamic names and symbols were written on the walls to establish a claim to wisdom, knowledge, understanding, and membership in a world community.

Lying around was widespread evidence of attempts to exert social control. Discarded

Building still occupied, Scudder Homes, Central Ward, Newark, May 1979.

Empty building, doors welded shut, Scudder Homes, Central Ward, Newark, July 1986.

One of the four buildings to be demolished still standing, Scudder Homes, Central Ward, Newark, September 1987.

Townhouses being built on the site where the four buildings were destroyed. Because of faulty construction, the townhouses were badly damaged during a windstorm and had to be demolished. Central Ward, Newark, February 1990.

Protesters voice scorn while housing officials on a specially built podium read their speeches. "Implosion Ceremony," Central Ward, Newark, June 1987.

Local politicians and housing officials applaud and congratulate each other as a cloud of white smoke completely covers a crumbling building, Scudder Homes, Central Ward, Newark, June 1987.

The land occupied by the four high-rises, and later by the townhouses, lies vacant, Central Ward, Newark, July 1992.

Townhouses rise again, Central Ward, Newark, January 1995.

missives from such institutions as the courts, the welfare department, and the public schools threatened the residents with the loss of freedom, income, and education. Teachers sent letters complaining about absences and poor performance, promising to fail those who would not work harder and show up for classes. Daily concerns got into class assignments; when a student in his homework for English 091–004 gave examples of the use of "to," "too," and "two," he wrote: "To: After the convict had done three years he finally went to court."

A surprising variety of colors of paint and wallpapers decorated the rooms. Light blue, pink, yellow, green, and, oddly, black—the latter for disco rooms where, with blankets covering the windows, young people could shut out the world. Painted against the black background were white spirals and dots of red, green, and yellow. "People stare at that stuff and the dots start to move," observed a neighbor. A cleanly picked pigeon carcass shared a sunny corner room with empty wine bottles, remnants of a squatter's meal.

The first of the buildings was demolished in 1987. Among those invited to the "implosion ceremony" were the governor, the secretary of HUD, the state commissioner of Human Services, the state's two U.S. senators, a member of Congress, and the mayor of Newark, none of whom came. The audience consisted mainly of neighborhood people, city and county officials, and the press. Near the podium, built especially for the occasion, were a large number of officials whose job it was to provide decent housing for poor people, blowing up an unpopular but solid building with two hundred apartments. The other three buildings were demolished at a later date and without a ceremony.

Newark Councilman Donald Tucker called the events "a tragedy" but Walter Johnson, the former manager of the Newark office of HUD, quoted Sophocles: "Though a man be wise, it is no shame for him to live and learn." Johnson spoke about the replacement of "failed housing" with "successful housing." A group of residents from the remaining Scudder Homes formed an impromptu "Greek chorus" in counterpoint to Johnson's words, chanting:

Do you live here?
You don't live here. You live on Easy
    Street.
It's easy to make that speech.

As another speaker came and called the demolition a "historic moment for Newark," the chorus changed to:

He doesn't live here either.
He may blow your home up. He may blow
    you up.
They have good homes, nice cars.
I'll take your home.
I'm going to blow up your home.

"Phoenix" was also flown in for the ceremony, and "renaissance" was dusted off. Then Ida Clark, an elderly resident of the Scudder Homes, pushed the "hell box," and sirens wailed. She pushed again, with two helpers this time; the crowd waited; then the building went. Several sharp explosions threw streams of dust out of the center of the building, then ripped out its "guts." The sides folded inward and the huge structure collapsed. Then came the acrid smell of explosives and a mortar and plaster cloud rose, covering everything with a pale dust. Someone coming up nearby Howard Street quipped, "They finally made a white neighborhood out of it."

The crowd went to see the remains. Shocked pigeons circled and fluttered above. A man picked up a brick to take home, and a woman said, "I used to live there." "Good riddance," shouted another, while a man shook his head slowly, and intoned, as if in a daze, "It doesn't make any sense."

Was the demolition necessary? Had a different population lived there, the buildings would have been considered aesthetically dull, yet adequate and decent. After all, other buildings in the complex, exactly like those destroyed, are still occupied by elderly tenants. These projects are well maintained and patrolled by police. And one should consider the New York City Housing Authority, which has many more high-rise projects than Newark, and has yet to demolish one single building.

The families who had lived in these build-

Torn and fading family snapshots pasted on a living room mirror. These eerie reminders of a recent past were left behind in a building scheduled to be dynamited. Columbus Homes, Newark, 1994.

ings spent much of their time and energy trying to survive and protect their property in an environment of fear and neglect. If the Newark churches, the Boy Scouts, the housing authority, and the police had been successful in helping to organize the tenants and create a sense of community, would the projects have been viable? Surely, had working families been encouraged to live in these buildings, they would have contributed to stability.

Newark is desperately struggling to change its dismal public image. After going through a "New Newark" and a "New, New Newark" campaign, now the city calls itself "Newark, A City on the Rise." From the official point of view, the empty buildings stood for shame. So the city is transforming its core into a middle-class enclave by building 1,250 townhouses and by expanding old institutions, turning vacant lots into parking lots, and building a new cultural

center. If the housing authority had rehabilitated the sealed projects and filled them with destitute families, it would have created places that consumed resources, caused problems, and discouraged investors and shoppers.

Destroying housing, on the other hand, may help a municipality to get rid of some of its poor if only by forcing them to become another city's burden. Uprooting them leads to the breakdown of their social networks and to homelessness, the spread of AIDS and TB, and to shelters and prisons instead of housing projects.

After clearing the rubble from the "overpowering institutional structures in high-density superblocks," the Newark Redevelopment and Housing Authority started construction of "lower-density housing built at a human scale." But before reaching completion, the shoddily built townhouses were severely damaged in a windstorm. Until 1994, the land occupied by

Columbus Homes, Newark, 1981.

Part of the ruins: upholstered sofas, the essence of domestic life. Columbus Homes, Newark, 1994.

four of the large buildings and later by the one hundred unfinished townhouses remained vacant.

REQUIEM FOR COLUMBUS HOMES

"DESIGNED FOR LIVING. You should see these low-rent, modern apartments before they are all rented. This is the Christopher Columbus Homes—High Street and Eighth Avenue, Newark, N.J. Visitors are impressed by the many modern conveniences it offers—closeness to churches, schools, recreational facilities, downtown shopping centers, and scenic Branch Brook Park." Thus reads a 1950s promotional postcard for the Columbus Homes high-rise public hous-

ing project. On March 6 of 1994 four of the project buildings were dynamited. The remaining structures are expected to be blown up before the end of the year. The *New York Times* and assorted public officials hailed the demolition as the close of a misguided era.

I had known these buildings for fourteen years, and though on my most recent visits before the demolition I hadn't dared to go inside, I was left uneasy by all of this. Razing housing projects has become increasingly common across the nation, justified by the argument that architecture—those "brick behemoths," as they are called—is to blame for intolerable living conditions.

When completed in 1956, the Columbus Homes consisted of eight drab buildings, each one thirteen stories high, a block long, and containing nearly two hundred apartments. By 1960 the complex was flanked to the east and to the

Left behind on a shelf: unmatched women's shoes and a portrait of Jesse Jackson. Columbus Homes, Newark, 1994.

Demolished building, part of the Columbus Homes, Newark, 1994.

west by three elegant glassy towers designed by Mies van der Rohe for middle-class professionals who wanted to stay in the city. Towering over it from a high point three blocks northwest is the neo-Gothic Cathedral of The Sacred Heart, finished around the same time as the Columbus Homes. Southward the project is separated from the downtown by Route 280 and by the Erie Lackawanna railroad line.

I started photographing the Columbus Homes in 1980. In 1981, I ran a summer youth employment program in Newark. Fernando, one of the teenagers assigned to me, lived in the complex. When I asked him to define the word "ghetto," he replied that "the ghetto is the projects." Fernando and his friend Hakim would go to the roof to admire the Manhattan skyline, and to throw eggs at passersby. He and his friend would laugh as yellow stains spread on people's clothes. By the time anyone could climb up to

investigate, the boys would be gone.

A year later, after a tour of the project, James Baugh, a high-level official at HUD, declared, "No human should ever have to live that way." He saw "hallways . . . littered with garbage, and leaking roofs, and falling plaster . . . breakdowns in elevator service . . . widespread deficiencies in maintenance." At that time about half of the high-rises had already been closed. Once the buildings themselves had been declared bad, plans to modernize them were scrapped. This did not, however, stop the Newark Housing Authority from collecting federal support until 1987 for apartments it never intended to rehabilitate.

I visited the project many times, including once with a public television crew in 1987. I still remember the guns of the two security guards that accompanied us. We struggled to fit the entire party and all the equipment into one elevator so that nobody would get left behind. I also remember a clean-cut teenager climbing the filthy stairs carrying a newly pressed suit from the cleaners on his back. While I was being interviewed against a backdrop of one of the buildings, a group of young boys kept yelling, "Why do you ask him? Why don't you ask us? We live here."

The dynamiting of half of the Columbus Homes prompted me to return there to survey the inside of the remaining high-rises. The hallways were like tunnels with pools of water on the floor. Although most of the doors throughout the buildings were welded shut, the rooms were connected to each other and to the hallways by large holes punched through the thin walls. The complete darkness of the stairways contrasted with the sunlit apartments. Hundreds of broken windowpanes had been replaced with tape and plastic; casement windows with broken handles were kept shut with wire, making them difficult to open—the kind of slapdash repairs that signal general neglect.

The two towers to the west had been cleaned of graffiti, apparently the start of an aborted modernization effort. Their windows were sealed with rusted metal coverings that flapped noisily against the metal frames, resembling thousands of misshapen wings struggling to lift the buildings.

The two structures to the east were a gold mine of scribblings. Most of the writing consisted of people's names, often arranged in lists. On the wall of a bedroom that looked out onto the remains of the demolished buildings, someone had drawn the outline of a small house with a smoking chimney; and within that frame was a poem, titled "All Alone":

> I am Sitting Here All Alone,
> Waiting, Waiting
> To Find a Home.
> At night I lie in bed and dream
> And sometimes i wake up and start to
>   scream.
> What is this fear I feel inside,
> Is it of being alone
> Or is it my mind?
> I am Sitting Here All Alone,
> Still Waiting To Find A Home.

As I walked from apartment to apartment I found more drawings and messages. Many were about love, or its disappointments. One inscription, signed Keyonnah, read: "Whoever invented mens ther need to be killed." By far the most popular saying was "Dee Dee [or another name] was here but now she's gone. / She left her name to carry on. / Those who knew her knew her well, / Those who didn't could go to Hell!!!"

People also left their writings behind. In a school notebook, Tawanda wrote to Joseph: "Who do [you] want, me, Ida, or Stevonne. If you want any of them you can have them. I am not saying this because you think I am jealous I am saying this because I love you and I care for you. I won't let nothing happen to you. If something ever happens to you, that would be the end of my LIFE. If you don't want none of them Please tell me and stop playing with them in a nasty way."

In a diary entitled "I'm Sorry We Quarreled," another resident wrote, "I got a Cutlass of my own. I am going to school. Why you didn't go to college." The notes deal mostly with two children who the author would like to take into her home and raise but is not allowed to by a judge because she doesn't have a husband. She complains, "Wilbert didn't Treat Kid Right. his wife too. his wife never cook and clean them's clothes for school. She let Wes beat Chris up for nothing."

Many of the books left behind were textbooks on business, math, and accounting. I also found a copy of *Waiting for Godot*, a book of poems by Sylvia Plath, *Gorky Park, The Invisible Man,* and a manual on the care of tropical fish. On the way out I stepped on an old urban planning book.

I came across many copies of the Bible, pamphlets from Reverend Ike, and dozens of religious images. The only traces of political activity were signs in English and Spanish from the Progressive Labor party recruiting people for a May 1, 1984, March on Washington.

A list of about twenty phone numbers written on a wall led me to Ahmed. "I knew everyone," he told me. "It was a dangerous place. You are talking about people who had no jobs, man. If you was a strange face you was done in. If you was a strange face walking in that area, you was robbed, man. Who is going to come down there? Are you going to come down there? No. Is someone off the street going to come down there? No. No one is going to pop up in that area, no way. If that was the case you was easy prey. 'Who is this here, Hakim? You know him?' 'No, I don't know him.' 'Jamal, you know him?' 'No, I don't know him. Just check with any other guy.' "

When I asked him if he had been affected by crime, he replied: "I had eight brothers with reputations and my girlfriend Cheri had seven brothers, so my family was cool with one another. We had cousins. As a matter of fact, to tell you the truth, my family and friends were the ones that really do it."

At the end of our conversation I asked Ahmed what he did for a living. "I sell drugs," he said. "I do very well. I probably drive a better car than you. I have a house."

On the occasion of the demolition, Newark's mayor Sharpe James, president of the National League of Cities, said, "This is the end of an American dream that failed." It would be closer to the truth to acknowledge that the dream was made to fail by high unemployment, mismanagement, corruption, and federal policies that concentrated the poorest of the poor in these projects.

Why should we bother to pause and think about these buildings and what they represent? Why pick among fragments to create an archaeology of doomed buildings? Because the projects were wide open. Because these musty, dirty places and the belongings and markings left behind convey some of the worst of the American experience. Because in their remains can be read the yearning for respect, for love, for a modicum of order and security. Finally, because it is here,

inside abandoned buildings surrounded by ruins, that we feel most intensely the need to create a better world.

The letters, notes, calendars, drawings, family snapshots, and old shoes that I came upon at the Columbus Homes took possession of me and demanded to be passed on to others. Together with the former residents, we need to write the history of our ghettos from the inside; otherwise, the official story will prevail.

Under the 1987 Housing and Community Development Act, local housing authorities must replace lost or vacated public housing units on a one-to-one basis. "The one-for-one rule is the life preserver for public housing," says Stephen Finn, the executive director of the Newark Coalition for Low-Income Housing.

Typically, the demolished high-rises are replaced by townhouses. One hundred shoddily built townhouses being completed on the site of four Scudder Homes—another dynamited project in Newark—were so badly damaged during a windstorm that they had to be razed. Another cluster of townhouses, left unfinished for several years by the developer and attacked by vandals, is now being completed. In rows of dwellings completed during the last five years there are already several boarded-up units.

The Columbus Homes high-rises were clearly unpopular, and the newspaper accounts tell of crowds cheering when the explosion of 3,800 pounds of dynamite brought them down. Twisted iron, broken bricks, and recalcitrant bits of buildings are strewn over twenty-five acres, presided over by a cathedral. What next—townhouses for all? And then failing townhouses? These are so flimsy that they will save the federal government the cost of dynamite.

Park Avenue, South Bronx, February 1979.

Park Avenue, South Bronx, May 1982.

PARK AVENUE, SOUTH BRONX

"The owners abandoned the houses; they now belong to the city. Scavengers came and ripped off the aluminum siding. I am not worried; I am moving out next week."

—Resident of one of the five occupied houses
left on Park Avenue after a fire, 1981

Victorian two-story, wood-frame houses are common throughout New York City, particularly in areas of the Bronx north of the Cross-Bronx Expressway. They are spacious and economical, frequently accommodating three families. Typically the owner lives on the ground floor and keeps the small backyard. With barely enough

space for an adult to walk between two adjoining dwellings, these structures bear witness to the desire for a free-standing house.

The rising cost of fuel and taxes eroded their profitability, and young families with small children often added to the wear and tear, increasing maintenance costs. As the owners moved away, these buildings became vulnerable. Houses like those in the photo sequence above were often taken over by the city for nonpayment of taxes and later sold to families lacking the resources to make the mortgage payments and to maintain them properly. This led to a second wave of abandonment.

Lack of central heat made people turn to dangerous ways of keeping warm, causing fires. The first of the houses on the street to be destroyed was consumed in an electrical fire, which disabled the boiler that also heated the ad-

Park Avenue, South Bronx, March 1990.

Park Avenue, South Bronx, March 1993.

joining house. Soon an unmarked moving van pulled up next door, and the house on the left was abandoned. The city acknowledged its derelict status by hand-painting its street address, in large numbers, on the metal seal covering the door.

In my conversation with the owner of the remaining house, he objected when I compared his dwelling to the other three that had disappeared. He advised me to look south instead of looking north, noting that those houses had survived.

178TH STREET AND VYSE AVENUE, SOUTH BRONX

"The building had more than sixty apartments, some had as many as seven or eight rooms. [It was destroyed] not by one fire, maybe a dozen fires. There was a lot of arson. The heat was off last year and the city brought a big truck [a mobile heating unit] to heat the building. This year I knew that we were going to have problems there. First the fires were in occupied apartments, then in empty ones. To heat their apartments people sometimes put a piece of tin on the floor and build a fire over it."

—Firefighter,
East Tremont, South Bronx, 1982

67

178th Street and Vyse Avenue, South Bronx, June 1980.

178th Street and Vyse Avenue, South Bronx, June 1982.

178th Street and Vyse Avenue, South Bronx, September 1984.

178th Street and Vyse Avenue, South Bronx, January 1986.

178th Street and Vyse Avenue, South Bronx, May 1991.

178th Street and Vyse Avenue, South Bronx, November 1993.

178th Street and Vyse Avenue, South Bronx, January 1983.

178th Street and Vyse Avenue, South Bronx, March 1988.

178th Street and Vyse Avenue, South Bronx, October 1994.

When I first saw it in 1980, the building on 178th Street and Vyse Avenue seemed like a castle of brick and iron, filled with Puerto Rican and African American children. The late seventies and early eighties were times of pervasive destruction. Walking along the streets I had a sense of impending doom. Yet this particular building was so large, so useful, and seemed so solid that its abandonment and destruction were unthinkable.

Fires began in the fall of 1980, in top-floor apartments. (This is a telltale sign of arson, because when a fire is started on the top floor it is understood that the residents will be able to flee, so that charges of murder will not be raised.) Then scavengers moved in to remove the pipes, radiators, and appliances, leaving the water running to flood the apartments below and force the tenants to move out. The building was completely abandoned in January 1983.

Continuity has been lost. In an extraordinary transformation taking place over thirteen years, a big, solid building with sixty-four apartments was replaced by four townhouses, built to accommodate eight families. Brick, iron, and stone was replaced by wood and plastic; dark brown gave way to light blue; and where a courtyard with two staircases and a balustrade ringed the entrance, there are small lawns and some pavement for the owner to park a car. Two Bronxes are visible in these photographs: one that died too soon and one too flimsy to last.

New Street and Newark Street, Central Ward, Newark, January 1980.

New Street and Newark Street, Central Ward, Newark, April 1985.

NEW STREET AND NEWARK STREET, NEWARK

"New buildings are for people with jobs."

—Alice Davis,
Newark, 1981

Three badly maintained two-family row houses near the old city jail were all that remained of a much larger group of dwellings that stood on Newark Street in 1980. The city demolished the rest, its bulldozers facilitating the work of scavengers who, the night after the demolition, stole the exposed pipes and began to chop the boiler into sections to sell as scrap. The following day the landlord, faced with having to do major structural repairs and replace the pipes, decided instead to abandon his buildings and to fill the

New Street and Newark Street, Central Ward, Newark, April 1986.   *New Street and Newark Street, Central Ward, Newark, August 1994.*

trunk of his car with anything of value.

Without a landlord the tenants lived rent-free in apartments lacking central heat. As people moved out, mattresses, furniture, rugs, and appliances were left in the front yard. Windowpanes were broken and replaced by cardboard; apartments were sealed; the foundations continued to rot; hedgerows in the front yard grew wild. Residents used sheets and black garbage bags to cover the broken windows. The city's role as a landlord was minimal, consisting principally in boarding up and demolishing units as they emptied.

There was a sense of inevitability in the gradual disappearance of these dwellings. Perhaps the only surprise was that they had managed to survive for so long.

For Alice Davis, one of the residents, the ever-present threats of fire, the cold winters, the broken windows, and the rotten floors were not her greatest concern. "My man is the problem," she said. "Last night he pulled a knife on me."

View along Charlotte Street, South Bronx, March 1981. Although running only three short blocks, Charlotte Street was the most famous ghetto street in the country. With great fanfare, Jimmy Carter (1977) and Ronald Reagan (1979) each visited this national symbol of "urban decay."

View along Charlotte Street, South Bronx, February 1985.

TOWNHOUSES

"Those people [who build townhouses] are eating up the whole Bronx."

—Pancho Rodríguez,
superintendent of an apartment building, South Bronx, 1991

"This is what people want. . . . They come around here and they weep for these houses."

I. D. Robbins, builder of the Nehemiah Houses,
East Brooklyn, 1983

Clusters of brightly colored houses, with patches of green grass and flowers, line up for blocks in dozens of poor neighborhoods, contradicting the usual ghetto image of neglect and destitution. New York City alone has completed nearly ten thousand townhouses as part of its ten-year housing plan. The greatest advantage of these developments is their cost; they are the most inexpensive means of reclaiming and repopulating urban land. This kind of private housing, moreover, attracts working families to ghetto neighborhoods while eliminating problems resulting from absentee landlords.

High-rise public housing projects and tenements coexist with private houses; one group living at or near the poverty level, while the other—with an income about five times higher—shares in the nation's stability and wealth. Neighbors usually welcome the townhouses. The new developments, with their fenced yards, watchful neighbors, and brightly lit streets, signal that the area is under control.

The appeal of the townhouses to both families and public officials was heightened by the failure of many large developments constructed between the 1950s and the 1970s. Dozens of ex-

View along Charlotte Street, South Bronx, August 1989. Ranch-style houses were built six to an acre on Charlotte Street. Upon completion of the first ten houses in 1985, former mayor Ed Koch remarked that the new owners would "defend these houses with their lives."

View along Charlotte Street, South Bronx, October 1994.

pensively built public housing projects and subsidized towers of this period became anonymous, dangerous "vertical slums." In 1979, the well-known planner Edward Logue expressed the need for drastic change, stating: "We need housing, but on a very much lower, much less dense, level. We'll never build another five-story walk-up, you can be sure of that. I doubt we'll build another single building with an elevator in it in the South Bronx. . . . We have to realize that we're talking about a suburban intensity of land use. We're talking about one-story buildings with room for expansion, with off-street parking and off-street loading."

The most famous of these developments is a tract of ninety ranch-style houses built by Logue in the Charlotte Street area of the South Bronx. The national media responded enthusiastically to Logue's vision of bringing the American Dream to a forgotten and desolate area, to

his transformation of a troublesome national symbol of urban ills into a quiet, ordinary neighborhood of private houses, unique only because of its location. With great satisfaction he reported the reactions of visitors: "You should've seen their eyes when they looked at these houses. I've never seen such an enthusiastic response to a development."

The emergence of prefab houses with white picket fences along a street that for over a decade had witnessed fire and abandonment, roving dogs and touring politicians, is today one of the city's curiosities. The trees along the streets are now fully grown. Homeowners have added decks, swimming pools, fences, and sheds; their Jeeps and boats are on display. Charlotte Gardens, as the ranch-style development is called, was followed by Salter's Square, a row of two-story townhouses, and many similar developments.

Thirteenth Avenue Presbyterian Church, Central Ward, Newark, October 1987. The church was built in 1888 in "Richardsonian Romanesque" style— brick and brownstone, with a domed apse, a tower that echoes its shape, and large cathedral windows. The church was small-scale, comfortable, ornate, yet unpretentious.

Entrance to the Thirteenth Avenue Presbyterian Church left standing in the middle of a large empty lot, Newark, February 1990.

Typically, clusters of townhouses have replaced four- to six-story apartment buildings, lowering the original density of the block by a factor of five. In the extreme case of Charlotte Gardens, the factor is closer to twenty. The most marketable locations to date have been those with the greatest supply of empty lots; most of the townhouses have been built in formerly violent areas that become relatively safe in recent years, after the population moved out and the old buildings were leveled.

Cities give land for these developments free of cost or sell it for a nominal price. In addition, depending on the safety and thus the marketability of the area, townhouses have received city and state subsidies averaging between $10,000 and nearly $60,000 dollars per dwelling in New York City, to $125,000 in Detroit's first new subdivision. But despite such liberal subsidies, the price of most of these dwellings often surpasses $100,000, and two-family houses sell for more than $150,000. In order to purchase them, families need a yearly income of more than $40,000. Townhouses are often affordable only for two-income families.

Certainly, compared to deteriorating projects and apartment buildings, clusters of townhouses look idyllic, offering a new beginning. "Something clean to live in," in the words of a Crown Heights, Brooklyn, resident, who explains: "You are not inheriting all the rats and roaches and everything else from everybody for a hundred years before."

In this increasingly polarized city, over four-fifths of the renters cannot afford even the cheapest of the new townhouses. Such developments exclude poor and dependent families and use large tracts of land on which the city could build mixed-income communities. Moreover, a large proportion of the new homeowners once

Entrance to the Thirteenth Avenue Presbyterian Church surrounded by new townhouses, February 1992.

Out of place and meaningless, the entrance to the Thirteenth Avenue Presbyterian Church stands by the side of a row of townhouses, November 1993.

had counted among the most stable families still living in the core ghettos; by moving out of their apartments and into the new houses, they destabilize their old buildings. For example, over four hundred Brooklyn families from nearby public housing projects moved to the 1,050 Nehemiah Houses in Brownsville, Brooklyn. About half of the vacated apartments went to families on public assistance, thus increasing the concentration of poor families in the troubled projects.

In these settings, individual effort shows and is emulated; looking after each other's houses, people cooperate for the common good. As the surrounding areas continue to deteriorate and buildings are abandoned and demolished, room is made for more townhouses, thus shrinking the area covered by traditional ghettos, restricting the city's options for places where they can add to the low-income housing stock. The unstated hope is that without a place to live, the

destitute would move to another city.

In suburban-type urban developments, individual families can shape the land, and even accumulate savings as they pay the mortgage and improve their dwellings. Their fate is not determined by that of their surroundings. Residents are able to create a secure zone for themselves, their neighbors, and their cars in the middle of a decaying cityscape.

Townhouses, while keeping some working families in the ghetto, do so by creating isolated, largely homogeneous communities. Instead of creating neighborhoods that exclude the poor, the challenge facing us is to build economically and racially integrated communities connected to the mainstream of our society.

An implant: row of pastel townhouses, parked cars, and narrow stripes of lawn contrast with the taller surrounding buildings and empty lots, South Bronx, 1992.

Imperial Gardens of the Los Angeles Housing Authority, South Central Los Angeles, 1992.

A rectangular enclave, consisting of twenty-six townhouses, built in the middle of a prairie landscape, Lawndale, Chicago, 1991.

In 1990 1,250 townhouses are being built in the Central Ward of Newark, west of the expanding corporate, cultural, and institutional downtown. A middle-class core, with its own private streets, is being created in an area that was the center of the 1967 riot.

Row houses reminiscent of those built next to factories in the nineteenth century. Yet the only "factories" in the areas now are junkyards, warehouses, sweatshops, a bottling plant, and a bakery. Nehemiah Houses, Brownsville, Brooklyn, 1994.

"He can afford to sell the stuff here. People who have no money can afford to buy for what he sells. You have a house full of kids and you have no money and the washing machine busts and the most you can give for a washing machine is fifty dollars, you see that man. The stove breaks down on you; it's no good; you have to feed the family; you see that man; you can get a stove off him. You have to clean it up, it has a ton of grease on it, but everything works all right, and you take that thing home, you clean it up, and you go on cooking. You get the mattresses, you spray a couple of cans of Lysol, you lay them out on the roof, you bring them downstairs and put them on the bed."

—NEWARK RESIDENT EXPLAINING
AN OUTDOOR APPLIANCE MARKET,
1992

FOUR

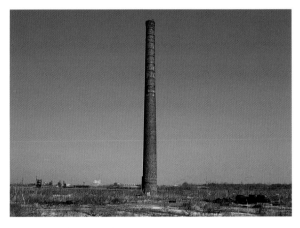

COMMERCE
AND INDUSTRY

Desolate section of West Madison Street, Chicago, 1988, the scene of two riots.

View east along Kercheval Avenue, Detroit, 1991. One of the city's commercial streets has taken on a rural look.

A distinctive characteristic of the modern ghetto is its commercial sector. The retailers still in business tailor their products to poor inner-city residents, rather than, as before, to the more affluent population of the entire metropolitan area.

Here, stores and businesses often sell different merchandise than is sold in the more affluent neighborhoods, and the buildings themselves are decorated and defended differently as well. Welfare allocations for furniture, funerals, and winter clothing have spurred local merchants to prepare and advertise packages for the exact amount of the allocation. Supermarkets offer large quantities of inexpensive foods such as five-pound plastic bags of frozen chicken wings, pigs' feet, or pork neckbone, items rarely sold in more affluent parts of the city. Here grocery stores sell brands of soft drinks—for example, Coco Rico and Shabazz Cola—not available elsewhere.

Living in a city like Camden limits the availability of products common in middle-class areas. According to local journalist Kevin Riordan, "There is no office supply store in Camden. If a woman wants to buy a business suit—and I am not talking a designer's suit—there isn't a place you can get one. There is no place where you can buy a white button-down shirt. I don't think you can buy such basic things as curtains, good-quality shirts or towels."

View north along John R., Detroit, 1993.

Washington Street, Gary, 1993, has the feeling of a frontier ghost town.

AVENUES OF MEMORY

"People talk about Broadway all the time even though it hasn't been a viable commercial street for fifteen years. The loss of it was really significant. Broadway symbolizes Camden for those who remember Camden. In the 1940s and 1950s Philadelphia was closed up on Sundays. People would come here and shop."

—Kevin Riordan,
journalist, Camden, 1988

"Blocks upon blocks of businesses have been destroyed and the grass is growing there."

—Rev. Bobby Wright,
describing Springfield Avenue, Newark, 1981

Long, broad commercial streets have traditionally formed the heart of American cities. Places of consumption and entertainment, they had stores, palatial dwellings, banks, restaurants, large movie theaters, car dealerships, and services that were central to the lives of generations of urban residents. People went there to march in parades and celebrations, to meet friends, to see shows, and to admire new products. The description of Euclid Avenue in Cleveland—"a seemingly endless vista of beauty"—applied to many magnificent urban thoroughfares throughout the United States.

Depleted by white flight and the competition from suburban malls offering the convenience of free parking in a secure environment, these avenues lost their customers, stores, and bright lights. Riots, frequent robberies, skyrocketing insurance rates, racism, and the angry black power rhetoric of the late sixties provided

A view south along Broadway from Sixth Avenue, Gary, 1994.

the final blow, convincing most of the remaining white-owned businesses that they had no future in the declining city.

What is left of these once-inviting streets has turned inward. The remaining businesses and facilities form strings of defended islands, boxy buildings surrounded by large parking lots where trading takes place from behind bullet-proof glass, directing products and services to those driving through. Corners and empty lots are used for peddling vegetables, used clothing, and appliances as well as for drug dealing and prostitution.

Additional factors contributing to the homogeneity of commercial strips in the ghetto are such franchises as Church's Fried Chicken, Gem, Stop and Shop, Value Plus, and Fayva Shoes. Their likeness is further reinforced by the many structures, once branches of national chains, that had a uniform look across the nation: Sears, Woolworth, and A. & P. Now, those recognizable structures, though often still substantial, have been abandoned.

Because of their high visibility, these main arteries became America's most prominent eyesores and most powerful symbols of urban decline. Their spectacular destruction signals daily to tens of thousands of drivers that the city is dying. Resurrecting a street that runs for half a dozen miles is a Herculean task consuming vast amounts of resources. And to keep the businesses profitable, the economic base of the city also needs to be revived. It is not surprising that even the most ambitious efforts at commercial reclamation have been limited to just a few blocks.

Officials are faced with the sad choice of leveling large sections of commercial streets to encourage development, or sealing and preserving the substantial yet semi-ruined structures that were once the pride of their city; in the latter case, the hope is that some day they will be recycled. Thus, the predicament is between something like a rural environment contained by a broken-down and overgrown city grid, interrupted by urban enclaves, and a city of ruins and ghosts.

Gary, Indiana's Broadway was once a major commercial street. It had three department stores—a Hudson's, a Goldblatt's, and one of the busiest Sears stores in the country—several theaters, and a large, first-class hotel. Since at least the late sixties, efforts to revive the street have included facade beautification, vest-pocket parks, street planters, banners, the building of two public libraries, and the rehabilitation of several vacant buildings for government offices and housing. The street continued to decline, however. Shopping malls outside the city limits attract customers from the city. At one point, Mayor Richard Hatcher refused to allow city buses to transport people from Gary to the malls. His rationale: "We certainly are not going to provide city services to help further destruction of our downtown."

Exceptional in its stubborn vitality and exuberant life is Harlem's 125th Street, a place where people go to meet one another, to observe the latest inner-city fashions, to preach, and to buy and sell. Ministers and activists address passersby, and the traffic barely moves through the rows of double-parked cars. The crowds are heterogeneous, a mixture of blacks from the U.S., Africa, and the Caribbean, and occasional tourists from Western Europe and Japan. From east to west the street is full of posters, signs, and images, while open-air stands sell books, cassettes, beads, and clothes. Several Korean shops sell toys, sneakers, vegetables, and bicycles.

The famous Apollo Theatre brings in large crowds. Restaurants and bars are lively; music shops play rap songs loudly into the street; and on Sunday storefront churches add to the general pandemonium with their rattles, choirs, and preaching. Drug dealing and prostitution thrive, less than a block away.

BUSINESSES

In ghetto areas, classical corner buildings, originally built as banks, are now likely to serve as storefront churches. Former Woolworth stores might sell used appliances, and once-thriving business hotels have been transformed into senior citizens' apartments. Meanwhile, car dealerships, business hotels, and stores selling jewelry, new appliances, and photographic supplies and processing have almost completely disappeared, as have banks.

The most common businesses are small food and furniture stores, fast-food franchises, dry cleaners and laundromats, gas stations, beauty parlors, check-cashing places, liquor stores, and bars. Street peddling, drug dealing, prostitution, and illegal gambling are very much in evidence. Recently video outlets and stores selling beepers have become a popular fixture of these communities, developing a reputation of being fronts for drug dealing.

Sodado's Market, which has been selling fresh-killed chickens in the Central Ward of Newark for more than two decades, illustrates some of the difficulties of doing business in a high-crime area. Senior citizens are the store's best customers, but most of them live in high-rises where security regulations prohibit them from buzzing in delivery boys. Instead, they have to come to the front entrance to pick up their chickens, wasting time and rendering the sale unprofitable. The store has been broken into several times; yet, because of strict health regulations, Mr. Sodado is unable to find a safer place to relocate. His equipment is obsolete, and cannot be replaced because it is not made anymore. He calls his trade "a business of days gone by."

Big, brash sign sweeps across the cinder-blocked windows, yellow brick facade, and traditional decorations of this clothing store, Brownsville, Brooklyn, 1994.

Sadie's "1" Stop Party Store, East Side, Detroit, 1994.

Used clothing store, West Side, Chicago, 1991.

Juanita and her grandson Javier tending her store. Among other things, she sells books, candles, statues, claws, and monkey and pigeon shit. Botanica del Gran Poder, South Bronx, 1988.

Art Deco movie theater converted into a supermarket, Oakland, California, 1985.

Four Brothers Grocery, Gary, 1994.

Tiny store offering six different services, Watts, Los Angeles, California, 1984.

Vacant lot along well-traveled Roosevelt Road on the West Side of Chicago becomes an extension of the "Community Resale Shop," 1993.

Second-hand appliance market on an empty lot, in operation for more than four years, Newark, 1988. Despite the lack of a building, this is a stable business.

Rummage sale along a busy street, organized by the First Mount Zion Baptist Church, Central Ward, Newark, 1987. After the city fenced the lot, the flea market was discontinued.

The Heavenly Missionary Baptist Church in Detroit runs a flea market and barbecue stand along Harper Avenue, 1991. Norma Sutton, a church official, accounted for their success by saying: "We don't charge people an arm or a leg. We don't sell junk."

A woman sells winter clothes and pots and pans on the parking lot of
a former shopping center on Forty-seventh Street, South Side, Chicago,
1992.

Rummage sale, Detroit, 1994.

Outdoor market, Robbins, Illinois, 1993.

Along Conant Avenue, Queen's Chapel stands out like the pink and white prow of an ocean liner. Detroit, 1993.

Hobbs Mortuary, nicknamed "The Orchid of the West" because of its use of purple for its fleet of Cadillacs, awnings, and trimmings. South Central Los Angeles, 1992.

"The oldest bank in Michigan" transformed into a Domino's Pizza, East Side, Detroit, 1991.

First Corinthian Baptist Church, Central Ward, Newark, 1993.

NEW USES FOR BANK BUILDINGS

"It is a good investment for the church; it requires little maintenance; it is made of the best materials: marble, stone, and walnut wood. We don't pay taxes on it."

—Church caretaker,
commenting on the advantages of having his church
in a former bank, Camden, 1982

"The notion of faith is an aspect that bankers and bank architects have always tried to understand and to express in their buildings; faith underlies both the building and the social practices of banking. Through buildings, banks try to convey to the public and particularly to their customers a sense of stability and trust."

—Ricardo L. Castro,
Design Book Review, 1991

Because of their sturdiness, size, and dignified appearance, former banks stand out. And because they are built as places of assembly, conforming to rigorous building codes and fire regulations, these edifices, more than any other type of structure, have been adapted as churches, Salvation Army missions, shelters, supermarkets, or drug treatment facilities. Yet their classical exteriors have barely changed, and even their safes and night deposit boxes remain in place. The strength of their construction and the cost of their original materials makes it prohibitive to

The former Clinton Trust Company, built in 1924, has been abandoned for more than a decade. Newark, 1993.

Untouched by time, these six colossal Doric columns have for three quarters of a century borne witness to the fortunes of the city of Camden. Once the home of the Broadway Trust Company, the building is now the James Apostolic Temple, 1993.

change their appearance to reflect their new functions.

There is no better illustration of the flight of capital from ghettos than the scarcity of operating banks and the large number of former bank buildings. Banks played a key role in the decline of Camden, according to former mayor Angelo J. Errichetti. In an interview in 1986, he called banks "absolutely worst" among the commercial enterprises, adding, "They made their dollars and made their wealth on the people of Camden for many years, but when it came time to move, they moved so damn fast it was unbelievable."

Between 1978 and 1990, according to a 1992 study by the New York City Department of Consumer Affairs, in the poorest fifth of the neighborhoods in Brooklyn 30 percent of all the bank branches were closed. This situation was even worse in similar areas of the South Bronx, where during the same period half of the bank branches closed.

In the inner city, a basic function of banks, to cash people's paychecks and government checks, is fulfilled by check-cashing places. These outlets often charge 3 percent and sometimes as much as 5 percent on the value of a

Bank, now a storefront church, East New York, Brooklyn, 1980.

A quarter century ago, this building was the Highland Park State Bank. Today as the Wood Six Twin it shows adult movies and live sex shows, male and female. Highland Park, Michigan, 1993.

check. Yet to cash a check in a bank, people need to have enough funds for an account, and for those who live from day to day, this is beyond their means. By the same token, banks gain little or no profit serving poor customers.

In addition to cashing checks, these outlets send telegrams, sell subway tokens and food stamps, accept payments on utility bills, and rent private mailboxes. Outside their doors, particularly on payday or when the welfare checks arrive, little marketplaces arise: the sale of food, clothes, and produce; begging, prostitution, and drug dealing.

Cashing a government check is a major event in poor, minority communities throughout the country. Usually on the first or last day of the month, entire families line up at private check-cashing outlets to get their money. The elderly and the disabled are delivered in vans driven by young, strong men who watch so that their charges don't get robbed. Drug dealers stand aside in groups waiting for payment on advance sales, while vendors hawk hot dogs.

Abandoned Banker's Trust building, South Bronx, 1980.

Stop 1 supermarket operating in the same bank building, 1992.

A former bank building now houses the "Church of God Prayer Tower," South Side, Chicago, 1990.

The Robert Treat Savings and Loan Association abandoned this building after the 1967 Newark riot. With painted-on crosses and windows, the structure houses the Church of Prophecy, but an incongruous life-size image of Robert Treat in his Puritan garb remains, 1992.

Griffins decorate this former palace of fantasy, now a ruin. The Riviera Theatre, Detroit, 1991.

Abandoned SRO, since demolished, Woodlawn, Chicago, 1987.

GONE OUT OF BUSINESS

"They were palaces, a great celebration for a boy. You had a feeling of entering a Las Vegas situation. There were bright moving lights; the colors were vibrant; there was a plush carpet. I remember walking on the carpet. No one at home had carpets like that. It was very sensuous, just grand; the impression was of great luxury. To go there it felt like you were getting a kind of a massage."

—Donald Moss,
remembering Detroit's Riviera Theatre in the 1950s, 1992

One would have expected most carefully constructed and richly appointed buildings to be those better able to endure neglect. Yet large, fancy structures were among the first to be abandoned, as their upscale residents and clients moved early to the suburbs. These fine buildings, because of their spacious quarters and high maintenance costs, pose the biggest challenge to finding new occupants with resources matching those of earlier tenants.

In ghettos, elegant office buildings, scores of business hotels, large movie theaters, Sears, Woolworth, and former car dealerships have remained vacant for decades. They are vulnerable. Their fine bronze fixtures and stained-glass windows are sold by landlords and strippers to suburban homeowners and antique dealers. Their commercial signs and cornices become a danger to the public and are often removed.

RKO Theatre decorated with giant cupids, Bedford-Stuyvesant, Brooklyn, 1989.

With its showroom windows sealed, this former Oldsmobile dealership is now a warehouse, Lawndale, Chicago, 1987.

Graffiti being scrubbed from a former Pepperdine University building. Its tower resembles a lighthouse. The building belongs to a church and is now sealed, South Central Los Angeles, 1992.

Ghost of a Woolworth's under the El tracks, Woodlawn, Chicago, 1987.

Alone in the middle of a vast empty area by the Delaware River, the gigantic smokestack of the former J. R. Evans Leather Company remained until it was dynamited a powerful symbol of an extinct industrial civilization. The factory closed in the 1960s. North Camden, 1982.

Abandoned parking lot once belonging to the Component Division of International Harvester, its plant now razed. At its peak, during the Viet Nam War, this division employed 3,500 workers. Ingersoll Products, in the background, with a greatly diminished labor force, is the last operating factory in this area, which once produced tools, farm equipment, metals, machine parts, and chemicals. West Pullman, Chicago, 1991.

INNER-CITY FACTORIES: FROM BOOM TO BUST

"For a hundred years Ingersoll Products Corporation has believed and operated on the concept that only the best is good enough.

Becoming the best has required the sweat, skill, perseverance, and teamwork of thousands of people, especially the employees, both past and present, of Ingersoll Products.

We, the employees, take great pride that our efforts have helped make the American farmer the most productive and respected member of the worldwide agricultural community."

—Sign, echoing feelings appropriate to boom times, posted at the entrance to the Ingersoll Products plant, a much-reduced survivor in an area of abandoned factories, West Pullman, Chicago, 1991

(Left) Like a survivor in a ruined city, a man pushes a shopping cart loaded with scrap metal to a nearby recycling place, against a background of industrial ruins and a tire dump, Lawndale, Chicago, 1988.

(Center) Same activity, against an ever-diminishing urban fabric, Lawndale, Chicago, 1993. Returning from the recycling place, a man pulls an empty cart. One large factory in the background has been demolished.

Just as elegant homes became rooming houses, and Woolworth stores became outlets for used appliances or storefront churches, factories, before being discarded, tend to follow a complex path toward abandonment.

The public usually learns of factory closings only when the owners decide to terminate operations completely. But industrial buildings are almost never abandoned all at once. Instead, their spaces are used successively by smaller and smaller businesses that pay low salaries and offer little job security. The result of the cycle is total abandonment. Because the cost of demolition is high and the value of the land is low, such structures often remain as features of the ghetto landscape. Residents regard abandoned factories as one of the many "messes" that are part of their daily lives.

Typically, the space once occupied by a single manufacturer becomes home to several sweatshops, and to carpenters and other skilled artisans, and the space left over is used for warehousing. New tenants have a high rate of turnover and eventually most of the space ends up being used for storage. After these structures are abandoned, cities find it almost impossible to secure such large buildings with so many openings. Thus, until they are leveled, these structures and their parking lots are used by squatters and illegal dumpers.

The ruined factories located in today's ghettos were part of a thriving industrial landscape once described with superlatives. For most of the century, their aggressively marketed products defined modernity and the promise of a better life. In 1908, John Kimberly Mumford, writing in *Harper's*, called the industrial area along the southwestern part of Lake Michigan "the greatest producing center in the world." Detroit was nicknamed "The World's Largest

Factory Town," and Gary was called "industrial utopia" and "Magic City."

Throughout the second half of the nineteenth century, optimism was pervasive; people felt that no problem resisted solution. The rapid growth of cities and of American power became synonymous with each other. Great productive centers were being created overnight; the land crisscrossed by railroads; noisy streets teeming with people.

An account of Pittsburgh in 1908 in *Harper's* by Charles Henry White reflects a fascination with the new environment created by heavy industry: "A spectacle never to be forgotten . . . these towering, flaming infernos . . . where forests of mammoth stacks are belching clouds of smoke." In this admiring account, even the shameful disregard for human life that characterized American industry before the rise of labor unions is depicted as unimportant and even hu-

morous. Describing a chance encounter with "a small, wiry man," White quotes him saying, as he points to a well-known factory: "Down there is the slaughter-house. . . . Fingers is going down there like bananas at a country fair."

To visiting European observers, the condition of industrial workers was appalling. Yet if workers, particularly those of immigrant origin, were victims of the system, they nonetheless shared the realistic hope of a better life for their children and grandchildren.

Supporters of capitalism were not blind to the poverty, preventable diseases, crime, and wretched working conditions that plagued the laboring poor, but they perceived these ills as temporary. Time would correct such aberrations, they argued, and asked their audiences to be patient. Growth would continue; immigrants would adopt modern American ways; and everyone would rise to undreamed-of levels of prosperity.

A fenced salt depot for the City of Chicago now occupies land used for dumping seven years before. An undefined zone has replaced the industrial neighborhood that was once there. Lawndale, Chicago, 1994.

97

Former Tiffany factory, a silverplate manufacturing operation, closed in 1984. The building is being converted into housing at a cost of $15 million. Inside there will be 129 new apartments, but the exterior's "Normandy towers" and ornamental brickwork will be preserved. Forest Hills, Newark, 1987.

Former American Bank Note Company, built in 1911. A massive factory in the South Bronx that printed stock certificates, lottery tickets, and the currency for several Latin American nations, it now hosts about a dozen sweatshops. South Bronx, 1990.

Typical of this view was a portrait of Chicago by Harrison Rhodes in a 1917 issue of *Harper's*. Countering those critical of the city, Rhodes stated that each moment of its history had brought improvement, and he encouraged readers to return in a few months to see its problems solved: "If everything in Chicago is not perfection it is only because there has not yet been time to make it so."

In Gary, the power of technology came together with an ideology of human improvement mixed with nationalism. Mumford gave an optimistic and racist view of the city. Gary was "so planned," he wrote, "that each generation shall have a chance to rise in intelligence, in comfort, in health, and in general well-being above the plane of its predecessor. It takes the human product of the Balkan states, brutal, unlettered, in some cases little better than a cave dweller; it

gives him a white man's house to live in, and hires people to teach him how to live the white man's way."

In this city, for the first time in their lives, multitudes of poor immigrants enjoyed running water, electricity, sanitary facilities, and medical care, yet differences in salaries and opportunities for advancement among workers were substantial from the start. Skilled laborers, mostly American-born, received housing from the company and much higher salaries than the sixteen cents an hour paid to the mostly foreign-born, unskilled workers.

The closing of factories in industrial cities, the loss of jobs and economic power, has been rapid, with devastating consequences. As part of efforts to revive the local economy, the federal government funded new housing and public works, supported training and employment pro-

The Lautner Humana piano factory until the early 1940s, this building later contained furniture and accessories shops. Totally abandoned in 1979, the building and grounds were sold for $500 at a public auction in 1982. Newark, 1982.

Newark, 1994. Twelve years later, the building shown in the preceding picture now functions as a homeless shelter housing eighty-two adults. Although bureaucrats refer to it as the "urban renewal shelter," a sign painted on the entrance door reveals little.

grams that continued to grow until the late seventies, creating a shadow economy that has been shrinking steadily for more than a decade. Today, among the largest employers in depressed cities are the boards of education, the hospitals, and city hall, places paying the majority of their employees only a fraction of the blue-collar wages industry once paid.

Often former industrial neighborhoods become ghettos. The new "industry" consists of services addressing urban ills and social problems. A labor force of security guards, social workers, nurses, doctors, and government officials commutes daily to work.

In new immigrant ghettos, sweatshops making clothing, jewelry, cutlery, and other products are common. It is frequent for people to do piecework at home, and for a middleman to bring the materials and pick up the finished pieces to be assembled at a shop by a regular workforce.

A powerful longing for the city of smokestacks and paychecks lingers among those old enough to remember. People recite like an incantation the names of nearby abandoned factories and the products they used to make. Joe Moody, a sixty-two-year-old resident of the Central Ward of Newark, gives his list: Tasty Bread, Bond Bread, Fisher's Bread, Krueger Beer, Fedders (air conditioners) and Emerson (air conditioners), Sylvania (television sets), General Electric (light bulbs). "You don't make nothing here now," he adds bitterly. According to Mr. Moody, without jobs people are not only poor, but their lives are rendered meaningless.

"One goes from one place that looks like a prison, to another place that looks like a prison."

—ADA,
South Bronx, 1993

FIVE

OUR FORTIFIED GHETTOS

Places we associate with awful events tend to remain in our minds with peculiar intensity. At 2258 Mack Avenue on Detroit's East Side stood a 120-year-old gray wooden cottage, a former farmhouse. The roof has black holes left from a fire that raged on the afternoon of February 17, 1993. Glass windowpanes are gone, but the metal bars are still visible. "A sad day," says Ms. Jones, a neighbor. "All I could see was the smoke. The bars stopped them, the smoke killed them. It made me sick. I had to go to bed."

Outside, around the cottage, are mementos placed there by people trying to come to terms with the tragedy: A red ribbon tied to the doorknob; stuffed animals arranged on the front steps; a bright yellow tricycle parked in the weeds; a table with a large clock, its hands stuck at two o'clock, the time of the fire; and next to it a neat line of children's shoes. A crude billboard depicts the faces of three angelic children; four ovals, each framing a cross, represent the others.

LaWanda Williams, nine; Nikia Williams, seven; Dakwan Williams, six; La Quinten Lyons, four; Venus Lyons, two; Anthony Lyons, seven months; Mark Brayboy, two—all died when left alone in their "prison house." In the preceding five months another six people in Detroit, most of them children, had died trapped by fires in barred and barricaded houses.

Fortification epitomizes the ghetto in America today, just as back alleys, crowded tenements, and lack of playgrounds defined the slum of the late nineteenth century. Buildings grow claws and spikes; their entrances acquire metal plates; their roofs get fenced in; and any additional openings are sealed, cutting down on light and ventilation. Glass windowpanes in first-floor windows are rare. Instead, window openings are bricked up or fitted with glass bricks. In schools and in buses, Plexiglas, frosty with scratches, blurs the view outside.

Even in areas where the statistics show a decrease in major crime, fortification continues to escalate, and as it does, ghettos lose their coherence. Neighborhoods are replaced by a random assortment of isolated bunkers, structures that increasingly resemble jails or power stations; their interiors effectively separated from the outside. Throughout the nation's cities we are witnessing the physical hardening of a new order, streetscapes so menacing, so alien that they would not be tolerated if they were found anywhere besides poor, minority communities. In brick and cinder block and sharpened metal, inequality takes material form.

The United States Post Office is the main symbol of the federal government in the ghetto. But where one might expect reassuring classical buildings decorated with eagles and images of the old Pony Express there are instead squatty concrete blocks with iron grating. The only unifying national symbols are the American flag on the outside, and on the inside, the FBI most-wanted posters.

In a truly democratic society there would be no great differences in the quality of the buildings the government constructs for the same purpose in different communities. Yet, in the ghetto form does not follow function as much as it does fear. A building's adaptations for survival announce the existence of a state of urban war, a fact that even Washington cannot ignore.

"Post offices should look friendly, identifiable, efficient, and stylistically typical of local buildings—not like factories," concluded a study reported in 1989 in *Progressive Architecture*. Certainly, the fortresslike ghetto post office is "stylistically typical." The same can be said of the most modest representation of the postal system: apartment-building mailboxes, which are often covered by a locked iron grid. In dangerous buildings in New York City, the boxes are kept in a separate locked room.

Commercial establishments are just as heavily defended. Already in 1975, businessman Phillip Cyprian of Gary, Indiana, figured that even if his clothing store were housed in an all-steel building with no windows or doors, burglars would still find a way to enter and clean him out. "They'd take cutting torches and do it and never get caught," he reasoned. So Cyprian decided to move out. Entrepreneurs who stayed behind have applied measures only a little less drastic than those in his bleak architectural vision.

"We try to block up anything at all that can give people the idea this place is an easy target," explained the owner of a warehouse in Camden, New Jersey. In Detroit, a fenced roof, blocked windows, and jail door help to make Singleton Cleaners a difficult target, while its bright colors announce to drivers that the establishment is indeed in business. At a Newark Kentucky Fried Chicken franchise, a large plastic menu is protected with Plexiglas and an iron grating, obscuring much of the writing.

Churches also turn into fortresses. In Brownsville, Brooklyn, St. Luke's Community Church, formerly a Jewish catering hall, had the misfortune to be located across the street from a rubble-filled vacant lot. After school, neighborhood children used to throw bricks at the church, breaking windows, so the congregation simply blocked them. The Lighthouse Gospel M. B. Church in Chicago gets a little daylight through a cross made of glass bricks.

The hardened exterior of these houses of worship often contradicts their appealing names. Churches are called Fountain Spring, New Light, Healing from Heaven, House of Blessing, and Pleasant Grove. Names evoking an aspect of Paradise are bestowed upon uninviting buildings, which are more a barrier against violent surroundings than an image of refuge.

Most of these structures are accented by razor-ribbon wire. It was not until the late 1970s that this wire, formerly common only in prisons and military installations, came into large-scale civilian use. First strung atop fences around warehouses and factories, more recently it has become a favorite device for domestic defense, separating roofs of adjacent apartment buildings, securing the space between structures, and protecting the perimeter. Yet despite awesome fortifications, buildings are still broken into and burned, and the streets, now invisible to those inside, are even more threatening.

Choice public spaces are open for only a few hours during the day, while others are allowed to fall into disrepair, to harbor drug dealers and to function as open dumps. In "people's parks"—places accessible only to those with a key—those enjoying the green grass, trees, and flowers seem to be themselves part of an exhibit for passersby. Fences dwarf the tiny spaces.

Within such environments, police are perceived as distant, taking a long time to answer calls and often refusing to come at night. Dogs and security guards protect the few who can afford them. And, if one is to believe residents, just about everybody keeps a gun. Thus, people defend their homes. Those living in townhouses and private dwellings surround the borders of their property with fences enclosing the house and the family car. In addition, they bar their first-floor windows and often install clearly visible burglar alarms, red lights blinking. The most effective defense, however, is not physical but social, as people watch after each other's dwellings, question strangers, and call the police.

In South Central Los Angeles a basic fortress is a bungalow with a small green lawn. The dwelling's first line of defense is an iron door, usually painted black. Metal bars on the windows add further protection, changing the once-friendly character of the wood and stucco houses. Less visible are the sharp black iron spikes to ward off trespassers.

In urban sections where apartment buildings are the characteristic abode, outsiders are discouraged from loitering in lobbies, harassing residents, selling drugs, and stealing mail by locked extensions made of iron fencing that jut out, removing sections of sidewalk from public use. Where there are courtyard entrances, these are closed off with heavy gates topped with razor-ribbon wire.

Inside buildings, a hallway dog chained to the stairway railings calls attention to suspicious movements. In dangerous projects, metal doors to apartments have as many as four locks, including one at the center that releases two cross-shaped bars. Between the dogs and the door locks, however, are often dark hallways, and little can be done to defend these.

Besides the profusion of physical barriers against crime, in violent neighborhoods in New York City, Newark, and Chicago, social arrangements have evolved befitting a state of war. Groups of disabled and elderly residents going from their secure buildings to check-cashing outlets and the supermarket require police or security guards for escorts. At the entrances of shelters and welfare offices, guards post photographs and composite drawings of people wanted for crimes.

Milagros Jimenez, a small middle-aged woman, the president of her building's tenants' association in the South Bronx, tells of her courageous struggle to save her building: "I would go with Gladys to the roof at two or three in the morning, to watch so that people would not go there to do drugs and to kick out those who were doing drugs. Since we were with God and I was with another brave person, I was not afraid."

People also resort to religion and magic. As protection against evil, Elizabeth Valentin, another resident of the South Bronx, keeps saints and voodoo statues by her bed. She credits these images with having saved her during at least five muggings.

Signs are widely used as warnings. A piece of cardboard on an apartment window of a Chicago Housing Authority project, Altgeld Gardens in South Riverdale, reads: "No Trespassing. Due to an epidemic of AIDS do not enter my apartment when I am absent. Game is over, dude." Other prominently displayed notices warn intruders that they will be attacked by dogs or even shot. A warning sign in front of a house on Hillman Avenue, in Youngstown, Ohio, reads:

> Yo' Homes, rock starz, body sellarz, bad
>   boyz
> DO *NOT*
> 1. "CHILL" Here
> 2. "CLOCK" Here
> 3. "HANG TUFF"
> 4. SELL rockz HERE
> 5. READ Too LONG
> In other words
> STROLL!
> Yes, this means you2

Ghetto schools in Chicago post signs at their entrances saying: "WARNING: SAFE SCHOOL ZONE. You have entered a safe school zone: Criminal penalties are severely increased for gang recruitment and the possession,

use, or sale of drugs and weapons. Project Clean." In similar neighborhoods in New York City, school entrances bear a sign reading: "Weapons are not permitted in New York City Board of Education facilities. All persons entering this building are required to submit to a metal detector scan, and to a personal search if necessary." Yet even these kinds of signs, as well as letters and numbers bearing the names, addresses, and purposes of edifices, are often stripped by thieves and vandals.

Interiors have also been modified. In businesses and public offices, bullet-proof Plexiglas separates attendants and clients; people are buzzed in only after being screened by a receptionist. Concern for security has led to a new brutalism. Fortification creates a conflict between the desire to make people feel welcome and the grim need for defense. Those who live or work in such buildings say that the outside appearance has little to do with the quality of what is offered inside.

The manager of a forbidding day shelter in Chicago declares himself proud of offering the best meals of any shelter in the city. A recreation worker at the Hillside Community Center, which looms like an arsenal on Milwaukee's north side, boasts that great basketball games are played inside. And a South Bronx resident comments that despite the menacing claws on the roof and metal shutters on the windows, her neighborhood public library is always busy.

Those involved in the erection of fortresses deny that their buildings are in any way extraordinary. A Salvation Army official who took part in designing a bunkerlike building in Chicago explained: "There are windows there, a clerestory window in the chapel above, and small windows along the side. We don't spend enormous amounts on large windows, but to call this building a fortress seems to be a little overkill. It is not like a Strategic Air Command blockhouse, where I served when I was in the service, where you work in the basement and you have to go upstairs to see if the sun ever came up that day." A guard at the Office of Family Services in the South Bronx laughed at a comparison between his workplace and a prison, saying: "Too small for a jail—it does not cover enough ground. In New York you never find a jail this small."

But a South Bronx resident was so surprised by the appearance of the Highbridge Branch of the New York Public Library that she "had to come here and check it out and take some books out." Another, commenting on the metal spikes that ring the roof's perimeter, said, "It is sad, isn't it. I guess they don't want people on the roof." Most people interviewed perceived that the defenses were there to protect them, and nobody expressed a wish that they be removed. Instead, people soften the unfriendliness of their environments, decorating homes and businesses with lively paintings, ornate wrought-iron designs, and plantings. But underneath the surface, the fortress remains.

Plans that a quarter-century ago gave rise to polemics against the "school of brutalism" that was so prominent in the 1960s have become widely accepted in ghetto neighborhoods. "It is strange that those designs that were made to provoke an outrageous response should become everyday normality—what you have to have to get through the day," remarks Marshall Berman, professor of political science at City College in New York.

What does it mean to live in a windowless world rimmed with sharp things that protect by threatening to cut, puncture, and impale? A world characterized by animals that bark and bite, crude warning signs, bars that keep some out but may also prevent escape? A world defined by security guards and razor-ribbon wire,

by streets, hallways, and nights that don't belong to you? People in these neighborhoods express their dislike of fortification, but accept it as inevitable.

Fortification has profound consequences. Where defenses are aggressively displayed they create bizarre, shunned streetscapes of distorted survivors and ruined losers. The time spent opening and closing so many locks and gates, connecting and disconnecting alarms, nervously looking over one's shoulder, feeding guard dogs, and explaining one's business to security personnel, can become exhausting and detracts from other activities. Blocking the openings in buildings forces people to consume more electricity for artificial lighting and cooling, while increasing their isolation and sense of imprisonment. Scarce resources that should be devoted to basic needs and services are used instead for security and fortification. And residents feel powerless to soften their cages because they believe that crime is out of control.

The house at 2258 Mack Avenue in Detroit has an aura. Terrible images pass through one's mind upon seeing the broken, old-fashioned cottage surrounded by tokens of sorrow. A few blocks east along Mack Avenue, on the corner of Meldrum, the writing on the wall of an abandoned building says: "We remember that when people lose their lives as a consequence of injustice, their spirit wanders, unable to pass over—seeking resolution." The message is repeated clearly and neatly several times to make sure someone notices.

DEFENDED HOMES

(Left) Belmont, South Bronx, 1980.

(Right) Same house, South Bronx, 1993. During the thirteen years that elapsed since the prior photograph this South Bronx house has taken down its decorations and raised its defenses. Mr. Pagan, the owner, admits that when he enters his house, he feels like he is going into a jail.

(Left) Basic fortress, South Central Los Angeles, 1992.

(Right) Gray and grim defended two-family house, Robbins, Illinois, 1993.

Cottage at 2258 Mack Avenue, Detroit, 1993, where seven children died, trapped inside in a fire.

A resident of this neighborhood of Miami remarked that Liberty City was a misnomer, because people lacked the freedom to walk the streets after dark, 1984.

Ruben Robles, day guard paid by the tenants, University Heights, South Bronx, 1990.

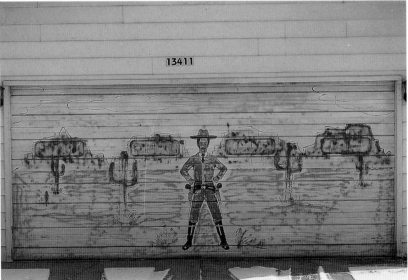

Garage door in Robbins, Illinois, announces to passersby that the resident is ready to kill in defense of his home, 1993.

(Above) Private altar placed in a hallway of an apartment building on Beekman Avenue, one of the country's deadliest streets, South Bronx, 1992. On the table, among flowers and religious items, are English and Spanish versions of a book entitled, You Can Live Forever in Paradise on Earth.

(Left) Warning sign in front of a house on Hillman Avenue, Youngstown, Ohio, 1992.

Iron cage protecting the light at the entrance of a high-rise part of the Tilden Homes, Brownsville, Brooklyn, 1994. The bulb had been broken repeatedly by drug dealers who prefer to sell under cover of darkness.

Padlocked Virgin Mary stands by the front entrance to a South Bronx house, 1990.

DEFENDED
INSTITUTIONS

Uninviting Hillside Community Center looks more like a bulwark than a building; the entry is on the side, Milwaukee, 1992. "That is an ugly damn thing, they ought to be ashamed of themselves. There ain't no doors, nothing. There ain't no style to it," said a ghetto resident upon seeing a picture of the center.

John F. Kennedy Recreation Center, Central Ward, Newark, 1994.

"One way in, one way out," Boys Club, South Bronx, 1987.

Sharing this citadel are the Crossroads Day Care Center, the W. L. Bonner Cultural Center, and the King Tut Dining Hall, Detroit, 1993. One of the church elders explained that fear of crime and riots had nothing to do with the look of the building. "That was Pastor Bonner's own design that he got from the Lord," he explained.

Social Security Office designed by James Stewart Polshek and Associates in 1973, South Bronx, 1990.

Walled Third Street Dental Group and Vision Centers of Wisconsin, Milwaukee, 1983.

For the membership of this Masonic lodge, fellowship and good cheer require the security provided by these grim bars and fences, South Central Los Angeles, 1992.

THE U.S. POST OFFICE IN HIGH-CRIME AREAS

Hub Station, designed for the dangers of the ghetto, South Bronx, 1988. A local resident commented, "It seems that they are afraid of thieves."

Located only two blocks west of the Hub Station, this classical building was formerly a post office, South Bronx, 1993. Its archways, windows, rooftop balustrade, and fine proportions bespeak a completely different way of life for the neighborhood.

Colonial Park Station, Harlem, New York, 1990.

Lincolnton Station, Harlem, New York, 1990. An elderly resident said: "Yeah, it had windows, I was here when it had windows. People used to bust in at night."

Clinton Hill Station, Central Ward, Newark, 1989.

Interior, Halsey Station, designed for a high-crime area, Bedford-Stuyvesant, Brooklyn, 1991.

In this drug-infested building, mail is delivered to a separate locked room, South Bronx, 1990.

Vandalized mailboxes, South Bronx, 1994. The residents of this housing project are forced to go to the post office to pick up their mail.

LOOKING FOR SECURITY, NOT APPEARANCE:

Day Care and Senior Citizens' Centers Resembling Prisons

"The elimination of windows is meant to say to the world, 'This is a bunker and we are sealed off,' and also meant to say to people: 'Don't worry, the world won't come in and kill you.' "

—Marshall Berman,
professor of political science, City College, New York, 1992

Office of Family Services, South Bronx, 1991.

Newark Pre-School Council, Head Start Center, 1994.

Omega Psi Day Care Center, Jamaica, Queens, 1992.

Social Services Center built like a fortress, East New York, Brooklyn, 1988.

Stapleton Center, East Side, Detroit, 1993. Here elderly people live behind a high fence topped with razor-ribbon wire.

A decorated fortress, North Avenue Day Care Center, Atlanta, 1980.

DEFENDED
COMMERCIAL FACILITIES

*"Buildings are vandalized; businesses are looted and robbed
until they leave the community or bar themselves in."*

—T. Willard Fair,
Urban League of Greater Miami, 1982

*Motel nicknamed "The Whorehouse," located along a busy prostitution and
drugs strip, South Bronx, 1991.*

*Singleton Cleaners, its fortified exterior painted in bright carnival colors,
East Side, Detroit, 1991.*

Carry-out Chinese food, South Bronx, 1994.

Defended truck, downtown Los Angeles, 1985.

Cardboard provides privacy and defense against rocks for a bus, Brownsville, Brooklyn, 1994.

The owner of this metal shop, North Newark, 1978, talks from behind iron grates, flanked by two German shepherds. He spoke of his shop's having been firebombed and of his desire to sell his business and retire to Florida.

"Hardened" pay telephone, North Newark, 1994.

DEFENDED CHURCHES

"We had to block the windows. This church was broken into twice; they took all the musical instruments, they took the ceiling fan, they even took the public address system we had bolted down to the floor."

—Al,
retired carpenter, Detroit, 1991

(Top) First Zion Hope Missionary Baptist Church, a former garage, Central Ward, Newark, 1980.

(Center) Eleven years later, isolated, sealed, and freshly painted white, "The Church with a Big Heart," First Zion Hope Missionary Baptist Church, Newark, 1991.

(Bottom) Fourteen years later, Newark, 1994, the outside shape of First Zion Hope remains constant even though its facade has been simplified for the sake of security. The recent addition of stone veneer adds a sense of durability.

The Light House Gospel M.B. Church, Lawndale, Chicago, 1989.

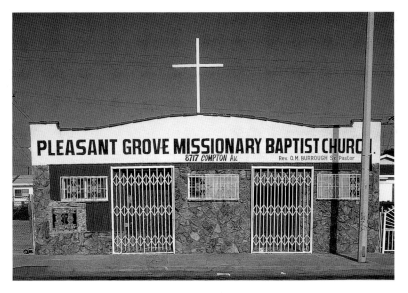

Pleasant Grove Missionary Baptist Church, Watts, Los Angeles, 1994. Gates and bars contradict the church's name.

Greater Holy Light Missionary Baptist Church, South Central Los Angeles, 1992.

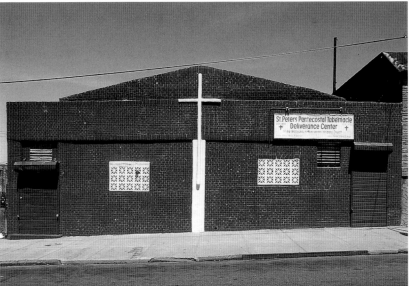

Designed like an open envelope, St. Peter's Pentecostal Tabernacle Deliverance Center, South Bronx, 1993, is sealed to the outside.

OLD PUBLIC BUILDINGS, NEW PUBLIC BUILDINGS

More than a century old, the large Holy Family Roman Catholic Church survived the Great Fire of 1871, which consumed everything around it. Today the church is under the shadow of the Chicago Housing Authority projects. An usher called Holy Family "the best and most beautiful thing in the neighborhood." Chicago, 1989.

St. Agatha Roman Catholic Church, Lawndale, completed in 1982. Resembling a power station, the building's religious function is revealed by the cross and the life-size crucified Christ. Chicago, 1990.

Bronx Borough Courthouse, South Bronx, 1986. A grand public building in the Beaux Arts tradition, it was executed by Michael J. Garvin, Architect, in 1906.

A huge, modern, impersonal structure to process people, nothing in the facade betrays the function of the Family and Criminal Court Building, Harrison and Abramowitz, Architects, 1977. South Bronx, 1988.

Englewood Family Center, Children and Home Aid Society of Illinois, built in 1925, has had grates put on the windows, bars on the door, and perimeter lights around its front. Chicago, 1991.

Impregnable building, Salvation Army Chicago Temple Corps, West Side, Chicago, 1992.

Eighty-six-year-old Saratoga branch of the Brooklyn Public Library, endowed by Andrew Carnegie. The building was closed two years ago after vandals stripped the copper flashing and gutters from the roof, causing it to leak. Failure to make repairs promptly led to serious damage. Bedford-Stuyvesant, Brooklyn, 1991.

Highbridge Branch, New York Public Library, Werfel and Berg, Architects, 1975. South Bronx, 1990.

CITADELS: HOSPITALS, COLLEGES, AND UNIVERSITIES

"This sleek, modern facility is an impressive architectural success—combining the functional utility of an efficient machine with a compassionate awareness of the people who will use it."

—Charles K. Gandee,
"A Major New Health Care Facility for Detroit: An Efficient Machine Designed with Compassion," Architectural-Record *(April 1980)*

Hard-edged and glassy citadels were often introduced to inner-city neighborhoods as a way to revitalize them. Others were old and prestigious institutions that decided to stay in the city. Surrounded by large parking lots, with entrances and perimeters tightly controlled by private security forces and electronic devices, they have expanded their facilities on adjacent land made available through the destruction of old neighborhoods. These nonprofit, tax-exempt institutions have taken the form of self-sufficient clusters, located near train stations and highways.

The University of Medicine and Dentistry of New Jersey rises like a gridded box at the center of an enormous parking lot in what once was the heart of the Central Ward, Newark, 1990. Reflecting the needs of the city, this teaching institution has become essentially an AIDS hospital. Newborns with AIDS were first diagnosed here.

Hard and shiny, Detroit Receiving Hospital was designed in 1981 by William Kessler and Associates at the cost of $125 million. Detroit, 1987.

Because of its industrial look, Woodhull Medical and Mental Health Center is known as "La Factoria" in this mostly Latino neighborhood, Bedford-Stuyvesant, Brooklyn, 1990. This facility, designed by Kallmann, McKinnel, and Russo, Architects, 1977, was the most expensive hospital of its time.

Lincoln Hospital, nicknamed "The Butcher Shop," South Bronx, 1992.

"People need to create their own history, to leave traces of themselves and of the meanings they generate in their lives. They feel a need to give expression to their community, to leave trails, to say, 'we are here,' to create beauty."

—SAM BECK,
professor of anthropology, Cornell University, 1991

SIX

WE ARE HERE

Helen Steiner in her living room with friend Alice Myers, South Bronx, 1994. During many years working for Good Will, Helen was able to select pieces that she liked from the many thousands of items for sale. To admirers, she responds that her apartment reflects her own taste, and that she does not read magazines on home decoration.

Life-size statue of San Lazaro and dogs, South Bronx, 1993.

Ghettos are always reacting. Life in these communities achieves an intensity that is reflected visibly inside buildings and out in the open. Doors, walls, even ceilings become places for dialogue and commentary.

Graffiti reveals a desire to be recognized, to lay a claim to the neighborhood, and to leave everything behind and begin again. Writing and sketching on walls preserve Black Power themes from the 1960s or memorialize the rise of Black Muslims in the 1970s. Some motifs remain perennially popular: names, love, sports, gangs, and drugs. Upon entering a building that has been sealed, one gets a glimpse of the past—changing names, gang territories, and cultural models.

In many housing projects and apartment buildings, thousands of individual pieces of writing form a palimpsest of names and nicknames, descriptions and advice, all blending together as one large tract covering most of the public space. One encounters depictions of local concerns, brief accounts of the peculiar conditions of the ghetto, and unexpected visions amid the surrounding decay.

RANCHO LUNA

SOCIAL CLUB

*Moonscape with a river,
South Bronx, 1972.*

FLEETING IMAGES, PERMANENT PRESENCES:

The Visual Language of the Latino Ghetto

*"Siempre ten presente que en esta pinche vida estamos de
paso."*

—Popular Mexican saying

*El sol, los muertos, el pueblo, la frontera, la familia, los ami-
gos, las mujeres, el ranchito, el carro, la droga, las flores, los
angeles, la cárcel, hijo de puta, los zapatos, los arboles, las
frutas, el fuego, la tierra, las estrellas, el mar, los indios, los
toros, los caballos, los perros, los pájaros, los gallos, las cucara-
chas, los cuchillos, las balas, las calaveras, la serpiente, Don
Quijote, Benito Juárez, Che Guevara, La Virgen de Guadalupe,
Jesucristo, San Lazaro, Santa Barbara, El Morro.*

—Basic Spanish

Driving on the country roads of northeastern
New Mexico in the summer of 1992, I heard on
a local radio station a group of women doing the
Via Cruces. A ritual at least three centuries old
in the pueblos of the area was being reenacted
once again: Women repeating Hail Marys in
monotone voices, the prayers punctuated by a
male narrator reciting descriptions of the Passion
of Christ. Caught beyond time and space, finding
myself transported in my imagination to the
small Chilean town of Rengo where I grew up,
I could not turn off the broadcast. The sounds of
an ancient religious practice, transmitted to a
lonely road I had never traveled before, told me

127

Moreno Auto Parts, Central Avenue, South Central Los Angeles, 1992.

that profound aspects of my culture were present here. I was surprised and moved.

The voices accompanying my travel epitomize the contradictory nature of the Latino expressions, their stability as images and their fleeting quality as presences. Individually their ephemeral character is manifested in voices traveling through space, or in materials that don't last, paintings that peel or are painted over, or in cheap objects that break and are discarded. Collectively, however, these types of images last because they are continually replaced by similar ones.

Contributing to their spread, popularity, and permanence is a growing population of new immigrants, many from small towns: men and women of rural origin, with little formal education, among whom mythical beliefs are strongest. Frequent trips to their countries of birth and a constant flow of visitors from home further

strengthen their roots. In addition, a slow rate of upward mobility among most Spanish-speaking groups contributes to their concentration in ghettos, where a separate identity is reinforced.

Surveying the breadth of the poor Latino communities of this huge nation, one encounters a rich culture. The images recent immigrants create reflect their varied geography, the struggle or fusion of Indian, Spanish, and North American culture, the prevalence of the Spanish language, and the influence of the Catholic religion.

There are, of course, the images of suffering Christ: kneeling alone at night in the Garden of Gethsemane, forsaken by his disciples; crowned with thorns, blood running down his pained face; crucified on a hill, between two thieves, only the light of heaven illuminating the crosses. The triumphant Christ, "Cristo Rey," is rare.

Then there is the ubiquitous San Lazaro,

*A memorial to father and son, Diz and Cojo (*cojo *means "lame" in Spanish). Depicted on the memorial is Lazarus walking on crutches through the graveyard, dogs licking his wounds. Sharing the wall is a memorial to June and Luis featuring a white BMW, a truncated obelisk, and a gigantic marijuana plant. Traditional and modern, weak and powerful, slow and fast, a crippled saint and a slick car emerge from a shared background of clouds. Both murals are the work of Paco. East New York, Brooklyn, 1993.*

depicted walking with crutches, dogs licking his bloody sores, a saint with a reputation for healing the sick. Another popular presence is the defeated Indian, grimly preserving his dignity despite his loss, his head brightly decorated with feathers.

Why is there so much suffering portrayed in these images? Why are the figures so meek and resigned? I would guess that they reflect the experiences of a poor population more used to pain and "desengaño"—disillusion—than more affluent Americans. There is the influence too of Spanish Catholicism's view of the world as a Vale of Tears, a troubled, temporary stage on our journey to eternal salvation or damnation.

Yet there are many joyful manifestations of the Latino presence. As if to reassure people that they will find what they need inside, grocery stores fill their windows with stacks of colorful merchandise: packages of diapers, boxes of

detergents, shaving cream, pots and pans, and stuffed animals. The signs display a curious mixture of Spanish and English, establishing the shopkeeper's ability to deal with clients in Spanish, to cater to Latino tastes, and to assist customers in getting insurance, filing income tax forms, and securing driver's licenses.

On three occasions, Hollywood crews have filmed the facade of Moreno's auto parts store on Central Avenue in Los Angeles. The owner, Jorge Moreno, originally from Mexico City, decided to decorate his business by neatly painting on his walls the products he sells. He is constantly cleaning off graffiti and adding pictures of new products, such as motor oils and axles, as they are introduced. Mr. Moreno's wife, an interior decorator, convinced him that it was much more effective to use images than words, since so many Latinos in the area come from the provinces and are illiterate. He is very pleased with

Puerto Rican flags, Mickey Mouse, and a Mexican sombrero are part of the decor of this living room, South Bronx, 1990.

the popularity of his store and the free advertisement he gets in movies.

Typically, the first Latino family on a residential block will announce its presence with loud, bright colors. People may not be able to afford to paint their entire house at one time, but the section painted will often be bright red. Light blue, green, and pink are popular choices for interiors, and for the gardens, climate permitting, geraniums, lilies, prickly pears, and palm trees.

For Puerto Ricans, their flag—waved in parades, displayed on their stores and homes, decorating hats, affixed as decals on cars or attached to the antenna—has the character of an obsession. The urge to display this emblem was forcefully illustrated to me during a salsa concert by the late Puerto Rican artist Hector Lavoe at Madison Square Garden in New York City. In front of a full house, a man ran from the audience, carrying a huge Puerto Rican flag to the

stage, eluding dozens of security guards, as if going through a battlefield. Representing a people, but not an independent nation, this ubiquitous symbol of identity is regarded as sacred.

Paradise is depicted on storefronts or apartment walls as the traditional "ranchito" built in a clearing next to a river or a lake, shown under the bright light of the sun or a full moon. Perhaps as a reaction to the crowding of the city, people are seldom depicted in such scenes. We see a rooster by a fence, a boat on a riverbank, a banana tree full of ripe bananas shading the house, a suckling pig roasting on a spit, a woman waiting by the door. In these depictions we are reminded of Don Quixote's El Dorado, a world made to please humankind, a paradise without cars, television antennas, computers, powerboats, guns, or other signs of modernity. There the abundant waters were crystalline and "sabrosas." To feed oneself it was necessary

Elizabeth Valentin keeps saints by her bed as protection against evil. South Bronx, 1991.

only to reach up for sweet and spicy fruits or to help oneself to the delicious harvest that bees had left inside a hollow tree or in the crevices of a rock. To build a house, to protect oneself from inclement weather, it was sufficient to lay the bark of a cork tree as a roof atop rustic posts. Here women would cover themselves with leaves and vines and men would respect them. A land of peace, friendship, and concord, in El Dorado the earth freely and willingly offered humankind its gifts.

Latino popular imagery is not politically correct. Women are shown only as good mothers and as objects of pleasure. Male dominance is unquestioned, and magic often takes precedence over more established religious practices. The conquistadors dressed in armor and Columbus and his ships are viewed with pride. (Mexican Americans, who make up half the nation's Spanish-speaking population, take pride in their Indian heritage, however.) Light skin tone is preferred. In inner city neighborhoods, where Spanish-speaking people have a choice of a reproduction of The Last Supper in light- or dark-skinned versions, they almost always buy the light one.

In city cemeteries, or in the less expensive sections of Catholic cemeteries, one finds clusters of Latino graves, their identity revealed by images, cards, and fresh flowers, signs that families still visit their dead. The same images of the Mother of God that one sees in the homes are placed on the stones: The Cuban Virgen de la Caridad del Cobre appearing to the three fishermen as their boat, rocked by huge waves, is about to sink; La Virgen de Guadalupe, indicating that Mexican Americans are buried nearby; La Milagrosa standing on the globe, a sign of those of Puerto Rican descent. A telling reminder of national allegiances in Latino neigh-

Unfinished mural of the Virgen de Guadalupe, East Los Angeles, 1985.

borhoods are the many funeral parlors advertising the services of shipping the deceased back to their countries of origin.

On walls in Spanish-speaking neighborhoods in Camden, Los Angeles, and New York City, memorials commemorate young people of the neighborhood who have fallen victim to the violence that characterizes their surroundings. "La Vida Loca," the brutal clash of U.S.-born Mexican American youths (*cholos*) and a system that fails to accept them, is vividly depicted by West Coast artists. In these works, exemplified by a series of paintings called "They Don't Want Me in My House" by Los Angeles artist Adan Hernandez, police brutality, drugs, and street crime create a chaotic vision of hellish violence.

Perhaps nowhere else is the presence of Latinos in the United States felt as strongly as on a summer Sunday at Coney Island. Escaping from their hot dwellings, a youthful crowd of more than a million Spanish-speaking people loudly enjoy the sun and sea. Rap music blends with salsa and Peruvian waltzes. In addition to the huge Latino crowd, West Indians, a sprinkling of non-Hispanic whites, and a surprisingly small number of American blacks share the miles of beach. In this southeastern corner of Brooklyn, the largest and most harmonious expression of the Rainbow Coalition basks in the sun.

Among Latinos, separation from the dominant culture is seen in attachment to roots and in the meager interest in mainstream symbols. They have asserted their presence with images that call attention to their diversity, yet which are not of a type that defines an aggressive, imperial nation. In the barrios and ghettos of the indifferent "giant of the north," a story of aspirations, poverty, endurance, violence, and exclusion is told in a visual language that, however ephemeral in individual expression, continues to endure in the culture.

DOMESTIC INTERIORS

"The poorest negro housekeeper's room in New York is bright with gaily-colored prints of his beloved 'Abe Linkum,' General Grant, President Garfield, Mrs. Cleveland, and other national celebrities, and cheery with flowers and singing birds."

—Jacob Riis,
How The Other Half Lives, New York, 1890

"In the inner city they don't feel like linking with Washington, Lincoln, or Roosevelt; they have their own heroes."

—Raymond,
school janitor, Central Ward, Newark, 1992

Berenice Davies's den, decorated with objects bought from Good Will, the Salvation Army, or second-hand vendors on the streets. Hough, Cleveland, 1985.

Family and religion are the main themes in this living room, Roxbury, Boston, 1985.

Baby J-Kuan Jimenez in his bedroom dominated by a plastic-wrapped banana, South Bronx, 1991.

Jamie's bedroom, Bushwick, Brooklyn, 1991.

Manuel, Confesion, and Maria in their living room, a wallpaper river running behind them, South Bronx, 1990.

Almost blind, hands and fingers like claws, feet covered by thick wool socks, Leola Robinson, age ninety-three, sits in her kitchen in Robbins, Illinois, 1994. Buckets on the floor collect leaks that come through the roof, the walls are darkened with smoke, a chair is falling apart, the sink is rusted. Mrs. Robinson was happy to be photographed. She said to me, "A record, now there is a record, people will see it."

Cats, goldfish, curtains, a crucifix, and flowers decorate this South Bronx apartment, 1990.

On this black-militant mural, painted faces are fading away, West Side, Chicago, 1986.

Screaming head of Black Panther leader Fred Hampton showered with drops of blood and framed by ailanthus trees, West Side, Chicago, 1989. Hampton was killed in a night raid by the Chicago police in 1969.

RESISTANCE TO DEGRADATION:
Representations of Black Power and Black Pride

"Now this is true artwork that I happen to be putting up in this cold-ass hall wall."

—Graffiti,
Polo Grounds Towers, Harlem, 1993

"I am somebody."

—Inscription below an anonymous face,
part of a mural in Ford Heights, Illinois,
the nation's poorest suburb, 1980

Revolution at home and the struggle against colonialism abroad, central themes of the late sixties, found expression in hundreds of large murals. In these paintings, people still holding their broken chains were reborn, their new freedom portrayed with an innocence and a feeling of hope that seem naive today.

Exposed to time and the elements, the existence of murals is precarious from the start. Typically they are painted on the exposed side of abandoned buildings, and destroyed with the demolition of their host structures. Those rare ones that survive become eroded—their paint fading, their bright colors muted, the plaster behind the paint showing, the composition breaking down into fragments, softening the stern faces and whitening the Afros.

Contemporary signs are nostalgic, constructing a remote utopian past, chronicles of lost battles, martyrs, victims, and dreams.

135

(Above) Slavery, the African past, and liberation are themes in this unfinished but arresting mural, Trenton, 1982.

(Left) Visions of Africa give a semblance of life and color to this abandoned building, South Bronx, 1989. Labeled "the beautiful tree people," by the artist, warriors, African kings, a black Madonna, and a lion decorate its facade.

Depicted as a lost paradise under a red-hot sun is a primordial Africa with giraffes, lions, and panthers running wild in a vast open landscape. In a world that was pure, maidens pour antelope milk from pitchers. And in a place where black men ruled, Zulu warriors, spears in hand, sit adorned in traditional attire.

Ancient Egypt, the biblical land of slavery, is seen as the birthplace of civilization—African civilization. Already in 1923, Marcus Garvey declared King Tutankhamen a black man, a source of pride. Today Egyptian symbols—queens with high headdresses, cobras, the Sphinx, the Pyramids, and even hieroglyphics—are all important elements in a struggle to forge an identity.

In poor, minority communities, popular images are offered for sale on the streets. These pictures—mostly color reproductions—are directed to the entire population as well as to overlapping subgroups within that population:

West Indians, Southern blacks, welfare mothers, and Latinos.

A theme often found is the "pantheon"—black leaders, popular entertainers, sports figures, and jazz musicians. The most frequently encountered black heroes are Martin Luther King, Jr., Nelson Mandela, and Malcolm X—"the founding fathers"—and the long-time favorite, Emperor Haile Selassie dressed in royal attire, standing by his throne, with the Lion of Judah by his side. There is co-optation of the symbols of white America: for example, a drawing of an imaginary black Mount Rushmore with likenesses of Frederick Douglass, Harriet Tubman, Martin Luther King, Jr., and Malcolm X.

Images of men, such as the Zulu warrior, his back against the red African sun, and a dark-skinned Arab noblemen represented inside a gilded palace, fully armed and elegantly dressed, are common. African American versions of

(Above) Harlem, New York, recreation center painted in the colors of the Afro-American flag and decorated with Egyptian symbols, 1992.

(Left) Bold African mask painted on an apartment door, Scudder Homes, Newark, 1987. Upon seeing this image, a neighborhood resident remarked: "Somebody who lives in the house may have said, 'I am this African, here is my family mark.'"

Adam and Eve are also very popular. A young black man, a white sheet barely covering his body, is portrayed above a sign stating: "Black Man the Original Man." A similarly dressed young woman is placed above a matching sign: "Black Woman the Original Woman."

The need to claim roots is a dominant theme in these essentialist images. In vacant lots, in the midst of devastation, one encounters images of the first man and the first woman, "the first queen" (Nefertiti?), and Jesus. The contrast could not be stronger between the degraded urban settings where these images are displayed and the lofty beginnings the residents claim.

Popular portrayals of women rarely depict a real person. One such image is known as "The West Indian Girl"—a tall, slender maiden dressed in white and carrying a basket of flowers on her hip, a popular symbol of purity. Another is an African woman standing atop a cliff, a

black panther by her side. Below, a version of earthly paradise unfolds: a vast plain with a river flowing through it, populated by elephants and giraffes. Another is a mysterious picture of a strong, beautiful woman, sitting barefoot on a ladder inside a dark barn, like a key scene in a play, an image replete with ambiguous allusions to slavery, religion, and sexuality.

In the exclusion of white leaders and of national symbols such as the Statue of Liberty, the bald eagle, and the flag of the United States, there is a sense of separation and rejection of white America. One white face is occasionally represented, that of John F. Kennedy, his assassination having confirmed for many that he was a friend of the black people.

Images require public support. Grassroots artists produce a variety of murals on city walls and abandoned buildings. It is a measure of their popularity that many endure for years without

Mural on a pawn shop on Forty-seventh Street celebrating the famous blues singers and performers who once played in the area clubs, South Side, Chicago, 1986.

Mural on a supermarket wall, portraying black celebrities and heroes, is dominated by a large image of the very popular former Mayor Harold Washington, Lawndale, Chicago, 1990.

Martin Luther King crucified, by B. Walker, South Side, Chicago, 1980.

Mr. Toy's pantheon has portraits of Nelson Mandela, Martin Luther King, and Malcolm X, surrounded by representations of purity, innocence, and motherly love. The images are contained by the outline of Africa and by the colors of the black liberation flag. West Side, Chicago, 1991.

Billboard depicting a child's view of a shooting. South Side, Chicago, 1994.

"CEASE FIRE," a billboard message displayed on Livernois Avenue in Detroit, 1992, seems more a cry for help than an appeal to reason.

being defaced. Local residents are quick to destroy any piece not to their liking. On the street stalls, if an image does not sell, it is quickly retired and replaced by a new one.

AMERICAN GRAFFITI

CRIMINALS
ROBBIN
INNOCENT
MOTHERFUCKERS
EVERY TIME

—Graffiti,
Bedford-Stuyvesant, Brooklyn, 1994

"Where is the money? I don't have it! I am going to ask you one more time. Where is the money? I don't have it! Boom! Boom! I ran. That was real stupid what they did. It makes no sense at all."

—Teenage girl describing to a friend
a killing she had just witnessed,
Brownsville, Brooklyn, 1989

"With the crome on my hips I come swiftly, some extra clips, now pop some ships cause madd confusion like my man on the block who shot that cop. Respect due to all the crews that is true, I say no names, careless about fame 'cause I know I am true to the game like Wu-Tang. I bring the rockus with the thorough heads. Nuff said I'll leave your fucking body red."

—Graffiti,
stairway, Garden Spires housing development, Newark, 1994

The "peace sign," billboard erected in Englewood, an extremely violent neighborhood of Chicago, 1992. Its message, designed by a former gang leader for a local Methodist church, is framed by gang symbols. The billboard's purpose is to spark a dialogue with local members.

Memento mori, Mexican style: skulls seem to dance above a quintessentially American pile of used tires. South Central Los Angeles, 1994.

Like empty seed packets placed on sticks to remind the gardener what lies below, billboards in the ghetto mark the terrain, telling residents and passersby alike that here is a special kind of ground, a place set apart from the more pedestrian territory of simple producers and consumers. In sections of Chicago, Newark, Detroit, and New York City where the murder rate has reached record highs, there are dozens of billboards designed solely to urge people to stop killing and to avoid getting killed. Mostly they are sponsored by churches and civic organizations—public service announcements for populations so dangerous and endangered that they constitute their own macabre advertising niche.

One popular sign admonishes, "Don't Let Your Child Be the Next Victim of Violent Crime," and urges people to get a booklet. Another, referred to as "the peace sign," reads, "It's Time for Peace, Stop the Killing," these words framed by the symbols of Chicago's major gangs. A billboard in Detroit, using red letters dripping blood, reads "Cease Fire," an injunction underscored in small print with the statement "Hundreds of our children are dying."

On the South Side of Chicago a sign saying "Take Crime Out of Your Child's Life" portrays one boy shooting another in the head with a gigantic revolver. Someone "completed" the picture by putting a sideways baseball cap on the aggressor, thus identifying him as a gang member.

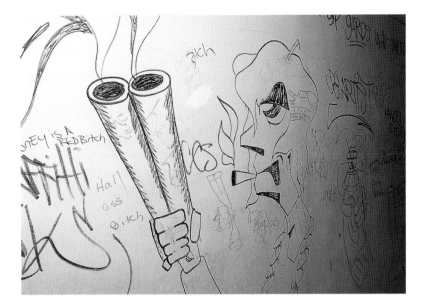

A warning: man holding a smoking, double-barreled shotgun. Graffiti, Martin Luther King apartments, Central Ward, Newark, 1991.

Large mural painted in a tense, aggressive, video-game style that underscores the fearsome imagery of fire and death. North Philadelphia, 1992.

Greg Turner, who manages a day shelter on Chicago's West Side, argues that these billboards, which began popping up in the late 1980s, were long overdue. "We should have been hollering a long time ago in our communities to stop this kind of behavior," he says. "Those are our offspring, those are our next generation and now they are killing each other. That is our future, and if we don't let them know how they should live, there will be no future for us."

For Reverend John Porter, whose organization placed "peace signs" in the Englewood section of Chicago, this is a way to communicate with the gangs. He explains: "The community has one of the highest homicide rates in the country. Young men cannot find meaningful work, and they [society] expect them to be functional. Men are in a position out there where they face other angry men, and angry men who are frustrated take their frustration out on the nearest target. And the nearest target to these men is not some social system that is very abstract, it is somebody that looks like them. White people don't have the same need for these signs." Indeed, white neighborhoods never display such billboards—not even those that preach brotherly love and urge an end to bigotry.

Graffiti is at the opposite end of the spectrum from the professionally designed billboards and signs sponsored by benevolent institutions. In semi-private spaces and on walls one finds murals pleading with criminals to stop (someone in Camden, New Jersey, wrote on a wall, "Peace Motherfuckers!"), threatening them with retaliation, or warning visitors of the general state of lawlessness. More common are signs seeking to silence neighbors and to claim territory through intimidation—graphic warnings depict executioners with smoking guns and reptilian eyes.

One day I would like to see these billboards posted in suburbs, airports, and other public places frequented by the affluent. They could bear inscriptions, like warnings on cigarette packages: "Neighborhoods with fine recreation facilities and schools are closed to the youth of the ghetto" and "In inner cities, a promising future is difficult to envision." Others would simply state, "No more ghettos."

STREET MEMORIALS:
"People Saying Good-bye in the Only Way They Can"

"OH MY BELOVED SON. There were times our eyes didn't meet. But through losing you I have tasted defeat. Luisa."

—"In memory of Willie," East Harlem, 1993

"Peaceful Journey."

"Here is something I can't understand."

—Inscription and added commentary on a memorial to a seventeen-year-old shot in 1992 in South Camden

Along the most violent streets in Camden, New Jersey; Compton, California; Chicago; and New York City, walls have replaced the cemetery as places to remember the dead. Memorials frequently commemorate young men who were involved in the drug trade, who died in the streets, hallways, and public spaces of their neighborhoods. Richie was one of these youngsters. "Everybody knew him around here; he was killed across the street," said a resident of East Harlem.

The imagery of faces, names, crosses, flags, guns, cars, angels, and city landmarks evokes the brief lives and violent deaths of young males, giving a glimpse of their lives, possessions, and surroundings, often a bleak geometric representation of the urban skyline. In these paintings we see imaginative yet almost illegible lettering styles, and products of our times mix with traditional symbols: crosses, images of Christ or Saint Lazarus along with automatic guns, sports cars, motorcycles, and razor-ribbon wire.

In ghettos, every day people walk by the spots where family members and friends have been murdered. A bus stop, a supermarket, a place on the sidewalk, elevator doors, or even a stop sign become reminders of death. During a recent tour of Larry Rogers's neighborhood, in Bushwick, he showed me the spot where his brother China was assassinated: an empty lot, half a block from his home, that once was the location of a particularly violent club. Rogers commented, "As soon as you walk out of your house, you see your brother right there. It is hard, it is really hard."

Using rectangular shapes reminiscent of flat grave markers for the memorial, Rogers, an artist and a neighborhood activist, painted a symbolic cemetery on the corner of an abandoned building. In these shapes, he wrote the names and dates of the dead who once lived in his immediate neighborhood. Soon, because so many people had died, he "had to find a bigger wall." Now, with the renovation of the building, his collective memorial has been destroyed.

Muralists often develop a reputation that goes beyond their communities, and receive commissions from the entire city. Patrons expect that local residents, finding the walls more attractive than before, will respect them. An additional reason to respect the art is the fear of retaliation from the dead person's friends.

Some of the meanings tangled up with these memorials became clear on December 9, 1994, when Father Rick Malloy, associate pastor of Holy Name Church in Camden, set out to paint over "The Lost Boys" mural in North Camden. Father Malloy believes that murals like this foster the drug culture and glorify its vic-

"In Memory of Wolf," Cabrini-Green Houses, Chicago, 1989.

"May You Fly Free," mural for Fernando, South Bronx, 1991.

Candles light the dark in a South Bronx corner, in memory of a Puerto Rican man shot by the police in Connecticut, 1994.

With a crown of thorns on his head and eyes closed, Chito is depicted as the suffering Christ. Brooklyn, 1991

tims, and his goal is to replace all of them with positive murals. "North Camden is not a cemetery," he says. "What should a community honor?"

Father Malloy began with a quick silent prayer, then coated with white paint a wall mural representing Gadget, Jay, Carlos, and So-Big. Present that afternoon were representatives of the press and the city police. Local youths involved in the drug trade, who stood by, were disturbed to see the obliteration of the memorial. After finishing the work, Father Malloy told Monica Rohr, a reporter from the *Philadelphia Inquirer*, "These aren't lost boys. These are dead boys. We don't want any more dead boys."

For the drug dealers and other neighborhood residents who knew the victims portrayed on the walls, however, the wall was a sign of caring. Carlos's brother objected, "This is like kicking over someone's tombstone. I don't like it at

all. I can't see him no more. That is all I see, all the memories I have from him. Now it's gone."

Father Malloy afterward felt ambivalent about the event and how it was portrayed in the press: Priest faces the rage of drug dealers. He thinks it was less a confrontation than a "heated discussion"—they were not calling him "motherfucker." He is not against memorials, but rather against the omnipresent drug culture.

There was something pathetic about "The Lost Boys." Jay sighted along the barrel of his gun. Carlos seemed to be caught in a reflective mood, leaning on a baseball bat. Gadget and So-Big just stared. They stood above the garbage and discarded cardboard boxes from the corner grocery store, a painted skyline of Philadelphia and the Delaware River behind them.

The inclined head of Christ suffering, a representation that is three centuries old in Western art, is part of the street scene in the South Bronx, 1994.

"We'll Remember You Always, Tony,"
Mott Haven, South Bronx, 1991.

Festive mural commemorating "Lil Big Man Manny," killed in a motorcycle accident. The Dominican artist wanted to include Manny riding the motorcycle in the painting, but his mother, who lives across the street, asked him not to. She said that seeing her son there would make her cry. Represented with its headlight on, the slick vehicle seems alive. East New York, Brooklyn, 1991.

Memorial to Hector, South Bronx, 1992.

Memorial by W. Cordero to Johnny, killed in this playground in the middle of the afternoon, Manhattan, 1992. "Somebody hit him with a baseball bat on the head," said a local resident.

"The Lost Boys" Gadget, Jay, Carlos, and So-Big, four teenagers from North Camden, portrayed in a mural by War against the background of the Delaware River and the skyline of Philadelphia, 1993.

Memorial to P.J., South Bronx, 1994. David, a neighbor, explained that murals like this are for the dead, to let them know that "they were loved, they were cool, they were popular, they had friends, they were respected and they lived in a community."

A mural by Vonce of Big El (murdered in 1992) as he zooms along, chatting on his cellular phone, on the way to visit to his parents, who are pictured on an adjoining wall. Directly above his head, a black angel guards the pearly gates of Paradise, now El's home—a place of fast machines, the latest sneakers, endless fun. Harlem, New York, 1994.

"Eugene" painted this car repair shop, a former High Speed gas station, and suggested to the owner that he rename it "Mister Fix It," Detroit, 1994. Among pictures of cars, automotive parts, and tools, Eugene included a Bible and a reference to Psalm 23, "Though I walk through the valley of the shadow of the death, I will fear no evil: for thou art with me; thy rod and thy staff they comfort me."

From donkeys to jumbo jets, transportation is the theme of Willie's Garage, West Side, Detroit, 1991.

COMMERCIAL SIGNS

"I wanted to capture the most interesting part of the ocean and put it on the fish house's wall. I would have liked to put lots of bubbles and more creatures from the ocean but I ran out of money."

—Mark Perrien discussing the mural he painted for the Clinton Fish Market, Lawndale, Chicago, 1990

In surroundings where commercial ventures tend to be short-lived, businesses use bright colors and animated forms to decorate their buildings. There are signs depicting animals, such as painted racehorses outside a messenger service, or pig heads outside of a butcher shop, and even a whale decorating the parking lot of a fish store.

Mural on the side of the Clinton Fish Market, Lawndale, Chicago, 1990.

Salem Travelers Bus, The Soulful Gospel, Lawndale, Chicago, 1990.

Festive colors dress up these stores on an otherwise dreary block, West Side, Chicago, 1988.

Skin revealed under fur, a white Rolls Royce at the center, an offering of play, pleasure, and prestige, Mr. G's Billiard Room, Detroit, 1993.

B & E Country Store, West Side, Chicago, 1987.

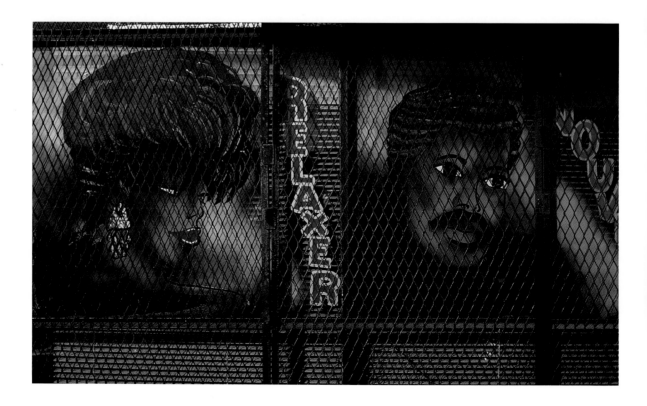

Painting of a farm on a Harlem, New York, food market, 1972.

*Faces of a young man and woman behind a thick iron
grate decorate the windows of Full Control Hair
Designs, South Side, Chicago, 1993.*

Storefront church, West Side, Chicago, 1985.

Mount Carmel Holiness Church, Newark, 1990.

STOREFRONT CHURCHES AS DESIGNS

"We wanted purity: the Lord has shown me white."

—Rev. Lilly Minnigan, *who painted the First Zion Hope Missionary Baptist Church white, Newark, 1987*

"I love blue, royal blue. Jesus is royalty."

—Apostle Pam Hill, *Spirit Vision Christian Church, Detroit, 1987*

The design of storefront churches is greatly influenced by the nature and size of the "host" building and the financial means of the congregation. The challenge lies in giving to what is typically a low, rectangular structure the familiar look of a church.

Movie theaters, union halls, garages, synagogues, Masonic temples, stores, banks, gas stations, and supermarkets are buildings that at one time or another have been converted into churches. Often their original functions remain only partially masked. These religious edifices are often stark; imprisoned in a shape that hugs the ground is a church trying to soar.

In the opinion of a Jersey City minister, the physical structure was not an important concern. She said: "It is not the building, it is the people together that make a church. Wherever you worship it is the house of the Lord even if it is in the middle of the ocean."

The skillful use of a few basic elements often succeeds in establishing a new identity—for

Refreshing Spring Church of God in Christ, Detroit, 1993.

"You Must Fight to Live Right," Spirit Vision, Detroit, 1987.

example, some lines from Scripture painted on the facade. The cross is the single most important symbol used to announce their religious function; also popular are images of the Bible, of Christ, of the Garden of Gethsemane, and of Paradise. Existing windows are made to look like stained glass, and a triangular shape is often added to the center of the facade to resemble a steeple.

The ministers, their wives, and other church officials who were interviewed lacked a design vocabulary, and attributed their formal choices to the will of God. Typically, they reported that inspiration came to them in a dream or from a biblical passage. Decisions that could not be attributed to a divine authority were often explained as practical necessity. Yet when asked about their own artistic abilities, church leaders claimed to have been good in art at school or to

be fortunate to have someone in their congregation gifted at painting and drawing.

Storefront churches tend to be short-lived. Buildings are expensive to maintain; congregations dissolve as their members grow old or switch their allegiances to other churches. If a pastor gets ill or dies, the building may simply be abandoned.

Churches that have a measure of stability tend to develop more sober designs over time. Striking reds and blues and yellows give way to more subdued colors. Congregations add towers, steeples, crenelated walls, and new carved doors, and to give an impression of solidity, the facade may receive a thin veneer of brick, stone, or wood.

The long, narrow slits serving as windows of the El Bethel Church are varied in length and placement. They create visual rhythms within the arched shape, Milwaukee, 1992.

Church, Englewood, Chicago, 1992.

Holy Communion Church, Compton Avenue,
South Central Los Angeles, 1985.

On Compton Avenue, Triumph: The Church and Kingdom of God in
Christ had, until recently, a mural facing its parking lot, South Central
Los Angeles, 1987. While traveling by boat on the Mississippi in 1905,
church's founder, Elias Dempsey Smith, had a dream in which an eagle
became a lion, master of the "jungle principle," higher than any other.
Painted by the artist Elliott Pinkney seventy years later, the mural
showed the eagle and the lion, with the Reverend Mr. Smith holding in
his right hand an eye symbolizing his visionary power. The modestly
clothed woman on the right represents the church, whom Jesus Christ
marries.

Christ, his apostles, and a saintly woman by the River
Jordan decorate the facade of this small storefront
church, Englewood, Chicago, 1992. One has to go
through Christ to enter the church.

Children playing among abandoned buildings, Public School 104, High-bridge, South Bronx, 1990.

Cement, graffiti, and bundled-up children, playground, Public School 53, Morrisania, South Bronx, 1990.

THE SPACE OF PLAY:
Parks, Playgrounds, Empty Lots, and the Streets

Clean, attractive, secure spaces for play are rare in ghetto areas. Improvised playgrounds are made in vacant lots; old mattresses are used for jumping and discarded crates for building playhouses. The most popular places for recreation are the streets, with their open fire hydrants for cooling off and their abandoned buildings and cars for exploration. Some games, such as setting trash fires and torching derelict structures, riding on the back of buses, throwing rocks at passersby, and breaking windows, are dangerous. The most deadly among these improvised activities consists of riding atop elevator cabs in highrise public housing projects.

Residents keep different hours from those living elsewhere, staying out until late at night. It is common, particularly in summer, to see children running and shouting in the early hours of the morning.

Victor and his brother, Polo, jumping on rusted springs in an empty lot, South Bronx, 1988.

Cooling off, Robert Taylor Homes, South Side, Chicago, 1988.

Schoolboys watching mating dogs, South Bronx, 1973.

155

Darleisha, Levita, and Gwendolyn jumping rope, sixteenth-floor walkway, Robert Taylor Homes, South Side, Chicago, 1988.

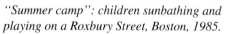

"Summer camp": children sunbathing and playing on a Roxbury Street, Boston, 1985.

Yvonne, Tammi, and Yolanda hanging out after school on the stairway landing of their Bushwick project, Brooklyn, 1990.

The Ark rises above a sea of weeds, Newark, 1987.

AN ARK IN WHICH TO FLEE THE GHETTO

"Forty days and forty nights, that was not so bad; look at what happened to this Ark."

—Kea Tawana,
Ark builder, Central Ward of Newark, 1987

"I dream about the Ark, about being on the deck of the Ark and I wake up and look down the hill and see that lot empty. Emotionally, it's still around. I'll get another ship; it won't be like the Ark for sure but I'll get me something on water. It ain't over by a long shot."

—Kea Tawana
after taking down the Ark, Newark, 1988

Sited on high ground, the sky visible between the bare beams of the hull, the Ark pointed toward downtown Newark and beyond, to the towers of the World Trade Center, and farther, past the Statue of Liberty, to the Atlantic Ocean and the freedom of the open sea.

The Ark was the creation of Kea Tawana, a carpenter, electrical worker, and scavenger who has a sixth-grade education. Kea, a Newark resident for twenty years, created a unique folk-art monument at the edge of a church's parking lot in the city's Central Ward. Unfinished, the boat possessed a rawness that sometimes surfaces in its stubbornly determined builder as well. For all the planning, hard work, and carpentry skills that went into it, the old-fashioned, sturdy, and reassuring presence of Kea's boat belonged to the realm of dreams and play.

Her boat was full of objects she had collected on her forays into abandoned buildings:

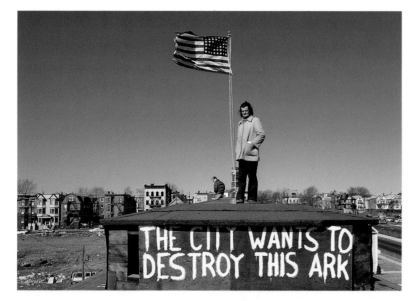

Forty-eight-star flag discarded by a Newark school flies on the mast of the Ark, Newark, 1987

Kea's compound: House, workshop, and warehouse built on trailers, ready to be moved, Newark, 1984.

the dark gray four-by-sixes that once supported houses were the ribs that gave the boat its shape. Hundreds of books and magazines, heaps of hardware, building ornaments, theater seats, bicycle parts, electrical equipment, radiators, window frames, shards of colored glass, buckets full of nuts and bolts, pots and pans, and parts of five pipe organs. To those puzzled by her eclectic collection of objects she said: "Everything has a purpose in this mayhem."

Scavenging is a common occupation in Newark, and some people have accumulated mountains of materials to sell: sinks, refrigerators, toilets, and pipes, which can be seen rusting in fenced lots throughout the city. Yet only Kea lent design and craft to her collection.

To a city that wants so desperately to start over again, the boat was an embarrassing nuisance, preserving as it did discarded pieces of Newark's history. It was a reminder of a race riot, fires, abandonment, and disinvestment, precisely what the city is trying to move away from so that it can become part of "normal America." In addition, city officials saw the Ark as an "eyesore," and, since it was built without a permit, as a prominently displayed challenge to their authority.

Officials harassed Kea for three years, tak-

When seven police cars, two firetrucks, and two bulldozers came to demolish her place, Kea barricaded herself behind her window protected by barbed wire and a thick wire mesh. She told the officers that her home was full of gasoline, ready to blow up, and that before they destroyed her home, they had to kill her. They re-treated. Newark, 1988.

Stained-glass window, made by Kea from old glass, Newark, 1987.

ing her to court several times, first to move the boat from the city's land and later to demolish it. After she took down the Ark, more than twenty police officers, fire fighters, and city workers with their cars, trucks, and bulldozers came to destroy Kea's shack, which she had built without a permit, but she locked herself in and refused to come out. Later she moved the house to another site where it was eventually destroyed.

For no one was the loss of the boat more painful than for Kea herself. The Ark could have become a museum of lost communities, and a place for racial harmony. It made peace between a transformed downtown and the disappearing world of the ethnic neighborhoods. It also be-came a meeting place for blacks and whites. For me, Kea's Ark symbolized an atonement for the burning of so much of the city. In Newark, tools, books, bottles, and other everyday objects not normally found in museums continued, until the spring of 1988, to be commemorated in the var-ied contents and noble form of Kea's Ark.

The power of Kea's dream lives with those who saw the Ark, observed her at work, and spoke to her. Faces would turn up to look at the ship, and people smiled with a sense of wonder as if seeing something that could not happen.

"Get off the streets and start thinking about your future.
Get off the streets and start thinking
Start thinking."

—SIGN ON THE DOOR OF THE INNER VOICE,
A DAY SHELTER FOR STREET PEOPLE
ON THE WEST SIDE OF CHICAGO, 1991

"The tension created in this area is unbearable. You are constantly
running into drug dealers, addicts, and into people with aspirations to
become something. Nobody is satisfied; they are all stalemated, fight-
ing each other."

—TIM HOBSON,
Crown Heights, Brooklyn, 1991

SEVEN

THE IMPACT OF ADDICTIONS AND HOMELESSNESS

In a society that puts low priority on providing housing for its poor and offers only a limited number of supervised facilities for those unable to live independently, homelessness is a chronic condition. The situation is made worse by drug addiction, and by a changing economy that creates few jobs in the inner cities.

The condition of homelessness is fluid. Homeless people are often those unable to pay their rent; those who have doubled up with relatives and friends; the victims of fires; and those who live in condemned dwellings. They are people who sometimes unexpectedly and for varying periods of time find themselves without a place to live. For others, homelessness is chronic.

To prevent people from sleeping in the open and freezing to death or from becoming nuisances in public facilities, cities across the nation have opened former schools, hospitals, armories, and other vacant buildings as temporary shelters. The mid-1980s saw the construction and rehabilitation of hundreds of permanent shelters situated in ghettos: shelters for AIDS patients, for the mentally ill, for pregnant women, for single women, for men who lived in single-room occupancy hotels that had been demolished and who could not afford comparable housing, and even shelters for those rejected from other shelters. The need to respond to a crisis situation has given rise to large, hybrid facilities, such as one in Brooklyn serving both men with AIDS and men with mental illnesses.

The stigma carried by shelters and drug treatment facilities is shown in the secrecy with which they are established. Most of these buildings—even those costing many millions of dollars, occupying nearly a city block, and visually very distinctive—lack even a sign identifying their function. A New York City Housing Authority employee in Brooklyn remembers being surprised at the sight of a group of teenagers hanging out in front of a townhouse that had been vacant. Asking her co-workers about this, she discovered that the building had become a shelter for juveniles.

Adding to the growing institutional character of poor urban areas, there is also an increasing number of difficult-to-detect "group homes" in houses and apartment buildings. Often accommodating fewer than ten unrelated individuals, these are halfway houses for victims of domestic violence, homes for foster children, the mentally ill, and those with AIDS. Yet like the larger institutions, these are insular, heavy users of services, places to house, feed, clothe, and change the behavior of destitute people, but do little to strengthen neighborhoods.

"TAP THE BOTTLE":
Chicago Billboards Advertising Liquor

"Colt 45: It works every time."
"Olde English 800: It's the power."
"Lord Calvert Canadian: When you call the shots."

—Billboard slogans,
Chicago

Like fragments of dreams, rising high above the empty lots and the ruins, the good life in the ghetto is represented by billboards advertising liquor, depicting young, sexy, and affluent men and women enjoying themselves. The glass or the bottle that appears in the scene seems to contain a magic potion having the power to lift people above their surroundings of despair.

The devastating effects of alcoholism have long been a major problem in poor communities. In *How the Other Half Lives* (1890), Jacob Riis mentioned a survey disclosing that Manhattan had 4,065 saloons for the nearly half million New Yorkers living below Fourteenth Street, or about one such establishment for every 120 men, women, and children.

Today, alcohol is just as plentiful. Before the 1992 riots, South Central Los Angeles, for example, had 728 liquor stores; in proportion to its population, that was almost seven times as many as for the state of Rhode Island. In the

"Powerful Pleasure," Woodlawn, Chicago, 1988.

Over a wrecked West Side neighborhood, a soft-focus dream of passion in sepia tones transcends the anonymity and devastation below, Chicago, 1991.

Rising above dreary empty lots and abandoned buildings, an invitation to enjoy warmth, intimacy, and a glass of cognac, West Side, Chicago, 1990.

Muscle and liquor, South Side, Chicago, 1991.

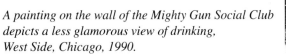

A painting on the wall of the Mighty Gun Social Club depicts a less glamorous view of drinking, West Side, Chicago, 1990.

burning and looting of the riot, 200 of these outlets were damaged or destroyed, leaving many community leaders and politicians elated and feeling ambivalent about permitting them to re-open. Many liquor stores sell food and school supplies, but liquor is by far their most profitable item. Calvin Sims, a *New York Times* reporter, wrote in November 29, 1992, "There is perhaps no other inner-city business that has been as lucrative as alcohol."

Malt liquors and inexpensive fortified wines, the intoxicants of choice among poor, inner-city youth in search of a cheap high, constitute a two-billion-dollar business targeted to the nation's ghettos. Malt liquors—beer brewed with sugar to boost the alcoholic content—were introduced in a large (forty-ounce) bottle in the 1980s.

Spokespersons for the brewers, distillers, and wine makers argue that targeting their products to ghetto youth is intended to preserve a market. The industry perceives any effort to restrict their advertisement and distribution as tantamount to limiting the local people's freedom of choice. Moreover, they argue, liquor stores provide jobs to the residents. Critics dismiss this view, comparing selling liquor to crack dealing and prostitution, activities that also generate employment. Cynical and exploitative in its linking of black success with malt liquor, the ads are helping to turn stressed youths into alcoholics.

Crack-addicted woman begging inside a check cashing place, Mott Haven, South Bronx, 1991. She claimed to make twenty-five dollars on a regular weekday and seventy-five dollars on Friday.

Mural on a wall of I.S. 148, South Bronx, 1993.

DRUGS:
Warnings and Addicts

"Here I am . . . high as hell . . .
not doing nothing but feeling swell.
Pollution . . . pollution . . . is everywhere . . . on you . . .
*   on me . . .*
that is the government you see . . .
Cancers, cancers Please go away . . .
'cause there is no one that wants you to stay."

—Graffiti,
South Bronx, 1989

"When a guy puts the needle in his arm, this is his choice and they should make it available to him. They shouldn't tell him you cannot do this. So what they are doing is restricting the use, trying to stop the supply by raising the price exorbitantly high. What does he do, he gets a gun, he goes and puts it into somebody's ribs and says: 'Give me what you got' and if they don't give it to him, he destroys them. Why? Because he thinks he is doing what he has to do in order to survive."

—Tim Hobson,
Crown Heights, Brooklyn, 1991

One never has to wait for long on a ghetto street before seeing evidence of the drug trade, drug use, and their consequences: crack vials strewn

This mural by M. Caton on the South Side of Chicago, 1982, is a power-ful personal representation of the disintegrating effect of drugs. Flanked by symbols of white cruelty and indifference as well as by idealized im-ages of African life, the drug peddler at the center deals death amidst chains, knives, and wilting flowers.

As one man moves fearfully away, another, eyes bulging, crawls toward the grim reaper's chain, symbolizing the horrors of addiction. Mural in East Harlem, New York, 1991.

on the sidewalks, vigilant dealers at their street-corner posts, unkempt, dazed addicts, the warn-ings and memorials on the walls. These and other signs form constant reminders of a way of life in which drugs play a prominent role.

Even though 70 percent of drug users in the United States are white, and a similar percentage have more than a high school education, are regu-larly employed, have an income above $25,000, and, moreover, live outside poor, minority com-munities, it is the ghetto where the domestic drug wars are fought. Twelve percent of drug addicts are black, reflecting their numbers in the total population. Yet for a variety of reasons de-riving from poverty, lack of political power, and the types, cost, quantity, and availability of the drugs consumed and sold, the impact of drugs in the inner city is devastating.

It is often noted by local residents and scholars alike that in a success-oriented society that places responsibility on the individual, pov-erty combined with bleak inner-city surround-ings contribute to depression. To find oneself and one's children at the bottom of the social structure, constantly facing random violence, and with little hope for anything better, leads many to rage, bitterness, and despair. Psychiatric help, antidepressants, and tranquilizers, all legal drugs regularly prescribed by doctors to the middle class, are in short supply among the poor, who cannot afford them or lack access to a doc-tor. It is not surprising that people who seek to escape loneliness and insecurity, who need to survive on the streets and to give meaning to their lives, resort to alcohol, crack, or heroin.

Because of their practice of sharing needles,

(Above) Drug-addicted woman sleeping on the roof landing of a South Bronx building, Mott Haven, 1989.

(Left) On this bulletin board, announcements of celebrations of Black History Month and invitations to participate in a garden competition share space with a skull, surrounded by warnings against the use of drugs. Thomas Jefferson Houses, East Harlem, New York, 1989.

intravenous-drug users run a high risk of becoming infected with AIDS. Nations with harm-reduction policies, such as England and the Netherlands, perceive the danger posed by the spread of AIDS as a much more serious problem than heroin use. To avoid higher rates of infection among heroin addicts, authorities in these countries make clean syringes available.

In the dozen years since 1981, the national drug control budget has grown by a factor of nine, to $12.7 billion, of which more than 40 percent is used for domestic enforcement. Between 1985 and 1990 alone, the number of people in jails and prisons has increased by an additional 450,000 inmates, raising the total imprisoned population in the nation to a record 1.2 million.

The drug war has had the unintended consequence of substantially increasing the propor-tion of incarcerated blacks. During the eighties, the proportion of blacks among those arrested for drug abuse rose from 24 to 41 percent of the total.

As many have come to understand, it is not the drugs that are killing and terrorizing the residents, but the confrontations between rival dealers fighting each other for territory, and the muggings and thefts committed by addicts in need of cash to buy drugs, that is, crimes resulting from prohibition. Making drugs available to the addicted on a controlled basis would greatly decrease the violence associated with their use, and would keep hundreds of thousands of people from going to prison.

Unmarked methadone clinic, serving three hundred heroin addicts daily, resembles an abandoned building, Brownsville, Brooklyn, 1988.

Anonymous methadone clinic, Harlem, New York, 1994. "NO ENTRY BE-YOND THIS POINT WITHOUT PROPER IDENTIFICATION" reads a sign on one of the doors.

METHADONE CLINICS, NEW YORK CITY

"Looks like an abandoned building. Like a snake in the grass, ready to ambush you."

—Local resident,
describing a clinic, Brownsville, Brooklyn, 1988

"Junkie treatment center, built like a crack den. If they put a sign out saying Drug Rehabilitation Center, they tell everybody what the thing is. It must make a junkie feel comfortable to go there to get their shit."

—Newark woman,
1991

A well-protected building that does not call attention to itself is considered the ideal location for a clinic in an inner-city community. Yet these structures are often both elemental and bizarre. The facades indicate former lives as theaters, banks, or garages. No attempt is made to mitigate the brutal look of their defenses. To house methadone clinics in improvised quarters in medium-sized buildings, the sponsor must block windows, secure the roof, and post guards at entrances. In the lobby, a clearly visible set of rules of behavior is displayed.

Addictions are a major force shaping the built environment of poor communities. One of the most common responses to heroin dependency is the synthetic substitute, methadone. It was introduced in 1967 to stabilize addicts, to stop them from committing crimes to satisfy their cravings, and to enable them to function in mainstream society. The drug is less addictive

Methadone clinic, South Bronx, 1991.

Methadone clinic named after St. Martin De Porres, a Peruvian who devoted his life to the sick and unfortunate, East New York, Brooklyn, 1991. The clinic is located in one of the most violent areas of the city.

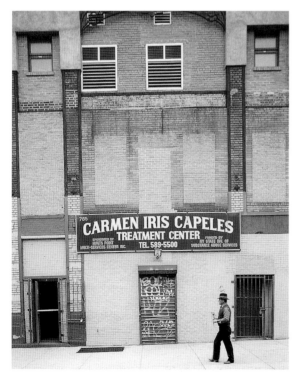

(Above) Methadone clinic, Crown Heights, Brooklyn, 1990.

(Left) Methadone clinic, South Bronx, 1991.

169

Narco-Freedom, Inc., South Bronx, 1992. "You see that razor-ribbon wire? There must be something important in there," a local resident commented.

To make Narco-Freedom more attractive, a pair of murals has been painted on its facade, one depicting a New York of skyscrapers, and the other Puerto Rico as a sunny island of palm trees, beaches, and love. South Bronx, 1994.

than heroin, and its effects last between twenty-four and thirty-six hours; by contrast, heroin is "effective" only for about six hours.

Outpatient facilities proliferated during the rapid increase of heroin consumption in the early 1970s. More recently, perhaps the most powerful argument for the use of methadone is to slow the spread of AIDS. Taken orally, the drug eliminates the risk of infection that comes from using contaminated needles.

Clinics, originally planned to provide coun-seling and job and housing referrals, now typically offer "no frills" service. Justified only in terms of the benefit they provide to the city as a whole, these shabby facilities are passionately resented at the local level. Neighbors perceive clinics as public nuisances, as magnets for troublesome strangers who disturb the peace. With their groups of addicts and former addicts loitering outside, selling methadone, pills, or other drugs, methadone outlets are a distinguishing mark of poor neighborhoods.

Michael Grave as an intense celebrant turned toward an imaginary congregation. Plastic containers are the sacred vessels, a discarded stereo console an altar, and the abandoned Thirteenth Avenue Presbyterian Church the temple, Central Ward, Newark, 1987.

ABANDONED BUILDINGS, A BILLBOARD, AND PARK BENCHES AS HOME

"We carry God's love to the community. These people need help."

—Activist affiliated with Mother Teresa discussing plans to open yet another shelter in the Mott Haven section of the South Bronx, 1989

It is common, in the morning, to see people coming out of abandoned buildings to wash up and brush their teeth in front of an open fire hydrant. In unexpected places I see large pieces of cardboard used to lie on, neatly packed bundles of clothes and blankets. And on landings and stairways I often encounter people sleeping.

Some homeless people squat in the Hayes Homes, an abandoned housing project in Newark slated for demolition. Their existence is revealed at night by a few unexpected lights shining through the windows. These buildings are structurally sound, and offer better shelter than other abandoned structures. Bobby Wright, a maintenance worker for the Newark Housing Authority, feels that even though most people would be terrified to live there, squatters have

Francisco, David, and Arnaldo, three Puerto Ricans living under a bill-board, downtown Newark, 1987.

Martha and Roman, squatters in a building on Home Street, South Bronx, 1990. The building was later razed to make room for townhouses.

become used to this way of life. They know and protect each other, and even though the officials try to keep them out of the buildings, they always manage to get back in.

In 1987, a box under two billboards along McCarter Highway in downtown Newark served as home for three Puerto Rican men. Using a combination of doors and blankets, they built a low, rectangular, makeshift structure no better than a doghouse. There were advantages to their location; their improvised dwelling was situated only a block away from a popular soup kitchen at St. John's Church and three blocks from the public restrooms at Penn Station. For

two months, from their "home," the men went to work as temporary laborers in local sweatshops.

Rich suburban communities avoid dealing with homelessness by banning the poor altogether, providing neither low-income housing nor shelters. Newark social worker William B. Watson notes that "if a homeless person or a family appears in one of those wealthy little suburban communities, like Short Hills or Millburn, they don't last long. They would be escorted to the nearest big city by the local police, explaining that there is where the facilities to accommodate them are located."

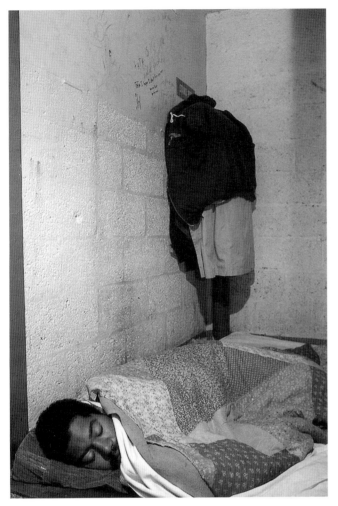

James sleeping on a mat, on a roof landing of the Patterson Houses, South Bronx, 1992.

The Thirteenth Avenue Presbyterian Church was home to at least five homeless men who sought shelter there, Central Ward, Newark, 1987. The men slept, cooked, drank, and kept warm in the church's apse; above them rose a vaulted blue ceiling sprinkled with stars.

BUILDINGS ADAPTED AS SHELTERS:
Hospitals, Schools, Banks, and Stores

"DEAR BROTHERS AND SISTERS IN CHRIST WE ASK YOU PLEASE TO RESPECT OUR VOLUNTEERS WHO MAKE MANY SACRIFICES TO COME HERE TO HELP US SERVE YOU. WITH-OUT THEM WE CANNOT KEEP OUR SOUP KITCHEN OR SHELTER OPEN. IT IS YOUR CHOICE. IF YOU CAN PUT ON A CHRIST-LIKE ATTITUDE TO THEM AND RESPECT ALL OUR VOLUNTEERS AND THEIR PROPERTY, WE CAN REMAIN OPEN. IF THEY HAVE TO SUFFER ACTS OF REVENGE AND ATTACKS WE MUST CLOSE DOWN.

    THE SISTERS"

 —Sign posted on the window of a shelter and soup kitchen, run by the Missionaries of the Charity, in the Mott Haven section of the South Bronx, 1992

Men's shelter in a former bank building, Central Ward, Newark, 1993. The sign reads on one side "St. Rocco Community" and "Bank on Jesus" on the other.

Blinded by its dark window gates, rust staining its pink walls, the Saratoga Respite Center is a shelter for sixty-six pregnant women. This fortress is located in a "killing zone," Brownsville, Brooklyn, 1993.

Trailers donated by a Virginia bank, used as emergency mobile shelters in Washington, D.C., 1991. A sign on them reads "Because We Care." Since the trailers are small and temporary, they generate much less neighborhood opposition than permanent shelters.

174

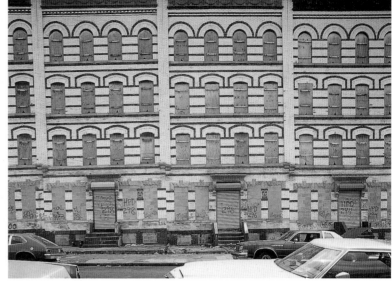

Inner Voice, an abandoned store, transformed into a small day shelter for homeless men, West Side, Chicago, 1990. A sign on the door reads "No Place Like Home."

Boarded-up buildings in Ocean Hill soon to be rehabilitated as a shelter for forty-five families, Brooklyn, 1991.

Franklin Armory, New York National Guard, built in 1910, is now a shelter for single men, South Bronx, 1994.

Former Female Guardian Society and Home for the Friendless, William B. Tuthill, Architect, 1901. Now, the building is a ninety-nine-bed AIDS shelter for families and individuals. South Bronx, 1990.

Former Philip Knitting Mills, a nineteenth-century textile mill, has been adapted as a shelter for 130 single women, South Bronx, 1991. Its foyer is decorated with colorful reproductions of impressionistic paintings of women dancing and of pleasure boats by the shore.

Twenty-third Regiment Armory, National Guard; Fowler and Hough, Architects, 1892. The largest and most dangerous of New York's shelters, the Armory, in 1991, offered temporary accommodations on the drill floor for one thousand single men at a yearly cost to the city of eighteen thousand dollars per person. This congregate shelter in the Crown Heights section of Brooklyn also serves as an assessment center for men. The Armory is an evocative castellated structure, that brings the look of the Middle Ages to an area of Crown Heights rich in landmarks. Instead of armored knights one sees homeless men.

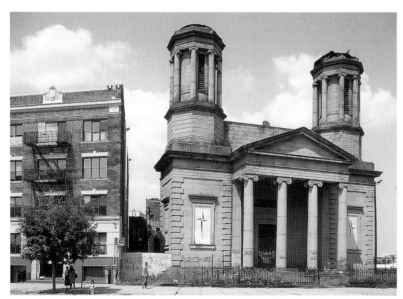

Once a landmark Presbyterian church, later a homeless shelter, and now a burnt shell, the building awaits demolition, Newark, 1993.

Room in the Lincoln Motel, downtown Newark, 1987.

NEW YORK'S NEW SHELTERS

"A shelter [in the neighborhood] is like spitting in your face."

—Michael,
retired teacher, Briarwood, Queens, 1991

"Every single area in which we site a shelter is drug-infested. This is not utopia."

—Official of the New York City Human Resources Administration, 1990

Sometimes occupying an entire city block, and built at a cost of between $13 and $20 million, New York City's new shelters are among the largest of their kind in the nation. They are remarkable not only for their size, but for the lofty ideals they embody.

Take, for example, the anonymous edifice on 138th Street and Jackson Avenue in the South Bronx, which resembles a civic building. Its two facing wings are linked by a cheerful squarish structure with a pitched roof and a windowed cupola that allows light to enter the lofty room it crowns. The orange-brick exterior, articulated with delicate latticework, contrasts with the pale green of the metal doors and roofs. Inside, alternating color patterns lend a sense of both order and variety. As with the other new family shelters for homeless people operated under the auspices of New York City's Human Resources Administration (HRA), nothing betrays its function. The architects (Skidmore, Owings, and Merrill) proposed placing a small bronze identification plaque at the entrance, but HRA declined.

The new shelters take the same basic design and adapt it to the conditions of the site. Ascending a flight of steps to the front entrance of the one of the appealing new city shelters, one could sit on a comfortable bench under a recently planted tree to mingle with the shelter residents. There is no better illustration of a new, friendly attitude toward the homeless than this little public space. The plaza was intended to bring together residents of the shelter and the neighborhood so that they could get to know each other. This concept clashed with the hard realities of the neighborhood and the financial hardship of the city. Once the buildings passed from the contractor to city officials, they were immediately filled to capacity, leading in some cases to the accommodation of families in rooms originally planned for services.

From the time they opened, these institutions were rejected by their neighbors. The city neglected to hire local residents to work in them, thus causing resentment. Without gardeners, the hedges grew wild and the yard became a place to throw empty bottles, cans, diapers, and newspapers. Vacant land adjacent to the shelters was similarly used to dump garbage, giving them a derelict look. Youngsters broke glass windows, forcing the city to replace them with Plexiglas; when the Plexiglas in turn breaks, it is taped or glued together. Recently a tall black fence has been placed around the perimeter.

The initial approach to homelessness characteristic of the administration of New York's mayor Edward Koch (1982–1990) was limited to providing minimal accommodations to those coming to the city for shelter. Critics labeled it the "bed of nails policy," arguing that the city had to furnish comfortable and secure accommodations and social services, not just a roof, to those seeking shelter. Officials responded that more pleasant facilities would serve as a magnet, attracting thousands of precariously housed families who would enter the shelter system as a route to obtaining permanent housing. The new shelters signaled the abandonment of this policy, a set of twenty buildings were commissioned by the city in 1987, and ten were built.

From 1983 to 1989 the area around Pennsylvania Station, a short walk from the media center of the country, was the most visible place for the temporary settlement of homeless families. Infamous hotels such as the Martinique, the Madison, and the Prince George are now closed. The new homeless capital is the South Bronx, which now contains almost half the new shelters and 44 percent of the recent permanent housing for the homeless. Other institutions, part of the poverty, prison, and drug-abuse "industry," and assorted NIMBYs, have been relegated to the same urban areas, making the new shelters with their massive size and large number of residents— regardless of their architectural qualities—the

HELP 1, Alexander Cooper, Architect, accommodates two hundred families at a cost to taxpayers of more than one hundred dollars per night, per family, East New York, Brooklyn, 1991.

With a capacity for 207 families, this HELP College Avenue family shelter, Alexander Cooper, Architect, is the largest and most expensive (over $20 million) of the new facilities built in the city. South Bronx, 1990.

anchors of these "institutional ghettos."

In 1994, the easiest way to find the most depressed, drug-ridden, and violent communities in all of New York City is to visit the area surrounding nine of its thirteen large new shelters (the other four are located in places usually referred to as "nowhere": semi-abandoned industrial areas, the landing path of JFK Airport, and alongside a busy expressway).

Large private shelters, on the other hand, are always separated and designed like fortresses, with stringent rules and more security guards. The first of New York City's large new private shelters, the HELP 1 facility depicted here, is located in an area of junkyards and huge public housing projects, notorious for having the highest homicide rate in the city. Lacking hospitals, parks, public libraries, movie theaters, or adequate shopping facilities, this bleak section of New York is not a neighborhood. These private structures provide temporary isolation from this bleakness. Their playgrounds, park benches, and plantings are behind fences and walls, and management maintains the perimeter, quickly replaces broken windows, and keeps out the local population. It is not surprising, then, that one resident of HELP 1 told me that at night, she saw the shelter as an island of light and security in the darkness of East New York.

Wrapped around the notorious corner of Saratoga and East New York avenues, this SRO, designed by Skidmore, Owings and Merrill, houses about two hundred homeless men, some with AIDS, some mentally ill. Brownsville, Brooklyn, 1991.

Homeless shelter for ninety-eight families, designed by Skidmore, Owings and Merrill at the cost of more than $12 million, South Bronx, 1990.

"Queen Robin, busting out of this hell to start it new and fresh alone, doing it right this time."

—GRAFFITI,
Martin Luther King Towers, Central Ward, Newark, 1991

"Indeed, the real tragedy surrounding the emergence of the modern ghetto is not that it has been inherited but that it has been periodically renewed and strengthened."

—ARNOLD HIRSCH,
Making the Second Ghetto, 1983

EIGHT

GHETTOS
TRANSFORMED

Sign beside the door to Stateway Gardens development reads: "Entry requires passing through metal detector." South Side, Chicago, 1993.

Ghettos are often portrayed as temporary aberrations, un-American violations of the nation's creed that could not endure. This optimistic view underlies such publications as *Newark: An American City* and *Detroit: An American City*, and it prompts such statements as "We're a city with a future, make no mistake," which appeared in an official Gary, Indiana, publication.

Nowhere does one find more public expression of this faith in new beginnings than in this country's ghettos. Even though residents commonly perceive their surroundings as unchanging or even deteriorating, new developments are given names such as "Genesis," "Phoenix," and "Renaissance." Street names are often changed, as if to free them from associations with their derelict past. The words "new," and "hope" form part of the names of many community organizations.

Contradicting this boosterism, local businesses and institutions drop stigmatized city names lest failure rub off on them. More general terms are brought in as substitutes. Thus, the Gary National Bank is now the Grainer Bank; the *Gary Post Dispatch*, the city's daily, has shortened its name to the *Post Dispatch*; and the Gary Symphony has become the Northwest Indiana Symphony. Until recently Tiffany's had a silverplating plant in Newark, but advertisements stated the location as Forest Hills, New Jersey, which is just a northern section of the city.

It is hard and even tragic to manage a city of mostly poor people. In 1986, as if destitution were a modern equivalent of the plague and Camden was in quarantine, Mayor Melvin Primas commented: "No community wants the poor. Whenever there is a problem with the poor, [they say] 'send them to Camden.' It is a rather grim scenario because all the poor are in one place. . . . The poor can't support the poor. The

Abandoned Art Deco building, South Central Los Angeles, 1992.

more services you have for the poor, the more poor you're going to attract."

To the nation, Los Angeles once symbolized being young, carefree, and playful: the delight of palm trees, small bungalows, and ocean, an irresistible combination of water, sky, sun, and advanced technology. Now, anger, fire, and homelessness invariably shape the city.

Chicago-Gary is home. I attended Notre Dame University where I was often bored, alienated, and lonely. I thought of the power and wealth of Chicago as a great spectacle. It was along Maxwell Street in Chicago, a quarter of a century ago, that I was given the first hateful look by a person I had never seen before. To the southeast, in the smoke and stench of the crowded city of Gary, its whorehouses and bars promised the pleasures of hell and its factories well-paying jobs. Today so many street signs in the city are missing that I often do not know

where I am and find myself driving the wrong way along one-way streets. To accurately label a photograph, I often drive for several blocks looking for the name of a street.

DISPATCHES FROM THE LOS ANGELES GHETTOS

"We can get along."

—Rodney King,
quoted on billboards throughout South Central Los Angeles, 1992

It is June 1994, the fifth time since 1979 that I am photographing poor, minority areas in Los

Man being handcuffed outside an abandoned bungalow, Watts, Los Angeles, 1994.

Couple on their way to Sunday services, Watts, Los Angeles, 1981. Upon seeing landscaped bungalows such as this, journalists were at loss to explain the anger that precipitated the 1965 Watts riot.

Angeles. I stand on the roof of a car to avoid filling my pictures with pavement and parked vehicles.

Skid Row is where my day begins. Along a sidewalk on Fifth Street, I photograph sanitation workers busy loading the shovel of a bulldozer with crates, cardboard boxes, rectangular pieces of foam rubber, plastic sheeting, and even a shopping cart. These are fragments of last night's homeless encampment, which must be taken down early in the morning. At the end of the day another set of boxes will be placed on the sidewalk.

I see a man and a woman frantically trying to save what is left of their belongings. As I take pictures, the worker closest to me puts his hand up, momentarily stopping the bulldozer and its infernal noise. The sanitation men turn away from the camera and the police move off from the scene. I can feel their shame. The five offi-

cers overseeing the operation are black- and brown-skinned like the vast majority of the homeless.

A few minutes later, a black policewoman approaches from behind to tell me to stop obstructing the street. She has the warmest smile and addresses me with the friendliest voice. Lights on, motor running, the bulldozer waits impatiently. Residents of SROs and missions across the street watch the scene.

The bulldozer is a Caterpillar IT28B, a machine that can scoop up a heavy concrete building. Yet here it is removing mere packing crates, old clothes, a picnic basket, a plastic colander, dishes, and assorted household articles.

Behind the workers, a mural on the building's wall depicts people lying inside boxes, some in fetal positions, outlined by light. The scene goes on: warming fires burn in garbage cans, and as one moves to the right, the flames

Bookcases contain used clothing for the needy, South Central Los Angeles, 1992.

View of Vermont Avenue and Eighty-fourth Street, South Central Los Angeles, an area severely damaged by the 1992 riot.

get larger and more menacing, reaching their climax with the burning of Los Angeles. Fire fills the windows of City Hall. Farther to the right a few people perch on platforms, with large red clouds in the distance: the homeless that God has chosen to save from the flames, I believe. On one of the platforms, a woman seen from behind sits by an hourglass, looking back over her shoulder at passersby.

The mural acquires a three-dimensional quality as boxes, people, and fires depicted on the walls merge with those in real life on the sidewalk below. The painting is well liked by the street population. The images have not been defaced.

L.A.'s Skid Row is the nation's premier homeless zone. It epitomizes the last stage in the disintegration of neighborhoods, in that residents live in single-room occupancy hotels, missions, and on the sidewalk, a place where many must build and take down their makeshift homes every twenty-four hours. The zone also has light manufacturing, several warehouses, a small park that closes at night, and an L.A. police precinct, a fortress among fortresses.

Over the boxes and the windowless walls behind them rise the tops of downtown skyscrapers: the crown of the tallest building in Los Angeles; the logo of the Crocker Bank; the Interstate Bank; and the pyramid of City Hall.

Public life on Skid Row is extremely disconnected. Most people look angry, tired, depressed, tense, and undernourished. Some stand in the middle of the street, others hang out in safer areas. Many stay inside their boxes or lie on the sidewalk covered by blankets, only their feet visible.

Signs of hard times are pervasive in South Central. On Florence and Normandie a handwritten piece of cardboard affixed to a lamppost

185

A daily Skid Row routine: Sanitation men, accompanied by a police escort, remove encampments that homeless people have hastily set up. Los Angeles, 1994.

reads: "Full employment equals empty jails." And a note on an old bookcase, stacked with used garments by the side of a house on Flower Street, proclaims: "Clothes for the whole family, everybody welcome." Forty-year-old buses with round backs take Latino and African American children to their shabby schools. In Watts, children walk to school past a stinking dead dog, eaten by worms, wrapped in an old rug.

The area has no plazas or squares, museums, or theaters, and lacks anything resembling a center. Absent are the signs of former wealth and power so pervasive in Detroit, Harlem, or Chicago's South Side. Only the streets have great names redolent of history: Normandie Avenue, Florence Avenue, Century Boulevard, Imperial Highway.

South Central lacks marble, bronze, and stone; columns and architectural decoration are a rarity, development having begun after a taste for ornament had waned and revival styles had gone out of fashion. A few exceptional examples of Art Deco architecture remain, mostly vacant, such as the former buildings of Pepperdine University.

Along tree-lined side streets, once-friendly bungalows have their windows sealed like dead eyes covered with black iron shutters. Doors are painted black and are also made of iron.

Even in a place where buildings are rou-

Mural depicting a colossal Christlike figure presides over an empty lot, Watts, Los Angeles, 1994.

tinely adapted to repel break-ins, the nameless blue-and-white cube on Main Street is striking. A high fence surrounds its parking lot, a video camera peers down from a corner, and 3201 is announced boldly on the facade. "You enter through the parking lot. You have to ring about ten bells to get inside. You go through four or five doors to get inside," explains the mail carrier. He tells me that the structure is "a place where they make jewelry."

"It is a nice, very nice, fence. Nobody can just jump over it," says a woman about the formidable ten-foot-high iron fence encircling the David Roberti Day Care Center on Vernon Avenue, where she works as an aide.

At the headquarters of the Watts Labor Community Action Coalition, a gasoline pump enclosed by an iron cage resembles a jailed robot.

Signs along the freeways are framed with razor-ribbon wire, and arched signposts along the side of the highway have double necklaces of coiled wire.

From the roof of the tallest building in South Central, on Forty-eighth Street, I can see only one smokestack spewing fumes. Along Sixty-first Street, a silvery food truck playing carnival music is parked by a sweatshop, next to a pile of discarded tires, in the midst of desolate industrial ruins.

Jewelry factory, a fortress that blends with the sky, Los Angeles, 1994.

Along commercial streets, on storefronts and walls, the image of Christ is popular, second to the Virgin of Guadalupe. So too, pictures of cows, pigs, chickens, and produce. Lively and brightly colored, these signs relieve the drabness of the streets.

Blacks to the south and Latinos to the north watch a Latino youth being dragged by a policeman out of an abandoned house on Wilmington Avenue and then handcuffed. I am amazed at how young he looks, but then he turns away from my camera.

I count three entrances to a small bungalow, a multifamily house in disguise. Behind the last dwelling is a garage, often also a family's apartment, and next to it, not much smaller, is a doghouse the size of the boxes in which the homeless dwell.

"We are built-up around here. We don't have bombed-out areas around here," says the manager of a housing agency. Yet I see many vacant lots along Central Avenue. Roses, laurel, ivy, and grass continue to grow alongside abandoned bungalows.

In a neighborhood where white kids are exotic, "Nobody's Born a Bigot" is the message on a billboard with a photograph of two children embracing, one black, one white. Found only in our nation's ghettos, this billboard seems merely to call attention to segregation instead of fostering racial tolerance.

A sentence from the 1965 McCone Commission Report on the Watts riots runs through my mind: "While the Negro districts of Los Angeles are not urban gems, neither they are a slum." This much-quoted statement lends nostalgia to the memory of minority neighborhoods—under stress, to be sure, but still ordinary—that composed the Watts of three decades ago.

Today industrial abandonment is almost complete. Poor, minority communities consist of derelict commercial streets and fortified clusters of old dwellings. Residents nervously watch their families and possessions.

Defenses continue to proliferate and to become more assertive. I see more razor-ribbon wire, iron bars, windowless buildings, dogs, and security guards than ever before. Popular colors used to paint the exterior of the most brutal fortresses are sky-blue and cloud-white.

Comparing photos taken two months after the 1992 riot with those taken two years later, I discover that rebuilding means a new Louisiana Fried Chicken, a Payless Shoes outlet, other franchises, a fenced parking lot, gas stations, a few hundred units of housing, new missions and single-room occupancy hotels. The empty block where I attended, uninvited, the ground-breaking for a Muslim complex and where I had the pleasure of shaking hands with Muhammad Ali, still lies empty.

Across from the Metropolitan Detention Center on Alameda Street, a homeless man approaches me as I stop to ask directions. "I bought a chicken, I have some tomatoes, I need three dollars for cooking oil," he tells me. 'If you help me I can stop now and go with my wife and have dinner." He opens a bag to show me a small raw chicken wrapped in plastic, and points toward a heavy-set woman standing like a statue by a street light. I give him a dollar.

On the banks of the Los Angeles River I meet a homeless man with a vision. He is a gatherer from East Orange, New Jersey. In his shopping cart he carries a bed frame he plans to sell for thirty dollars. He hopes for rain to raise the water level and transform the river into a conveyor belt, bringing him an endless supply of empty cans. In the green shallow stream, used to dump sewage, he has seen flamingoes and herons.

By the Sixth Street Bridge, a man methodically sets fire to the weeds sprouting out of the concrete riverbanks. Their fuzzy tops burn with a bright short flame, and much smoke drifts from their green stems.

Near the Hollywood Subway Tunnel, where Glendale Avenue dead ends, I speak to homeless men and women living in an abandoned power station. Used to film crews, they know how to pose for photographers and hope to be discovered by movie producers. At the same time they live in fear of being killed by gangs.

I did not go to visit the "Consejera de Terremotos" on Figueroa Street, who offered "Free Earthquake Counseling" but I would have liked to stop by. Feeling that I had witnessed the effect of an economic earthquake, I could not understand why I felt good about the future of the Los Angeles of the poor. It moves, it is lively, it is young, it sings.

I had a long conversation with Noe, a Latino school aide from South Central. Feeling sorry to see me spending so much time in ghettos, and afraid that I was getting the wrong impression of Southern California, he urged me to "see something pretty; go to Disneyland."

VISIONS AND SHADOWS:
"Reinventing" Chicago and Gary, 1994

"We dream of a city free of racism, poverty, crime, and corruption."

—Richard Hatcher,
former mayor of Gary, 1984

"Why when things are broken do they seem like more than when they're together?"

—Thomas Berger,
Crazy in Berlin, 1958

In the ruined neighborhoods and downtowns of the once-richest nation on earth, I see poor people, vacant land, abandoned buildings: former banks with classical porticos boarded up; Art Deco automobile showrooms, their wrap-around windows cinder-blocked; splendid hotels with large ballrooms; neo-Gothic churches. With

511 Browning Street, part of Ida B. Wells development, South Side, Chicago, 1987.

511 Browning Street, South Side, Chicago, September 1991.

so many of the surrounding buildings leveled, these substantial "leftover" structures, too costly to demolish, dominate the streetscape in isolated grandeur. Common wisdom tells us to relocate the people, demolish the remains, and rebuild. Structures that lured immigrants from the entire world, that survived riots and decades of disinvestment, soon, indeed, will be leveled. Why is it so difficult for us to accept that beyond their immediate meanings of neglect and failure, these ghetto cityscapes can nurture our imagination?

Chicago, a still-vital city, exhibits bizarre patterns of development. Moribund Gary is leveled by the pull of gravity and the work of scavengers. A tour of their poor, minority communities reveals a little rebuilding, signs announcing future development, but, most often, impending demolition. In these two cities the new American ghetto, with its contradictions, inequality, and tragic allure, reveals itself to us.

CHICAGO

Chicago has lost about nine hundred thousand people since 1950, more than 23 percent of its population. During the 1980s alone, the city lost one hundred thousand African Americans. Among those fleeing in 1992 were over twice as many residents of wealthy neighborhoods as of poor communities. "The strongest force behind that migration today," according to a December 1993 *Chicago Tribune* study, "is fear of crime." Asked to comment, Mayor Richard M. Daley replied in his usual telegraphic style, "You're going to have a smaller city, better quality of life. . . . The city will get smaller and then reinvent itself. You'll start planning it differently in a way. It's going to be much smaller, which is good for us." Meanwhile, Daley keeps the demolition crews busy, clearing space for Chicago to "reinvent itself."

*511 Browning Street, South Side,
Chicago, August 1994.*

Alongside thoroughfares like West Madison Street in Chicago, I travel through a familiar cityscape: a particular building I have stared at so often I can even recall the faded name on a former dentist's office; a busy intersection where I photographed the structures that stood on a now-vacant corner; children coming home from school; men in small groups hanging out in front of liquor stores; and prostitutes, visible from a distance along stretches of empty lots, soliciting passing drivers.

Once one of the nation's most important commercial streets, after two riots and four decades of disinvestment, West Madison is mostly gone. Moving west from the Loop, a buffer zone of institutions and housing leads to five miles of large-scale abandonment, and then on to "normal" Oak Park, where one sees what things used to look like when they cohered.

Bearing a sign that reads "Chicago Works," a few new structures are rising. Large buildings seem to have been dropped amid ruins, parking lots, and vacant land. Among such projects is a formidable cylindrical library whose pillars, leading to the entrance, seem designed to stop car bombers. Nearby is the massive Chicago Stadium, consisting of layer upon layer of concrete, and the Police Communications Center, otherwise known as "the 911 building." South of these public structures are two new additions to the huge West Side medical complex. This area of the Near West Side has experienced rehabilitation, and new housing for middle-income families is expected to follow. So far, only one apartment house has been erected.

The process of abandonment, fire, and demolition is repeated throughout Chicago's ghettos as it was in the South Bronx a dozen years ago. This is happening at a time of particular economic hardship: 21 percent of the population

Arresting murals on Forty-seventh Street, South Side, Chicago, 1993.

falls below the poverty level—four times the number of poor than in the ring of suburbs surrounding the city. Shortage of inexpensive housing combined with a scarcity of rent subsidies is forcing destitute residents to double up. At the same time, widespread poverty limits rebuilding and reduces expenditures for upkeep. Community development corporations and private entrepreneurs often are unable to manage even the buildings given to them, because they can't charge rents sufficient to pay the mortgage and carrying costs.

In many areas of Chicago, according to an official of the Buildings Department, "a building that is not occupied has a very short life because of the scavengers that will come in, strip the plumbing, and cause fires." Yet the city is very slow in transferring the rights to abandoned

buildings to nonprofit community groups willing to rehabilitate them. Why this is so is a matter of speculation, but many suspect a hidden "clearance" policy. In any case, consensus holds that if a structure is not going to be rehabilitated soon, it should be demolished. Structures meanwhile continue to deteriorate, substantially increasing the cost of future rehabilitation should funds become available and limiting the number of buildings that can be saved. Vacant and abandoned structures become focal points for gang-related activities such as drug peddling. Children are often hurt in these buildings. Finally, empty shells are a strong disincentive to people who might otherwise invest in the area.

In 1993, the city approved a fivefold increase in the demolition budget, raising it to $10 million. Hundreds of substantial edifices bear an official sign rationalizing their destruction. A note on the abandoned "House of God" on Roosevelt Road reads:

NOTICE

This building has been determined to be a hazard to the community and has been referred the Demolition Court of the Circuit Court of Cook County as part of Mayor Richard M. Daley's Focus Demolition Program.

An official of the Demolition Program explains, "The mayor keeps riding around the city and keeps seeing these buildings, and doesn't know 'where they are at,' so that now they decided to post them, to tell the people they are in court."

"Abandonment is old. It may be picking up speed now, but this has been going on since the 1950s," says Professor Charles Hoch of the University of Illinois. This time, however, nobody seems to be surprised that so much of the city is disappearing. "To the banks, to the people who own those buildings, their value in money terms is insignificant even though their value as shelter is still great. Capital is into new edge cities, not into restoration, protection, or preservation."

As privately owned apartment buildings disappear, the only large investment in low-income housing comes in the rehabilitation of projects belonging to the Chicago Housing Authority (CHA), an institution that has long being associated with mismanagement, semi-abandoned high-rises, concentrated poverty, gangs, and crime. Because it provides housing of last resort, the CHA has often been called "Chicago's unofficial shelter system." For nearly three decades, CHA developments, widely resented as "places to load down poor people" and as "hellholes," have defined the city's worst ghettos.

A large banner addressed to the drivers along the Eisenhower Expressway hangs from the windows of a building, part of the Rockwell Gardens project; the inscription is: "WE'RE PART OF THE SOLUTION, Residents of the CHA." For Vincent Lane, chairman of the CHA, the solution is to create "normal neighborhoods," that is, communities of mixed-income residents. He equates his program to "a revolution."

To deconcentrate poor people, Lane wants to build scatter-site housing for families now living in developments, while at the same time making the high-rises attractive to working families. Patrick T. Reardon, the *Chicago Tribune*'s urban affairs writer, calls his plans "seeds of the future stabilization of Chicago." Yet these seeds need a lot of costly protection just to survive. Reclaimed buildings have a thick iron grid on their ground floors with a sign saying, "ENTRY REQUIRES PASSING TROUGH METAL DETECTOR." Guards sit in the lobby. Visitors have to be escorted by residents and sign a register. Typically, the higher stories of these edifices were where vacancies concentrated, but now for security reasons the situation is reversed: in rehabbed buildings the top floors are again occupied, and it is common to find the ground-floor windows bricked. At night some visibility is maintained with powerful lights placed high above the ground. The CHA's attempt to create "normal neighborhoods" has resulted in buildings that resemble fortresses under siege.

Lane's most ambitious design is to create an economically integrated community in the infamous Cabrini-Green development. Through a combination of demolition and new construction, he plans to change the population mix from one in which 92 percent of its families receive public assistance to one where the poverty rate is 25 percent, slightly above the citywide average. The cost of the physical transformation of Cabrini-Green's 3,600 apartments is $350 million, $50 million of which has been approved by HUD. Within two years, the CHA expects to receive another $50 million from Washington and to leverage the rest from private investors. Cabrini-Green, bordering the affluent North Side of Chicago, may become part of an expanding and prosperous Loop.

One Chicago housing official, who prefers not to be named, is highly critical of the expensive rehabilitation of complexes that had become unmanageable, while many much smaller buildings scattered throughout the city are demolished. The official explained, "If any reasonable individual would have been in control of the situation, that individual would probably said, 'No, let's start disinvesting in these enormous high-rises and divert the money into rehabilitating an equivalent number of units in some very high-quality buildings that happen to be vacant.' "

When I asked why this was happening, he reminded me of the 1966 Gautreaux class action suit that charged the CHA with discrimination and Washington with financing segregation. A federal court decision in 1969 stopped Chicago from building public housing in poor, black communities, a practice that historian Arnold Hirsch called "reinforcing the ghetto." It is tragic that a quarter-century later, when economic segregation is seen as a far worse evil than racial segregation, the Gautreaux decision forbids the CHA to rehabilitate vacant buildings in depopulated black neighborhoods, where they are plentiful.

Small "public housing villages," consisting of rehabilitated apartment buildings and new townhouses in areas where little survives, would have been much more attractive and less expensive to secure and maintain than the high-rise complexes. As plans to house project residents outside the city's ghettos meet strong opposition from neighbors, the CHA efforts are primarily directed to the land and the buildings under its immediate control.

In addition to the rehabilitation of CHA buildings, recent development on the South Side is exemplified by gigantic churches surrounded by vast parking lots. In their lack of religious symbolism these structures resemble convention centers or gymnasiums. With room for as many as five thousand people, and pastors who are radio evangelists, these houses of worship draw their flock from the African American population of the entire metropolitan area. Like sports stadiums and hospitals, such churches form enclaves that have little connection to their surroundings of devastation.

On Forty-seventh Street, renamed Muddy Waters Street, arresting murals on an abandoned building announce the "Roots Festival" and the coming of the Lou Rawls Theatre and Cultural Center. The ground floor is decorated with large-scale, colorful faces of great blues legends belting out songs and blowing the horn. On the upstairs windows is a very different style of art, depicting an elegantly dressed audience of faded ghosts in black and white. The contrast between the musicians and their spectral audience in the windows could not be greater.

Likewise, the Chicago Bee building, a green-and-gold Art Deco landmark that formerly housed an African American newspaper, is being rehabilitated with a grant from the city. Dempsey J. Travis, a black developer, greets with skepticism the plan to turn this section of the South Side into a tourist attraction. "I can't see how it will work," he says. "Who wants to look at a historical building on Martin Luther King Drive, marvel at it, and then get shot?"

GARY

In the Chicago metropolitan area, Gary ranks first among the nation's cities in terms of population loss during the 1980s. At the National Black Political Convention in 1972, an event held at a time of hope, the 3,500 delegates and alternates were enjoined to "Come Home to Gary." In 1994, Richard Hatcher's successor, Mayor Thomas V. Barnes, still wants people to return. Banners strung along Broadway read "Come Home . . . to Gary."

In his five terms as mayor, Hatcher linked the city's downtown to the interstate highway system, cleared dozens of acres for reconstruction, and built the Genesis Convention Center. He stated his intention to build at the city's most prominent intersection a Civil Rights Hall of Fame; that spot still remains vacant. This is the city that Hatcher wanted to make the capital and economic center of black America. During the first fifteen years of his administration, Gary re-

Survivor in a tough city: the Blackstone building. Gary, 1993.

ceived $300 million from Washington. In 1976, federal funds accounted for 36 percent of the city's entire budget. On the other hand, U.S. Steel Works in Gary, the company that created the city, eliminated 20,000 jobs during Hatcher's tenure in office.

Steel City looks desolate. Viewed looking north from Washington Street, the ruined downtown rises like a mirage above large snow-covered fields. A few prostitutes with harsh faces, working out of semi-abandoned buildings, are what remains of a once-legendary red-light district. Street dogs trot over the empty lots. Plywood nailed across openings of vacant buildings has gone from brown to gray and the boards are falling off, leaving the vacant structures accessible to squatters and scavengers. Malfunctioning streetlights are sometimes cut off as if they

were trees stricken by a deadly disease, their jagged aluminum stumps left embedded in the cement. Overgrown sidewalks line streets that have lost their traffic signs and sometimes even their names. Trees grow from the roofs of abandoned buildings, and in parking lots wild shrubs break out of the cement. Broadway, the city's main commercial street, has only one building undergoing rehabilitation, a former Sears. "Fifty years ago, during the war, this was one of the busiest places on the planet," says James B. Lane, a professor of history at Indiana University Northwest.

Visions of renewal involve the development of resorts by the waterfront; the transformation of Gary's airport into the third airport for the tristate region; a minor league stadium by the Indiana Toll Road; and casinos to attract gamblers from the Chicago metropolitan area.

A $300,000 abandoned farmer's market built in 1976, used for a few months, then abandoned, Gary, 1992. An architect's fantasy, made of elegant steel triangles, open to the sky, the structure is now a large (and inspiring) outdoor sculpture.

None of these would directly affect the city's downtown or Broadway, its major commercial street. These plans remain on paper.

How will these cities cohere? In Chicago, Mayor Daley waits for his city to "reinvent itself" while increasing the demolition budget. The "City of the Broad Shoulders" disappears from the West Side and South Side while growing in size and prosperity in the Loop and North Shore. Heading a program to house the poor and the homeless, Vincent Lane at the same time struggles to create "normal neighborhoods." While Gary vanishes, Mayor Barnes pleads for people to come live in his city. Torn between helping people escape the ghetto to find jobs, better schools, and a more secure environment in the suburbs on the one hand, and fostering the development of the inner cities on the other, HUD Secretary Henry Cisneros chooses both.

In Chicago, Gary, and other older cities, boarded-up, roofless, and charred structures that were once the physical basis of much of our prosperity are now obsolete, unproductive places. Ghettos are increasingly seen merely as stepping stones from which "normal people" move to better places, as others did before them For those who have no choice but to stay and for those who are sent there, enlightened commentators ask that they be provided with better schools, prisons, housing, and social services in hope that they will eventually be fit to move out. Ghettos are seen as dubious incubators to "rebuild" men and women as well as to warehouse those deemed too old, too ill, or too hopeless.

Under the supervision of social workers, teachers, prison guards, security personnel, and the police, and with the help of the wonder drugs of our pharmaceutical industry, ghettos continue to expand with Washington's support.

Few deny the absurdity, expense, and hopelessness of this system, yet we are told to accept it as inevitable. Affluent suburbs are closed to the poor and the institutions that serve them. The economy is not producing enough entry-level jobs that pay enough to support a family. Drugs and violence have gotten so out of hand that it would take at least another generation to heal the damage they have caused.

Nationally, we seem unable to achieve the consensus needed to rebuild our cities, but as we see in Chicago and Gary today, we can surely blow up and bulldoze structures that we consider useless. Our extraordinary ruins represent a short transitional period when stately structures built for the affluent became the homes, churches, and businesses of the poor, and after decades of neglect and disinvestment were discarded. As municipalities, with help from the federal government, increase their demolition budgets, they will be able to level their more substantial "eyesores."

Large-scale leveling of cities will, of course, not mean the end of abandonment. Yet the next crop of discarded buildings, farther removed from the downtown, some even beyond the city limits, will not be as substantial or have the historical echoes of our present ruins. Brick, stone, and reinforced concrete will be replaced by basic frame structures. Classical ornamentation and lavish decoration will rarely be found.

America does not share Europe's respect for ruins. From a distance, they are perceived as messengers of bad news. We either ignore them or react to them with anger, resentment, guilt, and despair. Ruins stand as witnesses of their own past, not doing what they were built to do, yet possessing an awesome power to stir the soul.

There is something inspiring about ruins. As witnesses of the urban condition, they urge us to ask: Is there no choice but to stand by and watch the destruction of our cities? Stripped down to their essences, leftover buildings and discarded spaces form cityscapes of great power. While they last, we have our ruins and the immense longings they instill in us.

Even at risk of bodily harm, we need to hear the elemental chant that comes from our skeletal neighborhoods. The "City of the Broad Shoulders," and "Steel City," sing about the shortness of life, the awesome beauty of our creations, and our abject failure to create a just society. With their chant they beckon us to come home and perhaps to try again.

"I see for Gary a future of rare commercial power and signal industrial greatness. . . . I see a city rise as if by magic, in proportions vast and splendid, with a hundred busy marts of traffic and trade, with palatial homes unnumbered and seats of learning multiplied. . . . I see countless toilers in factory, mill, and shop—bare-bodied men who move like specters amid the heat and glow of furnace and forge, of molten streams of metal and red-hot, yielding, lapping sheets of steel—and heaving wharfmen loading cargoes on far-extending piers."

—GOVERNOR J. FRANK HANLY,
Gary, Indiana, November 25, 1907

NINE

CONCLUSION
No Solution in Sight

This miniature ruined castle seems to be in the middle of a wilderness, not downtown Detroit. Woodward East, Detroit, 1994.

The Puritans' godly "city on the hill" evolved through many stages to the progressive "wonder city" of the first half of the twentieth century. Now, urban America includes, inextricably, the image and the reality of ruins.

Lacking a shared vision of the value of our cities, we accept their destruction and fragmentation as inevitable. Urban landscapes, once central to the life and identity of the nation, are vanishing. We find that the stone, steel, marble, and brass that shaped "cathedrals of business" have disappeared without a trace. First-rate skyscrapers that defined a downtown, having stood vacant for a decade or longer, are leveled to make room for parking lots. Times are frustrating for activists, organizers, and advocates for the poor. The people to whom they must go for support—bankers and business executives—are not interested in experiencing first-hand the conditions that so urgently need changing. Showcase devel-opments create urban subdivisions that cast out troublesome residents and leave most of the city untouched. Programs such as homeless shelters, substance abuse treatment centers, soup kitchens, and needle exchanges do improve people's lives and reduce the damage that they may inflict on themselves and others, but hardly form a basis on which to rebuild the economy.

RUINS

"How long? Not long—How long? Not long—How long? Not long—How long? Not long—How long? Not long— How long? Not long—How long? Not long—How long? Not long—How long? Not long—How long? Not long."

—Inscription on an abandoned house,
Mack Avenue and Meldrun, Detroit, 1993

200

Overgrown Victorian ruin, part of Woodward East, a disappearing historic district, Detroit, 1991. In 1886 Edmund Kirke, in Harper's, *referred to houses in this neighborhood as "rows of private palaces, overhung with great trees and seated amid beautiful grounds that are parks in miniature."*

Three and a half years later, having lost its green covering of leaves, the ruined state of this once elegant Victorian house is revealed. Woodward East, Detroit, 1994.

America leads the world in urban ruins. We find them raw and unsettling, signaling things "ruined" more than ruins, a civilization wasted before its time. Unlike Romantic ruins, ours dominate a still-urban landscape. Ruins stretch for miles at a time, laced with streets, power lines, billboards, expressways, as components in a succession of derelict and semi-abandoned buildings, occasionally interrupted by a citadel-like edifice designed to resist a similar fate. Discarded buildings, ruins, are sacked for anything of value; nature grows wildly on and around them; surfaces collect dirt; structures split into fragments.

Some building is done in vain, its products serving their intended purpose briefly or not at all. Near downtown Gary, Indiana, lies a late sixties ruin. Along railroad lines without trains, flagpoles without flags, and people crossing the flat open land stand two giant triangles made of steel bars that once supported a farmers' market. The electric cords that supplied power and light to the stands now drop like dead snakes from the triangular roof, and plants push through the market's cement base. Its central fountain has not spurted water for seventeen years; the fixtures were removed from the restrooms, which now store garbage.

Huge factories lie silently rusting. On the outskirts of Gary, the large enclosed space of the former American Bridge plant leaves a profound impression. Under a huge steel roof, in a semi-deserted space big enough to park ten 747s, a few dozen men gather around metal planks, making armor for tanks. Light flowing through openings in the roof gives an air of sanctity to their work, their quiet observation and measuring. In the enormous plant, they may strike the observer as visitors from another planet, investigating the remains of a civilization whose popu-

Abandoned bungalows, East Los Angeles, 1994.

Former train station, Detroit, 1991.

lation of giants was felled by a neutron bomb.

When factories are razed, they leave behind a treacherous subterranean labyrinth of tunnels lurking under paved surfaces, parking docks, roads, and railroad tracks. Polluted fluids—mixtures of oil, rainwater, solvents, and chemicals used during their years of operation—are visible through the open sewer holes, their covers stolen by scavengers. Among ruins one is often startled by strangers or street dogs, and by inanimate dangers as well: floors about to cave in, beams, stones, or bricks falling from above, nails underfoot.

For public officials, these derelict structures are a source of shame, something that gives journalists material for critical articles that keep investors away from the city. Merely empty land, on the other hand, means opportunity for development.

To soften the dreariness of abandoned

buildings, cities have designed cheerful coverings to hide the holes left where windows once were. As part of a program called "The Occupied Look," New York City created a variety of bright plastic decals decorated with flowerpots, curtains, and shutters. Newark used crude pieces of painted cardboard for the same purpose. And on Forty-seventh Street, in a historic section of Chicago's South Side, artists painted elaborate window scenes that manage to surprise and delight.

For indigenous artists, ruins provide astonishingly strong imagery and an awesome wealth of materials to create works that make the ghetto accessible to outsiders. Yet this display, transformation, interpretation, and preservation of ruins enrage city hall. There was the case in Newark's Central Ward of Kea Tawana's Ark, perhaps the purest and most elegant of our folk art environments. The Ark soared in the midst of an apoca-

Ruined townhouses along Washington Street, seen from Broadway, Camden, 1993. If there were a guide to "all-American ruins," these blocks of downtown Camden would be included.

Only the charred and weakened shell of this former synagogue stands, a refuge for street dogs, Central Ward, Newark, 1991.

lyptic landscape of empty lots and abandoned buildings. It was made of the nerves, bones, and muscle of a once-powerful industrial city: bolts, nails, pieces of marble, wire, vintage glass, tools, toilets, statues, books, even a telephone pole serving as a mast. Under a court order that threatened demolition, Tawana was forced to dismantle her own masterpiece. With the destruction of the vessel we have lost an inspiring monument that made peace between a struggling city and the disappearing world of the old slums.

On the East Side of Detroit, Tyree Guyton imaginatively used discarded objects to dress up ruined houses, streets, and empty lots. His assemblages are disturbing: his red paint resembles blood, wood pieces have been charred, dolls are mutilated or placed in unstable positions. Shoes by the hundred line Heidelberg Street, standing in for their former owners. Guyton's work, widely seen as a commentary on the recent his-

tory of Detroit and celebrated in the press, was nevertheless almost completely demolished by the city in 1991. Lost were the photographs of young white women, taken from a former beauty salon, that Guyton hung along alongside an abandoned house, suggesting an exhibit about an extinct species.

Although Kea's Ark and Guyton's Heidelberg Project are among the most extensive and best known examples of public art, one frequently comes across anonymous assemblages of discarded objects in the ghetto. They are works of art because they seem designed solely to engage in a formal and thematic dialogue with their collapsing surroundings. On a corner of 139th Street in Robbins, Illinois, for example, in the space once occupied by a house, I found what is perhaps an altar to lost domesticity: a mound of cinder blocks surmounted by a black armchair, with a Eureka vacuum cleaner stand-

"Built to last" in the 1920s, the City Methodist Church included among its members Elbert T. Gary, the city's founder and president of U.S. Steel. Mr. Gary donated all the steel for the construction. By the 1980s the building was abandoned, and by 1993 it had become a ruin, its copper gutters stolen, and trees growing on its roof. Gary, 1993.

Fake windows, part of "The Occupied Look," a program of the Koch administration designed to cover the dark apertures of city-owned buildings in New York. South Bronx, 1986.

ing on that; placed on the side of the mound, a pair of sneakers on a small rug; and at the bottom, a discarded couch. I made inquiries of two neighbors, neither of whom had ever noticed the structure.

With their aura of mystery and decay, ruins have become a fashionable setting for movies, television dramas, and rap videos that center on crimes, gang rituals, and drug deals. For the movie *Wolfen* (1981), filmmakers selected "the big hole" along Charlotte Street in the South Bronx, surrounded by derelict tenements, as a place to erect a brand-new burnt-out church, an instant ruin, as a home for man-eating wolves. Urban ghettos are striking locations and backgrounds for the entertainment industry.

To visitors and residents alike, ruins are very important. They point to both the seriousness of the community's current problems and the fact that things were once better. Residents

regard them as proof that "the world is down on you," as symbols of whites walking away from their property and of Washington's neglect. The legacy of racism adds another dimension to ruins. Why should buildings that recall white supremacy be preserved? Why should officials in a predominantly minority city spend scarce resources to reclaim buildings that excluded them—a club that did not admit blacks as members, a hotel closed to people of their race, restaurants that made them feel unwelcome? Suburbanites, on the other hand, usually interpret ruins as an index of local mismanagement. The value of our devastated landscapes is thus limited to serving as useful exhibits focusing attention on the reasons for decay, on the plight of the residents, on the need to begin rebuilding. At the same time they demonstrate the futility of meeting the challenge: Why try to save what cannot, or perhaps should not, be saved?

Amid rubble, the makers of the movie Wolfen *built an artificially ruined church as a lair for werewolves. South Bronx, 1980.*

Abandoned and overgrown Harlem townhouses, New York, 1989.

Our ruins are not there to serve as models for new buildings and institutions. Unlike picturesque English monasteries and abbeys, preserved as testaments to the ancient lineage of the local nobility, for example, American ruins are perceived as useless, dragging cities down, standing for failure.

We are too close to our ruins. Strong feelings of anger, guilt, and despair prevent us from seeing them as they are. They stand as witnesses of their own past —not doing what they were built to do, yet possessing an awesome power to stir the soul. Historical precedent implies that it will be a long time before we can look upon these ruins with anything resembling appreciation. In England, for example, a century elapsed after the abrupt termination of the monasteries in the sixteenth century before observers could view them with interest and aesthetic delight.

Increasingly, ruins herald the coming of the post-urban era. The world economy has bypassed many American cities. Contradicting a long-held vision of our country as a place of endless progress, ruins were unforeseen and then often denied, but surely they are here to stay and spread, leaving us with the question of what things mean when they are no longer used.

As the millennium approaches, we may find ourselves staring at our throwaway structures with increasing fascination, being profoundly moved by them and asking, as the members of London's Metaphysical Society did one hundred and twenty years ago: "Are not ruins recognized and felt to be more beautiful than perfect structures? Why are they so? Ought they to be so?" But even after we acknowledge their power, what do we do with them?

View west along Watson Street, Detroit, 1993.

DETROIT WAITS FOR THE MILLENNIUM

"Let the future begin."

—Dennis Archer,
mayoral candidate (now mayor), Detroit, 1993

"DUST!"

—Graffiti on abandoned buildings,
Detroit, 1994

The city is quiet, the air clean; large open fields and derelict factories are everywhere. The Detroit River is wide and calm, its surface turquoise green. Tugboats and cargo ships cruise slowly by. "We got the water; we may not have the gold, but we have the water," says Michael Goodin of *Crain's Detroit Business*. "There is

no other city in the area that can boast of an international waterway, a fresh water supply like ours."

Detroit is a city whose economic power disappeared quickly, leaving it isolated, fragmented, and nearly bankrupt. During the decade beginning in 1968, the year after "the riot," the city lost 208,000 jobs, one-third of its total employment. By 1990, about a million people lived in the city, about half its 1950 population, and of those nearly one-quarter were on welfare. At the same time, well over 10 percent of the city's 140 square miles of land was vacant.

Once the largest factory town in the world, a mixed ethnic blue-collar city, Detroit is now an African American metropolis that can no longer sustain itself. More than three-quarters of the residents are black, with roots in the Southern states, particularly Alabama, Georgia, the Carolinas, and Mississippi. Compared to other large

Stone Hedge, a "castle" west of Woodward Avenue, is only a block away from an abandoned house. Detroit North, 1991.

Renaissance Center, completed in 1977 at a cost of $350 million. Henry Ford II, its main sponsor, spoke of it as a "catalyst that may change the whole tone and lift the spirits of a city and a downtown area that sorely needs a boost." At the Center's opening, Mayor Coleman Young referred to it as proof that cities were "on the upsurge." Detroit, 1991.

American municipalities its population is homogeneous and dwindling.

"People are running: there is nothing to do here; there is no jobs here. People have to get some money somewhere," says Al, a retired carpenter. Residents have been fleeing Detroit at the rate of about twenty thousand a year since 1950. Those I spoke with insistently warned me against "dumping on us and our city," and against looking at Detroit in isolation. "You cannot write about Detroit as if it is in its own little niche, its own little corner, just because it's black," Goodin emphasized.

Detroit confronts the visitor and resident alike with ubiquitous decay. The numerous churches that stand alone in open fields, their neighborhoods gone, are still imposing and attractive. Green historical markers commemorate the past in official prose on buildings that are themselves ghosts. Vehicles speed past the van-

ishing neighborhoods of single-family houses. Detroit's famous freeways—five of them, more than in any city of similar population—seem to be waiting for the city to wake up and form traffic jams once more. Unlike New York City, where the poorest parts of town have been marked by ever-greater concentrations of destitute people and facilities, Detroit is becoming increasingly barren.

After World War II, the construction of those five highways, ramming through hundreds of blocks of houses, sometimes at stretches of nearly ten miles, destroyed more than twenty thousand homes, contributing to the decline of the city by providing easy access to the suburbs. Already two decades ago, according to the city assessor, Detroit had more than five thousand abandoned commercial buildings, "which if lined up would occupy 60 of the city's 175 miles of business thoroughfares." The degree of

Typical of the strange juxtapositions found in our new ghettos: an Art Deco building behind a tall blank wall on Livernois Avenue, Detroit, 1994.

shrinkage is unprecedented. In 1989, a block-by-block survey by the *Detroit Free Press* found more than fifteen thousand derelict buildings. Asked to explain, Mayor Coleman Young replied that no city in the Western world has endured so much white and middle-class flight: "One million folks have abandoned this city in less than forty years."

Every neighborhood in the city has "For Sale" signs, sometimes a few to a block. Most neighborhoods have boarded-up houses and many have wide-open buildings, sitting vandalized and partially burned amid weeds. Families residing next to abandoned houses see their lives turn to fear—especially fear of fires and of drug dealers and addicts who use the dwellings.

Abandonment in a city that had such a strong belief in progress and growth has meanings that everybody understands. According to the *Free Press*: "The vacant buildings are the most visible evidence of the city's social and economic problems. The ugly confines of an abandoned house give shape and substance to every nebulous complaint about Detroit."

There have been many proposals to restore economic health to the city. The City Planning Department's 1985 Master Plan proposed that Detroit, while retaining industry, should compete with Chicago, New York, and the Bay Area in international banking, tourism, robotics, and other high-tech ventures. The plan envisioned a service-oriented metropolis, a cultural and information center linked with the rest of the world by fiber optics. This image of the city already fits the reality of its thriving and expanding mostly white suburbs.

With a population of more than three million, these suburbs are among the richest in the nation. On a late summer afternoon, the winding tree-lined streets of Bloomfield Hills are full of

208

children playing. No fences separate the well-tended lawns or the large and comfortable houses. Only lawnmowers break the sounds of play and conversation. Beyond the residential enclaves lie the research and development outfits, corporate headquarters, financial centers, shopping malls, developers' offices, and architectural and engineering firms that sustain this pleasant way of life.

Like earlier dreams of renewal, the Master Plan proceeded from a faith that some well-considered investments would set Detroit on a path toward reclaiming its importance in American economic life. In another era, large downtown projects providing jobs were the preferred heralds of "salvation." The most important of these grand designs was the Renaissance Center, a riverfront complex planned and built twenty years ago to "rejuvenate the city's image" and to draw people from the entire metropolitan region. Boosters still call Detroit "Renaissance City."

The Center was designed by Atlanta architect John Portman and sponsored by Henry Ford II with the support of the chief executives of the city's largest corporations. In 1972, Ford viewed the Renaissance Center, while it was still on the drawing board, as a "catalyst that may change the whole tone and lift the spirits of a city and a downtown area that sorely needs a boost." Portman echoed his patron, saying: "That is what architecture should do, it should lift people; it should make them feel good; it should make them want to be around and not to leave the area." At the Center's opening in 1977, Mayor Coleman Young presented it as a turning point in the history of urban America. Young declared: "We have here a monumental statement that speaks for itself. . . . The cities are on the upsurge."

Conceived when the 1967 race riots were still fresh in people's memories, the Center stands like a fortress high above the streets, separated from the rest of downtown by a broad boulevard, East Jefferson. Five large glass towers, the tallest seventy-three stories high, with a hotel, offices, shopping, and commercial facilities, were completed in 1977 at a cost of more than $350 million. Two more towers were added in the early 1980s. A local developer character-ized the choice of the Center's location and design as a strategy to attract tenants: "They were saying, 'Move on over to us; we are very safe, they can't attack us from the river side, they can't attack us from East Jefferson.' "

On a visit to the Center fifteen years ago I saw Tiffany's, F.A.O. Schwartz, and a shop being readied for Christian Dior. Today, these commercial symbols of wealth and sophistication are not there or anywhere else in the city. The most prominent commercial tenant now on the building's ground floor is a Burger King. Overall, the complex has a 5 percent vacancy rate because of the bargain rents they offer tenants. By contrast, the vacancy rate among other office buildings still operating downtown is 22 percent. Yet despite this abundance of available space, two large commercial buildings were recently completed. Both are elegant postmodern structures, similar to those in Battery Park City in New York or the new buildings in Chicago's Loop. Several subsidized middle-income housing developments have also been built along the river.

Winding alongside the Renaissance Center and making a 2.9-mile loop around the downtown area is the People Mover, a Disney-type train connecting thirteen individually designed stations. This federally funded above-ground rail system had the potential to contribute to a cohesive downtown. Yet by the time it was completed in 1987, at a cost of $210 million, a huge section of the downtown was already obsolete.

"I used it once; it don't go nowhere," said Frank, a maintenance man in a downtown office building. The original plan, vetoed by the state legislature, was to build a regional transportation system connecting Detroit to its suburbs along Woodward Avenue. The People Mover was a compromise, allowing the city to spend federal funds already allocated for a small, experimental, downtown transit system.

Whites are reluctant to walk most of the city streets, feeling safe only inside their cars, windows rolled up, doors locked. A few black pedestrians walk or socialize on its wide sidewalks and elegant plazas. A racial mix is achieved in a few places: near the Detroit River, on a narrow strip about two blocks wide, and in

One of the strangest sights in America: an empty monorail circling a skyscraper graveyard, the Detroit Opera under construction on the right, Detroit, 1993.

Greektown, a small enclave of ethnic restaurants and shops.

The Renaissance Center, the People Mover, the renovated Fox Theatre (an Art Deco landmark on Woodward Avenue where The Supremes, Stevie Wonder, and Marvin Gaye often played), and a neighboring theater turned dance hall—despite these attractions, the center of the city remains a desolate place. New construction, when sound existing buildings were in dire need of tenants, has resulted in the emptying of older structures more distant from the river, thus accelerating the demise of the north section of the downtown. And the new developments have not increased the number of commuters coming to the center city each day—still about one hundred thousand.

For a month I lived in the city's desolate northwest section, immediately west of Grand Circus Park, once a major entertainment and rec-

reation area, a regular stop for big bands and jazz groups and the nightclub set. The area was known for its hotels, theaters, restaurants, and specialty shops. Now two of the best-known and largest hotels are empty, and a third was recently demolished. Of five big theaters, only two are operating, and not a single specialty shop remains.

Underfunded service organizations predominate. Landlords undertake frequent raids to lure tenants away from neighboring buildings. Battles rage for the rent money of the American Civil Liberties Union, Planned Parenthood, Family Services, and employment training programs.

The sinister Book-Cadillac Tower, one of the tallest buildings in the area, looks like something out of a science-fiction novel. With almost no tenants, its 350-foot height serves mainly to support communications equipment. A brilliant

Frank J. Hecker House, Woodward Avenue, Detroit, 1995. This palatial residence of 1890, inspired by the Château de Chenonceau near Tours, is on the National Register of Historic Places.

white dish antenna on its classical temple top seems like a gigantic, wide-open eye surveying the city. A forest of rusting metal poles rises from the roof.

On the streets, wanderers and madmen sit on the sidewalks or push shopping carts. Those buildings that are still open are often cleaned and tended by Serbian women who barely speak English. Late at night, the People Mover, reduced to one brightly lit car, loops around completely empty, as if carrying a party of phantoms from station to station.

A quaint red trolley imported from Lisbon links this part of town to the Renaissance Center, its route ending on Washington Boulevard, once the most exclusive commercial street in Detroit. In the early eighties city planners decided to transform part of the boulevard into a "people's place," in a $5 million beautification project. Half of the street was given over to a raised rect-angular mall, with plantings, benches, and over-hanging iron fountains, pouring water into a crystalline stream running over a bed of stones.

The People Mover, the Lisbon trolley, and the Washington mall came too late. This is a large downtown mothballed, a stage set waiting for a replay of the 1930s, a place to wait for the millennium amid the homeless, the Serbian women, pigeons, and bats.

Detroit has great gaps. As nature takes over, the landscape begins to resemble a wilder-ness interrupted by citadels, small groups of houses getting smaller, and huge industrial ruins held together by rusting iron framework. Adding to the fragmentation, urban segments are sepa-rated from one another by wide radial highways and beltlines.

"Detroit is reverting to a farm," said Cor-inne Gilb, former director of the Planning De-partment and a professor of urban history at

Exemplifying the decline of Detroit is this building constructed in the late 1940s in a bold modernistic style. From housing in its heyday a Firestone tire dealership, it became a garage, then a one-story hardware store, and soon will host a car wash. The painted signs represent work-in-progress by Eugene. Grand River Boulevard, 1995.

Wayne State University. City residents, she says, are fortunate to have an environment for which white people travel far and pay dearly to enjoy. This observation was not well received by Detroiters who perceive derelict spaces as dirty and dangerous. "Nature" is what grows in places that people leave behind: the grass that sprouts in the cement cracks along the sidewalk, the hardy weeds and trees that push their way through the polluted floor of a razed factory, the tall plants that cover rusted metal, mattresses, rugs, bottles, and tires in empty lots.

A popular saying in the city goes, "The last one out, turn off the lights." After so much talk of extinction, the city's endurance has become a source of pride. "I am not leaving, I am a Detroiter," says Al. "Why not stay here and make it better?" asks Father Charles Denys, a Belgian priest whose parish, Our Lady of Sorrows, is in the poorest section of the city. He adds: "We are

just holding on. You have a lot of good people left. They don't want to leave. You cannot desert the people."

The adaptations needed to survive, though, are drastic. The Stapleton Center, a senior citizens' complex occupying an entire block, is enclosed by a tall iron fence topped with a row of razor ribbon wire. "It is reality today," says Father Denys. "The complex was built at a better time; the fence came later." A local teenager conceded that the complex looked like a jail for old people, but explained that these were measures designed "to keep people from going in, robbing them or something." Another teenager commented wistfully, "The churches take care of these old people. They got everything they need in there."

Middle-class blacks who can afford to live in the suburbs do so in the tens of thousands. But according to Evelyn Brown, a community

The blind angel of Detroit: head shaped like a bullet, dollar sign for a heart. Graffiti in the former Michigan Central Station waiting room, 1995.

development expert, "a pool of leadership stays here, people who are the future." For Arthur Johnson, vice president for community relations at Wayne State, there is no place he would rather live. "I was not in it," he says of the robust and thriving Detroit of the 1950s, and notes that white people forget how segregated "thriving" Detroit was.

"Why do so many black families who can leave decide instead to stay?" asks Johnson. Comparing the city to a big mansion left for a poor family to keep, he views Detroit as both a prize and a burden: "They cannot heat it, they cannot provide air conditioning, they cannot paint it or keep up the grounds because they don't have the means to do so. As long as they stay they prevent the fixtures from being stolen, the pipes from freezing; they are the ones who keep the water running and put out the fires. If they manage to preserve it, it would be for those

who stay." But asked when the city is going to turn around, Elizabeth Brown replies: "If I answered this question, I may not like the answer and go somewhere else."

Motor City is now spread throughout the world. Lacking a replacement for its automobile industry, Detroit must inevitably shrink. Only two assembly plants are still in the city from a total of about thirty in 1907. General Motors' Poletown and Chrysler's Jefferson North plants are automated, operating with less than half the labor force of the plants they replaced. Research and development and data processing have also moved out of the city. A widespread view is that this former "factory town" will eventually stabilize at a population of 200,000, slightly more than in such Michigan cities as Grand Rapids and Lansing.

Michael Goodin of *Crain's* expresses a profound faith in the city, saying: "I don't think

The splendid Michigan Railroad Station, Warren and Wetmore Architects, 1913. The main entrance leads to a vaulted waiting room filled with light streaming through enormous windows. If you are down and out or mentally ill, this is a place to buy tickets to nowhere, to draw angels or write graffiti, to pace, to stay out of the rain and wind. More than any other derelict space I've seen, this fine neoclassical structure says, "We were once a great city." Detroit, 1994.

Detroit is a dying city. All the stuff of life is here. It is a city in transition. Right now crime seems like it is out of control. Of course, I know it is not, but it seems like it. It seems that there is desolation and unemployment everywhere. I know it is not, but it seems like it. It seems that there is nothing but poverty and decay; it just seems like it. I think Detroit is like a drunk who has to take all the blows before he will reach out and seek help and do what is necessary to get off the bottle and regain the strength." "Whites living alone or whites who segregate themselves can prosper and there is nothing in my mind that says that blacks living segregated cannot prosper among themselves. And if that is going to be the city's destiny, then that is how the city will begin to reemerge and develop itself."

The powerful spell of this magnificent skeleton city by the river forces us to go beyond the issues of blame, anger, and hopelessness to ask questions about our national goals. I can think of no better place for meditation. Visits to Washington and New York City, our imperial capitals, should be followed by a visit to Detroit, a place for reflection.

Upon leaving Detroit, tired and bewildered, I saw a large male pheasant fly low in an arc over the freeway, landing on the grounds of a semi-abandoned housing project. The energetic clapping of its wings, the rich browns of its plumage, its long tail passing so close to the dull cement of the highway—an unlikely phoenix.

AMERICAN ACROPOLIS OR VACANT LAND?

The Future of Detroit's Pre-Depression Skyscrapers

"Jesus ✡ 7-6-92

Jesus ✡ Son of God 4-30-92

Messiah ✡ 5-29-92

Jesus ✡ 12-7-92

J.C. ✡ 8-4-93

J.C. ✡ 1-28-92

J.C. ✡ 1-20-93

Jesus ✡ 9-12-91

J.C. ✡ 11.11.92

12-26-91 ✡ J C

Jesus ✡ 7-11-93

7-12-94 ✡ Messiah"

—Graffiti on building,
Michigan Avenue, Detroit, 1994

Detroit's downtown moves me like no other place. There, for the first time in history, large numbers of skyscrapers that were planned to last for centuries are becoming derelict; a cluster of semi-abandoned structures rises like a vertical no-man's-land behind empty lots. Supposedly immutable structures of reinforced concrete are falling into decay, occasionally breaking their silence by shedding a gargoyle, an Indian chief, the arm of an allegorical woman, or a terra-cotta flower.

As Reverend G. Jackson of the Heavenly Mission Baptist Church recently remarked to me, Motown's core looks "kind of down and out, not housing anything, not worth anything, and decaying on the inside." Nevertheless, new

meanings can be found in the presence of these crumbling forms. I propose that as a tonic for our imaginations, as a call for renewal, as a place within our national memory, a dozen city blocks of pre-Depression skyscrapers should be left standing as ruins: an American Acropolis.

In Detroit grass, reeds, and even trees growing on a buildings roof indicate by their height and density how long the building has been abandoned. Peregrine falcons nest on the tallest of the city's great old towers of commerce. Words have faded on the billboards; the marquees of darkened theaters are blank. The city's core was once saturated with names and images of consumer goods; now, having lost the power to sell, the downtown goes mostly unclaimed. Also long gone are the floodlights that pierced the sky from rooftops and the huge blinking neon signs that signaled commercial activity. As buildings are picked clean of brass, marble, and loose decorations, the place is becoming anonymous. At the same time, it is taking on a universal character.

Many of the downtown buildings were designed by nationally known architects: Daniel H. Burnham, George Post, Albert Kahn, and McKim, Mead & White. The David Stott building (1929), resembling Eliel Saarinen's famous entry for the 1922 Chicago Tribune Tower Competition, is one of the most remarkable. The visionary architect Hugh Ferriss included a drawing of this skyscraper in his 1929 book, *The Metropolis of Tomorrow*, describing it as possessing "truly great proportions," and as one of "the forerunners of the future city."

A profusion of historical markers and statues reveals in brief texts the significance of places: the long disappeared workshop where, in 1892, "Henry Ford began experimenting with the motorized vehicle"; the vacant Schwankowsky Temple of Music, founded in 1879, where brass concerts and recitals took place; the statue of Mayor Hazen Pingree sitting on a giant chair, a sign on the pedestal proclaiming, "The Idol of the People." As if built to tour this

"The work of giants moulders away." Downtown Detroit, 1991.

extraordinary zone, Detroit's jewel of a mono-rail, neatly painted white, green, and yellow, takes the visitor around.

In Detroit, as in other cities, decay renders even the most ordinary buildings picturesque. The allure of structures in a derelict state is often the result of grime, broken windows, loss of ornament, and sheer bulk. As they lose their original features and gain a covering of dirt and plants, edifices achieve boldness of form and richness of colors and textures.

In historical photographs taken at night, light flooding out of the buildings broke up their mass. Nowadays they are dramatically lit from below by street lights, and from above by the moon and the stars. Shadowy structures, silhouetted against the sky, loom like huge, undefined forms. Yet immense aspiration remains embodied in these monumental old edifices. They recall the words of Ayn Rand's novel *The Fountainhead*: "The greatest structures invented by

men . . . the tallest structure in the city . . . my last and greatest achievement."

Comments Bill Kellerman, an Episcopal theologian: "The skyscraper, from a biblical perspective, may be as much an act of pride as—you think of the Tower of Babel. They are huge projections; they have a life and history; they may even be synonymous with idolatry. If they level those skyscrapers, I can imagine the huge psychic toll that it would take on the city."

The spasms of the millennium are being felt in the city of Henry Ford, Rosa Parks, Diego Rivera, "Raw Dog," "Ghetto Killer," and "The Beast 666." One wonders about the meaning of the scrawlings found on the walls of different floors in Detroit's abandoned train station: "Today's Menu: Wombat Dick Stew." "Today's Menu: Orangutan Asshole." "Today's Menu: Afterbirth Cooked in its own Juices." To me this is the right language to deal with the disrupted lives, the lack of future, and the city's destruc-

View south along Grand River Boulevard, Detroit, 1994. Few cars traveling the wide street, no pedestrians on the sidewalk, closed stores, a smokeless factory chimney, flagpoles without flags, vacant lots, make a fitting approach to the desolate downtown.

tion. Cryptic expressions such as the frequently encountered "Murder Hope in the Hopeful!" stay in your mind as incantations and color your impressions of your surroundings.

The writings on the walls of Motown pose desperate questions: Why are we surrounded by so much decay and death? How much longer will this go on? But another inscription quotes a reassuring line from Psalm 23:

> "The LORD is my shepherd; I shall not want.
> He makes me lie down in green pastures; He leads me beside still waters.
> He restores my soul; He leads me in paths of righteousness for His name's sake."

In 1994, the Land Use Task Force recommended to Mayor Dennis Archer the demolition of "structures which are functionally obsolete and have no viable reuse." Two of the most re-

markable, vacant for over a decade, are Hudson's Department Store, the largest and most central of Detroit's downtown buildings, and the twelve-hundred-room Book-Cadillac Hotel, once the city's most elegant place to stay, Detroit's Waldorf Astoria.

At first sight, Hudson's resembles a big, clumsy, red-brick fortress, but later the building seems reassuring, as it was in the past, a friendly box full of good things. The giant store, completed in 1924, was cherished by generations of residents in southeastern Michigan. A common happy memory is of having been taken there as a child to see Santa Claus. "There is a big nostalgia, every time news reporters ask, 'What do you think about Hudson's?' to the man on the street, all they want is for it to be the great department store it was in the fifties and sixties," says Romeo Betea, a member of the Mayor's Land Use Task Force.

Also completed in 1924, the twenty-nine-

Surprising view of major thoroughfare empty of traffic, Clifford Street, Detroit, 1993. A woman walks while a man pushes himself in a wheelchair by her side.

When architectural ornaments began falling from this empty Detroit skyscraper, making it a public danger, the city forced the owner to strip the rest. Downtown Detroit, 1992.

story Book-Cadillac was then the tallest hotel building in the world. Its facade brings together Antoine de la Mothe Cadillac, founder of the city of Detroit; Navarre, his lieutenant; Pontiac, an Ottawa Indian chief in the French and Indian War; and General Anthony Wayne, who negotiated a peace with the Northwest Indians in 1795. Crowning its roof are two bronze pyramids topped with enormous lanterns. In 1993 the city proposed to spend four to five million dollars in state funds to demolish the Book-Cadillac, but decided at the last minute instead to help upgrade some struggling downtown buildings that still had tenants. The State of Michigan lowered property taxes in 1993, reducing downtown development money, so that now demolition projects are on hold.

Another of the skyscrapers, the David Broderick Building, has only one tenant, a restaurant on the ground floor. For Jessie, its

seventy-two-year-old caretaker, the edifice is not dead. "They are going to do something with the building. It is going to be housing." "Everything works in here," he tells me proudly, but when I walk onto a tiny terrace on the thirty-fourth floor he warns me not to lean on the corroded iron railing. The structure is still useful, he says. "It has Motorola radio relay equipment for beepers on the roof."

So far, most of the city center has been "saved" by the lack of funds for demolition. The costs are high because so many of the structures have asbestos insulation. It has been estimated that nearly $200 million—a fortune for this impoverished city—is needed to raze all the troubled and vacant buildings in downtown Detroit and to dispose of the debris. On the other hand, the renovation of a single building can cost as much as $100 million, so that the total could run to several billion dollars. And if these buildings

One of the many faces looking down at you from the ceiling of the former Michigan Theatre, Detroit, 1995.

Extreme contrasts abound in the former Michigan Theatre, now a parking garage, Detroit, 1995. Where plush rugs once were is now pavement; older, pinked-toned marble columns face three parking floors supported by steel and concrete beams. The garage's ceiling is reminiscent of a rococo palace minus the chandeliers. An Austrian architect commented, "They would never have done this in Europe. They would have either demolished the building or restored it."

were rehabilitated, who would occupy the space?

Yet this, the third largest concentration of pre-Depression skyscrapers in the world after Manhattan and Chicago, could become a source of pride for Detroiters. These oversized towers, cathedrals and castles of commerce, erected for the advancement and glory of industrial capitalism and its champions, give me pause. Is this a collection of irrelevant symbols, icons of a dead civilization? Their powerful forms in constant flux indicate that we are in the presence of something momentous.

Contemplating a visit to Detroit, my mind fills with projects: opening a bakery and letting the smell of fresh bread fill the streets; planting red geraniums to contrast with the gray of the surroundings; going through the street ringing bells. At night, I would like to project movies on the sides of skyscrapers to recapture the faded energies of the city: old-fashioned locomotives,

steam billowing upwards; Ford Trimotors going a full speed. The great ghosts of Detroit would salute, speak, and fight: Chief Pontiac, Walter Reuther, "Detroit Red," and Joe Louis. The streets would resonate with the voices of Aretha Franklin and Stevie Wonder.

These emerging ruins are becoming "ripe ruins," like Highgate Cemetery and Abney Park, the much loved monumental resting places of London. After half a century of neglect, these cities of the dead have become pleasant places to pick berries, stroll, and birdwatch. Americans can learn how to live well with their symbols of decline, their ruins of past grandeur. We can learn to perceive them as contributing to the diversity and architectural richness of the nation.

What would be lost if these symbols of wealth, gentility, and boundless ambition were torn down? If birds went flying through the released space where thick walls once stood? We

Entrance to Metropolitan building, once the jewelry center of Detroit, 1993.

Above the Fisher Freeway, Detroit, 1994, stretches a raw cityscape of vacant land, taxi and parking garages, drug treatment centers, flophouses, and abandoned buildings.

should let this environment age "naturally," or, whenever economically feasible, we should restore them to their original splendor. To build pre-fab townhouses, parking garages, green belt systems, or simply to clear the land in the hope development will come is short-sighted and wasteful.

A starting point would be to place a moratorium on the razing of skyscrapers, our most sublime ruins, and instead to stabilize them. For the cost of repairs needed to avoid accidents from falling fragments, we could transform the nearly one hundred troubled buildings into a grand national historic park of play and wonder, an urban Monument Valley. The People Mover could carry visitors around this precious space.

After all, large fields in Pennsylvania have been set aside to commemorate the Battle of Gettysburg. Why not secure the blocks with the tallest and most notable structures, those around Grand Circus Park, along Woodward Avenue, Griswold Street, and Washington Boulevard, and transform the space into a memorial to our throwaway cities?

This fantastic cityscape rises in a spectacular setting between midwestern prairie to the north and the Detroit River to the south. Midwestern prairie would be allowed to invade from the north. Trees, vines, and wildflowers would grow on roofs and out of windows; wild animals, goats, squirrels, possums, bats, owls, ravens, snakes, insects, and perhaps even an occasional bear would live in the empty behemoths, adding their calls, hoots, and screeches to the smell of rotten leaves and animal droppings.

I presented a brief description of this plan for a skyscraper park to a journalist, an architectural historian, an architect, a university administrator, and several homeless men—all familiar with downtown Detroit. Their response was not

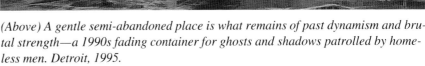

(Above) A gentle semi-abandoned place is what remains of past dynamism and brutal strength—a 1990s fading container for ghosts and shadows patrolled by homeless men. Detroit, 1995.

(Left) A cross between a factory and a castle, Hudson's occupies an entire block at the center of Detroit. Once one of the largest department stores in the nation, it is now vacant, 1994.

encouraging.

Michael Goodin of *Crain's Detroit Business* rejected my proposal as "absurd and ridiculous—the sad state of the city preserved as a tourist attraction!" He railed, "For the city to set itself up as the world's symbolic ruin—that is not going to attract tourists from Peoria, Illinois. This is the seventh largest metropolis in the country. You are not going to attract first- and second-tier suppliers to downtown Detroit or health field corporations or other automotive entities to a downtown that is composed of permanent ruins. There is no benefit to do that. The Romans, that is a dead civilization. Americans are not a dead civilization. Buildings have to be retrofitted for a new use, maybe residential, maybe office, but unlikely retail, but they have to be retrofitted for another use that creates a tax base and produces some form of employment." Goodin's arguments have been held as articles of

faith for decades by the local business community. Still, there is no demand for this space; the suppliers, the health field corporations, the automotive concerns are not standing in line to set up offices in downtown Detroit.

Architectural historian Carol Willis recently toured these "gray haunting monuments," finding them "the most depressing sight in urban America . . . a tremendous presence." Willis found my suggestion to leave the core of empty structures in the middle of the city "a poetic idea, the impressions of an eighteenth-century aesthete musing on the process of decay." She criticizes me for telling people what emotions to feel. "Buildings," Willis says, "represent an economic structure, not a romantic evocation of the past." She would like to see businesses operating there even at the cost of large public subsidies.

Stabilizing the skyscrapers may be cheaper

Book-Cadillac Hotel, Detroit, 1991.

than demolition, but, according to Willis, it would be more expensive in the long run. She asks me to be practical: "To allow buildings in the middle of the city to remain empty means accidents waiting to happen. How are people going to be prevented from going up and falling, are the floors going to be torn down? Soon the city will have to put a fence around the area." I could not see how securing the edifices would force us to render them hollow. It is possible to limit access to only some of the structures and to design safe paths into and around buildings to minimize the chances of people getting hurt.

"This is not a European country," said David Schervish to my suggestion. Schervish, an architect who hopes to raise $200 million to create new uses for a few of these buildings, explains, "If a building is sitting there and does not fit into the scheme of things, it is going to be demolished."

Arthur Johnson, vice president for community affairs at Wayne State University, wants me to know that not all is "abandonment and neglect," the city managed to preserve the landmark Fox Theatre when it was about to be demolished to make room for a fast food place, and Orchestra Hall, famous for its acoustics. Johnson is proud of the ongoing reconstruction of the Broadway Theatre, which will house the Detroit Opera. He is "willing to wait for life to be restored" to these skyscrapers. He understands the feelings of those eager to "destroy the signs of our abandonment," yet he believes that several of these buildings deserve to be kept alive. During our conversation, Johnson paused for a moment whenever I tried to relate Detroit's core to the Roman Forum or other famous ruins, as if seeing that there was after all something in what I was saying, but he never acknowledged it. He stressed repeatedly that our abandoned structures

The jewel of the downtown skyline, the exquisitely proportioned red marble and stone David Stott Building, was hailed by Hugh Ferriss, as a harbinger of the city of the future when it was completed in 1929. Bankrupt, in its new urban context, it still is. Detroit, 1995.

are "a sign of failure that has more to do with race than anything else."

In the derelict core many homeless men wander the streets and alleys day and night. For one named Leon, "It is getting to be a ghost town downtown." When I suggest preserving the skyscrapers as a ruins park, Cal disagrees, saying, "It is believed that the city is going to be reborn." Eddie would like to turn some of the buildings into shelters, "give them to the homeless, put some mattresses on the floor, put some heat in there, don't let anybody sleep out there in the cold." He likes my suggestion of letting plants grow on the buildings because it would create jobs: "Somebody would have to take care of them."

I am disappointed by the reaction against the ruins park. Michael Goodin adamantly maintains a commonsense position that has been argued for decades, namely that something compa-

rable to high-power professional offices and corporate headquarters of the 1920s should happen again in this downtown. Only now it resembles a local version of a national urban "cargo cult"—where locals wait for investors who have the capital and ideas that will return these cities to their former preeminence. Carol Willis eloquently describes the power of downtown Detroit's derelict cityscape, yet she insists on rehabilitation as the only option. Arthur Johnson resists the allure of these tall structures in their neglected state, preferring instead to discuss them as a consequence of racism, an understandable obsession for him and many others in this city. Against all these objections, can we imagine the possibility of a future that includes these skyscrapers as great ruins to experience?

A world ended in Detroit, leaving the setting awaiting another "Metropolis of Tomorrow." A memorial to a disappearing urban civili-

Obsolete cityscape of pre-Depression buildings, Detroit, 1995. Only two recent structures appear in this large panorama.

zation is a realistic alternative. Costing little in comparison to the expense of rehabilitating or demolishing the old downtown, a ruins park would occupy only a minuscule fraction of the city's idle space, estimated at more than fifteen square miles. Not a firm basis on which to re-build the local economy, but it preserves a won-derful space, a key to understanding an essential part of our recent past. If visitors come, new signs of life might accompany them.

Yet, on a visit to Detroit in December 1994, I saw buildings badly trashed, not the "ripe ru-ins" I had envisioned. I expected signs such as the one saying, "Danger Falling Bricks," in an alley by the Metropolitan Building. Yet much more destructive than the passing of time was the work of scavengers. The ground floor of some of the buildings was open; carpet had been ripped up, floorboards broken, and shards of glass were everywhere. The sight of once-attractive buildings like the Lafayette ransacked is a powerful inducement to cross to the opposite side of the street. Undoubtedly, the work of scav-engers will increase the numbers of those clam-

Eyes staring outward, blood dripping down his face, lips parted in address, the Christ of The Inner City Crossover Ministry is still talking to us. The artist, I was told, is in jail. Detroit, 1994.

oring to raze the buildings. But where would the money come from? From the budgets of the schools, the health department, neighborhood projects?

I left Detroit thinking what we have now is perhaps the closest we are going to get to an American Acropolis. We may never see the buildings losing their stigma under the cover of nature: structures part manmade, part organic, their supporting frames exposed, their sides buckling, squirrels climbing the vines, and as the seasons change, yellows, reds, and greens would

again be part of this treeless zone. All I can do is record the fading splendor of the buildings and the disjointed and anguished cries of those who try to make a home among them.

Meanwhile, the wind moans through narrow canyons, and the near-empty People Mover creaks and curves along. People tell stories of deer swimming from Belle Isle across the river to roam the empty streets under the shadows of skyscrapers. As officials plan to level the downtown, a space, capable of restoring our souls, waits to be discovered.

"That little world between the railway lines, with many others of its kind, has now been swept away. Except for a factory here and there, desolation remains. Perhaps the next generation will landscape it and there will be fields again, trees, flowers, a stream maybe—much as it must have been two centuries ago. And all that dark excrescence of an industrial age, like the poor folks who lived and toiled there, will have vanished like a lost medieval village."

—Robert Roberts,
The Classic Slum: Salford Life in the
First Quarter of the Century, 1971

APPENDIX: THE NEW AMERICAN GHETTO ARCHIVE

I have paid longer and more sustained attention to the South Bronx, Harlem, north central Brooklyn, Newark, and Chicago than to any of the other urban areas selected for documentation. I have covered these places on foot, marking a local area map so as to achieve completeness.

South Bronx, New York

The area photographed is located south of 182nd Street and the Bronx River. I have followed the elevated tracks of the Lexington Avenue IRT along Jerome Avenue to Burnside Avenue, and the tracks of the #2 train along Westchester Avenue and Southern Boulevard to West Farms, taking pictures from moving trains and from subway platforms. Other elevated viewpoints include a parking garage on Third Avenue and 152nd Street, the roofs of about three hundred buildings (half of them York City Housing Authority projects), and the Cross-Bronx and Bruckner expressways.

Since 1979 I have taken special care to photograph developments taking place around Charlotte Street. My photographs show the emergence of ranch-style houses from the ruins of apartment buildings; the recently developed townhouses to the south (part of "Townhouse Mile"); and a few surviving apartment buildings.

During the past seven years I have photographed the relocation of homeless families and the building of homeless shelters and drug treatment facilities in the South Bronx and other similar areas of the city. The South Bronx file is the oldest and largest of the archive, containing more than three thousand slides, at least four hundred of them time-lapse views.

Harlem, New York

The Harlem file covers the major boulevards that run north and south from 110th Street to 155th Street. Many cross streets are also included, particularly 110th, 116th, 125th, and 145th. The area has been photographed from more than eighty apartment buildings—projects throughout Harlem—the Metro-North Railroad Station at Park Avenue and 125th Street, North General Hospital, Harlem Hospital, and the YMCA.

I started documenting Harlem in 1977; the file consists of eleven hundred slides, one hundred and sixty of them time-lapse views.

North Central Brooklyn, New York

The area of Brooklyn I have documented includes the poorest sections of the borough: Brownsville, Williamsburg, the southern part of East New York, the eastern section of Bushwick and the northeastern part of Bedford-Stuyvesant. The major streets covered are Pitkin, Alabama, Sutter, Saratoga, Fulton, Dumont, Snediker, Belmont, Junius, Georgia, Pennsylvania, Broadway, and Troutman.

Much of this area has been photographed from the LL subway line that divides East New York from Brownsville; from the IRT line that moves north from Brownsville to East New York; and from the Jamaica line that crosses Bushwick and parts of East New York. Most importantly, I have photographed the neighborhoods from the roofs of more than eighty public housing buildings, fifty of which I have revisited.

The north central Brooklyn file was started in 1979 and consists of about eleven hundred slides, one hundred and fifty of them time-lapse sequences.

Newark, New Jersey

The area covered includes the entire city, particularly the Central, North, and South Wards, and within these commercial streets such as Springfield Avenue, Clinton Avenue, and Broadway. I have photographed Newark from the roofs of housing projects, apartment buildings, and downtown skyscrapers.

In the Central Ward of Newark, I have documented the striking change involving the destruction of the old riot-torn urban core, the displacement of the remaining residents, and the creation of a new suburban-style neighborhood anchored around expanding institutions.

A unique feature of the Newark file is the group of nearly thirty photographs taken inside abandoned public housing projects. I have documented objects left behind—furniture, murals, photographs—and copied poems and messages. I was able to visit twelve hundred apartments in two buildings of the Scudder Homes days before their demolition in 1987, and in 1994, four buildings of the Columbus Homes, also about to be razed.

The Newark file, began in 1979, includes at least one hundred examples of time-lapse photography. Some series consist of a dozen or more observations made at regular intervals. The file consists of eleven hundred slides, one hundred and twenty of them are time-lapse views.

Chicago, Illinois

I started documenting this huge city in 1980 using a car and the elevated train. I began photographing along two major commercial thoroughfares, West Madison Street and State Street, and from public housing projects: Cabrini-Green, Henry Horner, Robert Taylor, Washington Park Homes, the Ida B. Wells Homes, and others.

Over time I added other large commercial streets: Roosevelt Road, Ogden, California, Pulaski, Kedzi, and Cicero avenues, the area surrounding the University Medical Complex, and Lawndale on the West Side. On the South Side I photographed Martin Luther King Boulevard, Cottage Grove, 47th Street, 63rd Street, and the area surrounding the University of Chicago, particularly Woodlawn. Recently I began to photograph the South Side communities of Englewood and South Riverdale.

In the summer of 1989 I was given permission to photograph from the tall buildings of the Chicago Housing Authority. The panoramas obtained from three dozen tall buildings give an excellent view of the poorest neighborhoods in the city. The Chicago file consists of about twelve hundred slides, one hundred and fifty of them are time-lapse views.

Gary, Indiana

I began documenting Gary in 1980, concentrating on a ribbon five blocks wide and two miles long on either side of Broadway and Fifth Avenue, the city's main streets. I have photographed the city from the South Shore Station, from two elevated parking garages, from the former Gary Hotel, the Grainer Bank, the former Knights of Columbus Building, and two housing authority high-rises. The Gary file consists of three hundred slides.

Camden, New Jersey

The focal points of the documentation of this city have been Broadway—the main commercial street stretching for more than three miles south of downtown—and North Camden, a former industrial area with a population of about eight thousand inhabitants, the most destitute section of the city and the entire State of New Jersey. The photographs of Camden include views from twenty-three-story Northgate II, a senior citizens' high-rise located at the heart of North Camden, Northgate I, and Camden's City Hall. The Camden file was begun in 1979 and consists of three hundred slides, forty of them time-lapse sequences.

Detroit, Michigan

Although I had spent more than two weeks photographing in Detroit, I did not start a separate collection for this city until I had a chance to spend an additional week there in August 1993. I selected two major areas of concentration: the semi-abandoned core of the city and its long, devastated commercial streets. My earliest photographs of the city are from 1987, and I already have twenty-five time-lapse photographs. The collection consists of two hundred and sixty slides.

Los Angeles, California

In 1994, with help and encouragement from Tom Reese and Fran Terpak of the Getty Center, I decided to add South Central and Skid Row to the rest of the collection. I had photographed in Los Angeles on five separate occasions during the past decade and a half, yet it was for the purpose of exploring the differences with other ghettos, not to develop a database on the city. Now I have started to cover the territory: photographing alongside the main commercial streets such as Central Avenue and Figueroa, the businesses, factories, and houses on the side streets. The total number of images is two hundred.

Other Urban Areas

I have a sizable group of slides from each of the following cities or sections of cities: Oakland, Calif.; Hough in Cleveland and Cincinnati, Ohio; Washington, D.C.; Liberty City in Miami, Fla.; Trenton, Atlantic City, and Paterson, N.J.; East St. Louis, Ill.; and South Boston and Roxbury in Boston, Mass. The total is about six hundred slides.

BIBLIOGRAPHY

ABRAMS, CHARLES. *The City Is the Frontier.* New York: Harper & Row, 1965.

———. "Housing Policy: It Must Offer a Way Out of Despair." *Architectural Forum* (April 1964): 34–38.

ADDAMS, JANE. *The Spirit of Youth and the City Streets.* New York: Macmillan, 1909.

———. "The Subtle Problems of Charity." *The Atlantic Monthly* (February 1899):163–178.

———. *Twenty Years at Hull-House.* 1910. Reprint. New York: Signet Classic, 1981.

ANDERSON, ELIJAH. "The Code of the Streets." *The Atlantic Monthly* (May 1994):81–94.

———. *A Place on the Corner.* Chicago: University of Chicago Press, 1978.

———. "Sex Codes and Family Life among Poor Inner-City Youths." *Annals, AAPSS* 501 (January 1989):59–78.

AULETTA, KEN. *The Underclass.* New York: Random House, 1982.

BALDWIN, JAMES. *The Fire Next Time.* New York: Dell, 1963.

BALLARD, J. G. *Crash.* New York: Farrar, Straus and Giroux, 1973.

———. *Hello America.* New York: Carroll and Graf, 1981.

———. *Terminal Beach.* London: J. M. Dent, 1964.

BANFIELD, EDWARD C., NATHAN GLAZER, MICHAEL HARRINGTON et al. "A Symposium: Nixon, The Great Society, and the Future of Social Policy." *Commentary* (May 1973):31–61.

BANHAM, REYNER. *A Concrete Atlantis: U.S. Industrial Building and European Modern Architecture, 1890–1925.* Cambridge, Mass.: MIT Press, 1986.

BARAKA, AMIRI. "Black Art." *The Black Scholar* (January/February 1987):23–30.

BARIDON, MICHEL. "Ruins as a Mental Construct." *Journal of Garden History* (January/March 1985):84–96.

BAUDELAIRE, CHARLES. *Les Fleurs du Mal.* Paris: Le Livre de Poche, 1965.

———. *Petits Poemes en Prose.* Paris: Garnier-Flammarion, 1967.

BEARD, RICK, ed. *On Being Homeless: Historical Perspectives.* New York: Museum of the City of New York, 1987.

BERMAN, MARSHALL. *All That Is Solid Melts into*

Air: The Experience of Modernity. New York: Simon and Schuster, 1982.

———. "Urbicide." *The Village Voice* (September 4, 1984):18–25.

BLONSTON, GARY. "Poletown: The Profits, the Loss." *Detroit Free Press,* special issue (Sunday, November 22, 1981).

BLUESTONE, BARRY and BENNETT HARRISON. *The Deindustrialization of America.* New York: Basic Books, 1982.

BOURGOIS, PHILIPPE. "In Search of Horatio Alger: Culture and Ideology in the Crack Economy." *Contemporary Drug Problems* (Winter 1989): 619–649.

———. "Just Another Night on Crack Street." *The New York Times Magazine* (November 12, 1989):52–94.

BRACE, C. L. "County Jails and Almshouses." *The Nation* (March 23, 1876):199–200.

BRATT, RACHEL G. "Controversy and Contributions: A Public Housing Critique." *Journal of Housing* (September/October 1985):165–173.

CARALEY, DEMETRIOS. "Washington Abandons the Cities." *Political Science Quarterly* 107 (1) (Spring 1992):1–30.

CARMICHAEL, STOKELY and CHARLES HAMILTON. *Black Power: The Politics of Liberation in America.* New York: Vintage Books, 1967.

CASTRO, RICARDO L. Review of *Money Matters: A Critical Look at Bank Architecture,* by Brendan Gill, Robert Nisbet, and Susan Wagg. *Design Book Review* (Fall 1991):40–42.

CATHCART, JAMES, FRANK FANTAUZZI, and TERRENCE VAN ELSLANDER. "Editing Detroit." *New Observations* 85 (September/ October 1991).

CATLIN, ROBERT. "The Decline and Fall of Gary, Indiana." *Planning* 54 (June 1988):10–15.

CITY OF NEWARK, OFFICE OF REAL PROPERTY. "Bright Future Property Action, Together We Can Do Anything." Mimeo. Newark, 1981.

———. "Newark's 'Expanding Metropolis' Property Auction." Mimeo. Newark, 1980.

———. "Properties for All Your Needs." Mimeo. Newark, 1982.

CLARK, KENNETH B. *Dark Ghetto: Dilemmas of Social Power.* New York: Harper Torchbooks, 1965.

CLAY, GRADY. *Close-Up: How to Read the American City.* Chicago: University of Chicago Press, 1980.

CURETON, GEORGE. "My Ghetto: A Backward Glance." *Partisan Review* (Winter 1993): 143–149.

DAVENPORT, W. H. "The Work House—Blackwell's Island." *Harper's* (November 1866):683–702.

Daedalus special issue. "Political Pharmacology: Thinking about Drugs." 121, no. 3 (Summer 1992).

DAVIS, MIKE. *City of Quartz.* New York: Vintage Books, 1990.

Detroit Free Press, Sunday special section "Pain and Promises: The Detroit Riot's Legacy." (July 19, 1987).

DIIULIO, JOHN J. JR. "There But for Fortune." *The New Republic* (June 24, 1991):27–36.

DOMOSH, MONA. "The Symbolism of the Skyscraper: Case Studies of New York's First Tall Buildings." *Journal of Urban History* 14, no. 3 (May 1988):320–345.

DRAKE, ST. CLAIR and HORACE R. CLAYTON. *Black Metropolis: A Study of Negro Life in a Northern City.* 1945. Reprint. New York: Harper Torchbooks, 1962.

DUBOIS, W. E. B. "The Dilemma of the Negro." *The American Mercury* (October 1924):179–184.

———. *The Souls of Black Folk.* 1903. New York: New American Library, 1982.

———. "Strivings of the Negro People." *The Atlantic Monthly* (July 1897):194–198.

EDSALL, THOMAS B. "The American Dilemma." *The New Republic* (May 27, 1991):35–38.

———. "The Return of Inequality." *The Atlantic Monthly* (June 1988):86–94.

ELY, RICHARD T. "Pullman: A Social Study." *Harper's* 70 (February 1885):452–466.

FERRY, W. HAWKINS. *The Buildings of Detroit: A History.* Detroit: Wayne State University Press, 1980.

FISHMAN, ROBERT. *Bourgeois Utopias: The Rise and Fall of Suburbia.* New York: Basic Books, 1987.

FOGELSON, ROBERT M. *Violence as Protest: A Study of Riots and Ghettos.* Garden City, N.Y.: Doubleday, 1971.

"Framework for Action: Recommendations of the Mayor's Land Use Task Force, A." Detroit, 1994.

FUERST, J. S. and ROY PETTY. "Bleak Housing in Chicago." *The Public Interest* 53 (Summer 1978):103–110.

GANS, HERBERT J. "The Failure of Urban Renewal: A Critique and Some Proposals." *Commentary* (April 1965):29–37.

GISSING, GEORGE. *The Nether World.* 1889. Reprint. New York: Oxford University Press, 1992.

GOLDSTEIN, LAURENCE, ed. "Detroit: An American City." *Michigan Quarterly Review* 25 (2) (Spring 1986) (special issue).

GRUNDBERG, ANDY. *Crisis of the Real: Writings on Photography 1974–1990.* West Hanover, Mass.: Aperture, 1990.

HALES, PETER B. "Landscape and Documentary: Questions of Rephotography." *Afterimage* (Summer 1987):10–13.

HANNERZ, ULF. *Soulside: Inquires into Ghetto Culture and Community.* New York: Columbia, 1969.

HARLEM URBAN DEVELOPMENT CORPORATION. *Bradhurst Revitalization: A Planning Document.* New York, n.d.

HALEY, ALEX. *The Autobiography of Malcolm X.* New York: Ballantine Books, 1965.

HARRINGTON, MICHAEL. *The New American Poverty.* New York: Penguin, 1984.

————. *The Other America: Poverty in the United States.* New York: Penguin, 1981.

HARRIS, MARLYS. "The Methadone Center Nobody Wants." *New York Affairs* (1974):16–31.

HAYDEN, TOM. *Rebellion in Newark.* New York: Vintage Books, 1967.

HILL, RICHARD CHILD. "Crisis in the Motor City: The Politics of Economic Development in Detroit." In *Restructuring the City: The Political Economy of Urban Redevelopment*, ed. Susan S. Fainstein and Norman L. Fainstein. White Plains, N.Y.: Longman, 1986.

HIRSCH, ARNOLD R. *Making the Second Ghetto: Race and Housing in Chicago, 1940 to 1960.* Cambridge: Cambridge University Press, 1983.

HOFSTADTER, RICHARD. *Social Darwinism in American Thought.* Boston: Beacon Press, 1955.

HOPPER, KIM and JILL HAMBERG. "The Making of America's Homeless: From Skid Row to New Poor." In *Critical Perspectives on Housing*, ed. Rachel G. Bratt, Chester Hartman, and Ann Meyerson. Philadelphia: Temple University Press, 1986.

JACKSON, J. B. "The American Public Space." *The Public Interest* 74 (Winter 1984):52–65.

————. *Discovering the Vernacular Landscape.* New Haven: Yale University Press, 1984.

————. *The Necessity for Ruins and Other Topics.* Amherst: University of Massachusetts Press, 1980.

JACOBS, JANE. *The Death and Life of Great American Cities.* New York: Vintage Books, 1961.

JENCKS, CHRISTOPHER. "Deadly Neighborhoods." *The New Republic* (June 13, 1988):23–32.

KAPLAN, JUSTIN. *Walt Whitman, A Life.* New York: Bantam Books, 1982.

KATZ, MICHAEL B. *The Undeserving Poor: From the War on Poverty to the War on Welfare.* New York: Pantheon, 1989.

KEISER, LINCOLN R. *The Vice Lords, Warriors of the Streets.* New York: Holt, Rinehardt and Winston, 1969.

KELLERMAN, BILL. "The Angel of Detroit." *Sojourner* (October 1989):16–21.

KELLOGG, D. O. "Penury Not Pauperism." *The Atlantic Monthly* (June 1884):771–779.

KIRKE, EDMUND. "The City of Cleveland." *Harper's* 72 (March 1886):561–583.

————. "The City of the Strait." *Harper's* 73 (August 1886):327–347.

KUSMER, KENNETH L. "The Functions of Organized Charity in the Progressive Era: Chicago as a Case Study." *The Journal of American History* 60 (December 1975):657–678.

LAMB, MARTHA J. "Newark." *Harper's* 53 (October 1876):660–679.

LANE, JAMES B. *City of the Century: A History of Gary, Indiana.* Bloomington: Indiana University Press, 1978.

————, ed. *Homefront: The World War II Years in the Calumet Region 1941–1945.* Steel Shavings, vol. 22. Gary: Indiana University Northwest, 1993.

————, ed. *Life in the Calumet Region during the 1930s.* Steel Shavings, vol. 17. Gary: Indiana University Northwest, 1988.

————, ed. *Life in the Calumet Region during the 1980s.* Steel Shavings, vol. 21. Gary: Indiana University Northwest, 1992.

LEMANN, NICHOLAS. "The Other Underclass." *The Atlantic Monthly* (December 1991):96–110.

LEONARD, JOHN. *Life Classic Photographs: A Personal Interpretation.* Boston: Little, Brown, 1988.

LEWIS, OSCAR. "The Culture of Poverty." *Scientific American* (October 1966):3–9.

LIEBOW, ELLIOT. *Tally's Corner.* Boston: Little Brown, 1967.

LONDON, JACK. *The People of the Abyss.* 1904. Reprint. Oakland: Star Rover House, 1982.

LYNCH, KEVIN. *The Image of the City.* Cambridge, Mass.: MIT Press, 1960.

————. "The Waste of Place." *Places* 6 (2) (Winter 1990):10–23.

————. *What Time Is This Place?* Cambridge, Mass.: MIT Press, 1972.

MACDONALD, DWIGHT. "Our Invisible Poor." *The New Yorker* (January 19, 1963):82–132.

MANHATTAN BOROUGH PRESIDENT'S ADVISORY COUNCIL ON CHILD WELFARE. "Failed Promises, Child Welfare in New York City: A Look at the Past, a Vision for the Future." Report. New York, July 1989.

MANHATTAN BOROUGH PRESIDENT'S TASK FORCE ON HOUSING FOR HOMELESS FAMILIES. "A Shelter Is Not a Home." Report. New York, 1987.

MARABLE, MANNING. "Black America: Multicultural Democracy in the Age of Clarence Thomas and David Duke." *Open Magazine Pamphlet Series* #16 (January 1992):1–16.

MATTINGLY, KATHARINE MEYER, ed. *Detroit Architecture, AIA Guide.* Detroit: Wayne State University Press, 1971.

MAYHEW, HENRY. *London Labour and the London Poor.* (One-volume abridgement of the four-volume 1851–1852 original.) London: Penguin Classics, 1986.

MOORE, MICHAEL. "In Flint, Tough Times Last." *The Nation* (June 6, 1987):753–756.

MUMFORD, JOHN K. "This Land of Opportunity: Gary, the City That Arose from a Sandy Waste." *Harper's* (July 4, 1908).

MUMFORD, LEWIS. "The Sky Line: The Gentle Art of Overcrowding." *The New Yorker* (May 20, 1950).

MURRAY, CHARLES. "In Search of the Working Poor." *The Public Interest* 89 (Fall 1987):3–19.

———. *Losing Ground: American Social Policy, 1950–1980*. New York: Basic Books, 1984.

———. "No, Welfare Isn't Really the Problem." *The Public Interest* 84 (Summer 1986):3–11.

NADELMAN, ETHAN A. "Thinking Seriously about Alternative Drug Policies." *Daedalus* 121, no. 3 (Summer 1992):85–132

NAUER, KIM. "Feeding Frenzy." *City Limits* (August/September 1994):22–28.

NEWMAN, OSCAR. *Defensible Space: Crime Prevention Through Urban Design*. New York: Collier, 1973.

NEW YORK CITY COMMISSION ON THE HOMELESS. "The Way Home: A New Direction in Social Policy." Report. New York, February 1992.

O'BRIEN, TOM, et al. "The Drug Problem: A Project Manager's Guide." Pamphlet. Narcotics Task Force, New York City Housing Authority, New York, 1988.

OGDEN, R. "The Panic and Poor-Relief." *The Nation* (June 7, 1894):423–424.

ORWELL, GEORGE. *Down and Out in Paris and London*. New York: Harcourt Brace, 1933.

PETERSON, PAUL E. "The Urban Underclass and the Poverty Paradox." *Political Science Quarterly* 106 (4) (Winter 1991–1992):617–637.

PLAGENS, PETER. "Los Angeles: The Ecology of Evil." *Artforum* (December 1972):67–76.

PLUNZ, RICHARD. *A History of Housing in New York City*. New York: Columbia University Press, 1990.

PUBLIC WORKS HISTORICAL SOCIETY. *Chicago: An Industrial Guide*. Chicago, 1991.

RAINWATER, LEE. "Fear and the House-as-Haven in the Lower Class." *AIP Journal* (January 1966):23–37.

———, ed. *Black Experience: Soul*. Transaction Books, 1970.

RAVAGE, M. E. "My Plunge into the Slums." *Harper's* (April 1917):658–665.

REUTER, PETER. "Hawks Ascendant: The Punitive Trend of American Drug Policy." *Daedalus* 121, no. 3 (Summer 1992):15–52.

RHODES, HARRISON. "The Portrait of Chicago." *Harper's* (June 1917):80–90.

RIEDER, JONATHAN. "Crown of Thorns." *The New Republic* (October 14, 1991):26–31.

RIEGL, ALOIS. "The Modern Cult of Monuments: Its Character and Its Origin." *Oppositions* (Fall 1982):20–51.

RIIS, JACOB. "The Genesis of the Gang." *The Atlantic Monthly* (September 1899):302–311.

———. *How the Other Half Lives*. 1890. Reprint. New York: Dover, 1971.

———. "The Tenant." *The Atlantic Monthly* (August 1899):153–163.

———. "The Tenement: Curing Its Blight." *The Atlantic Monthly* (July 1899):18–28.

ROBERTS, ROBERT. *The Classic Slum: Salford Life in the First Quarter of the Century*. Middlesex, England: Penguin Books, 1971.

ROSENBERG, WILLIAM G. "Downtown Adaptative Reuse Project Signals New Public/Private Partnership." *Journal of Housing* (August-September 1981):437–443.

ROSSI, PETER H., J. D. WRIGHT, G. A. FISHER, and G. WILLIS. "The Urban Homeless: Estimating Composition and Size." *Science* 235 (March 13, 1987):1336–1341.

ROTHMAN, DAVID J. *The Discovery of the Asylum: Social Order and Disorder in the New Republic*. Boston: Little, Brown, 1971.

———. "The Rehabilitation of the Asylum." *The American Prospect* 7 (Fall 1991):118–128.

RUDWICK, BRACEY MEIER. *The Rise of the Ghetto*. Belmont, Mass.: Wadsworth Publishing, 1971.

RULFO, JUAN. *Pedro Paramo*. Mexico D.F.: Fondo de Cultura Economica, 1986.

RYAN, WILLIAM. *Blaming the Victim*. New York: Vintage Books, 1971.

SCHOENER, ALLEN. *Harlem on My Mind*. New York: Random House, 1968.

SHANLEY, CHARLES DAWSON. "The Small Arabs of New York." *The Atlantic Monthly* (March 1869):279–286.

SKOCPOL, THEDA. "Sustainable Social Policy: Fighting Poverty Without Poverty Programs." *The American Prospect* 2 (Summer 1990):58–70

SLAYTON, ROBERT A. "The Reagan Approach to Housing: An Examination of Local Impact." Chicago Urban League, mimeo (1987):1–23.

SMITHSON, ROBERT. "A Tour of the Monuments of Passaic, New Jersey." In *The Writings of Robert Smithson*, ed. Nancy Holt, pp. 52–57. New York: New York University Press, 1979.

SOJA, EDWARD W. *Postmodern Geographies: The Reassertion of Space in Critical Social Theory*. London: Verso, 1989.

STOTT, WILLIAM. *Documentary Expression and Thirties America*. Chicago: University of Chicago Press, 1986.

STRACHEY, LYTTON. *Eminent Victorians*. 1918. Reprint. New York: Viking Penguin, 1987.

THANET, OCTAVE. "The Indoor Pauper: A Study." *The Atlantic Monthly* (August 1881):241–252.

THERNSTROM, STEPHAN. *Poverty and Progress: Social Mobility in a Nineteenth-Century City*. Cambridge, Mass.: Harvard University Press, 1964.

THOMSON, M. W. *Ruins: Their Preservation and Display.* London: A Colonnade Book, 1981.

TRACHTENBERG, ALAN. *Reading American Photographs.* New York: Hill and Wang, 1989.

TREUHERZ, JULIAN. *Hard Times: Social Realism in Victorian Art.* London: Lund Humphries, 1987.

WACQUANT, LOIC J. D. and WILLIAM JULIUS WILSON. "The Cost of Racial and Class Exclusion in the Inner City." *Annals, AAPSS* (January 1989): 8–25.

WADE, RICHARD C. "Why It's Harder to Leave the Ghetto." *New York Daily News* (September 3, 1989):41.

WALD, LILLIAN D. "The House on Henry Street." *The Atlantic Monthly* (March 1915):289–300.

———. "The House on Henry Street II: Children and Play." *The Atlantic Monthly* (April 1915): 464–473.

WARNER, CHARLES DUDLEY. "Studies of the Great West: Chicago." *Harper's* 76 (May 1885):869–879.

WHITE, CHARLES HENRY. "Pittsburgh." *Harper's* 117 (November 1908):901–908.

WHITE, NORVAL and ELLIOT WILLENSKY. *AIA Guide to New York City.* New York: Macmillan, 1978.

WIDICK, B. J. *Detroit: City of Race and Class Violence.* Detroit: Wayne State University Press, 1989.

WILSON, WILLIAM JULIUS. "Another Look at the Truly Disadvantaged." *Political Science Quarterly* 106 (4) (Winter 1991–1992):639–656.

———. "Race-Neutral Programs and the Democratic Coalition." *The American Prospect* 1 (Spring 1990):74–81.

———. "Studying Inner-City Dislocations: The Challenge of Public Agenda Research." *American Sociological Review* (February 1991):1–14.

———. *The Truly Disadvantaged.* Chicago: University of Chicago Press, 1987.

WIRTH, LOUIS. *The Ghetto.* Chicago: The University of Chicago Press, 1928.

WOODS, ROBERT A. "The Social Awakening In London." *Scribner's* (April 1892):399–424.

WRIGHT, CARROLL D. "Are the Rich Growing Richer and the Poor Poorer?" *The Atlantic Monthly* (July 1897):300–308.

WRIGHT, RICHARD. *Native Son.* 1940. Reprint. New York: Harper & Row, 1966.

WYCKOFF, WALTER A. "Incidents of the Slums." *Scribner's* 30 (October 1901):486–492.

ZOLA, EMILE. *Le Ventre de Paris.* 1874. Reprint. Paris: Le Livre de Poche, 1966.

ZUBE, ERVIN H., ed. *Landscapes: Selected Writtings of J. B. Jackson.* Amherst: University of Massachusetts Press, 1970.

ABOUT THE AUTHOR

Camilo José Vergara received his M.A. in sociology from Columbia University. His numerous articles on life in poor, minority communities have appeared in the *New York Times, The Nation, Metropolis,* the *Village Voice,* the *Atlantic, Columbia Journalism Review,* and *Architectural Record.* He is also coauthor of *Silent Cities: The Evolution of the American Cemetery.* In 1993 his work was the subject of a BBC documentary.

He is the recipient of several awards, including grants from the New York Council on the Arts and the National Endowment for the Arts. His photographs have been widely exhibited here and abroad, and portions of his archives are represented in the collections of Avery Library at Columbia University, at the Getty Center, and at the New Museum of Contemporary Art in New York. The Author lives in New York City.